Neural Network Programming with Java

Unleash the power of neural networks by implementing professional Java code

Fábio M. Soares

Alan M.F. Souza

[PACKT] open source*
community experience distilled
PUBLISHING

BIRMINGHAM - MUMBAI

Neural Network Programming with Java

Copyright © 2016 Packt Publishing

All rights reserved. No part of this book may be reproduced, stored in a retrieval system, or transmitted in any form or by any means, without the prior written permission of the publisher, except in the case of brief quotations embedded in critical articles or reviews.

Every effort has been made in the preparation of this book to ensure the accuracy of the information presented. However, the information contained in this book is sold without warranty, either express or implied. Neither the authors, nor Packt Publishing, and its dealers and distributors will be held liable for any damages caused or alleged to be caused directly or indirectly by this book.

Packt Publishing has endeavored to provide trademark information about all of the companies and products mentioned in this book by the appropriate use of capitals. However, Packt Publishing cannot guarantee the accuracy of this information.

First published: January 2016

Production reference: 1060116

Published by Packt Publishing Ltd.
Livery Place
35 Livery Street
Birmingham B3 2PB, UK.

ISBN 978-1-78588-090-2

www.packtpub.com

Credits

Authors
Fábio M. Soares
Alan M.F. Souza

Reviewer
Saeed Afzal

Commissioning Editor
Amarabha Banerjee

Acquisition Editor
Rahul Nair

Content Development Editor
Riddhi Tuljapurkar

Technical Editor
Vivek Pala

Copy Editor
Tani Kothari

Project Coordinator
Kinjal Bari

Proofreader
Safis Editing

Indexer
Hemangini Bari

Graphics
Disha Haria

Production Coordinator
Nilesh Mohite

Cover Work
Nilesh Mohite

About the Authors

Fábio M. Soares holds a master's degree in applied computing from UFPA and is currently a PhD candidate at the same university. He has been designing neural network solutions since 2004 and has developed applications with this technique in several fields, ranging from telecommunications to chemistry process modeling, and his research topics cover supervised learning for data-driven modeling.

He is also self-employed, offering services such as IT infrastructure management as well as database administration to a number of small- and medium-sized companies in northern Brazil. In the past, he has worked for big companies such as Albras, one of the most important aluminium smelters in the world, and Eletronorte, a great power supplier in Brazil. He also has experience as a lecturer, having worked at the Federal Rural University of Amazon and as a Faculty of Castanhal, both in the state of Pará, teaching subjects involving programming and artificial intelligence.

He has published a number of works, many of them available in English, all including the topics of artificial intelligence applied to some problem. His publications include conference proceedings, such as the TMS (The Minerals Metals and Materials Society), Light Metals and the Intelligent Data Engineering and Automated Learning. He has also has published two book chapters for Intech.

> I would like to give a special acknowledgement to God for having given me the opportunity to get access to rich knowledge on this theme, which I simply love doing research on. Special thanks to my family, my father, Josafá, and mother, Maria Alice (in memoriam), who would be very proud of me for this book, and also my brother, Flávio, my aunt, Maria Irenice, as well as all my relatives who always supported me in some way during my studies. I would also like to thank the support of my advisor, Prof. Roberto Limão. I am very grateful to him for having invited me to work with him on many projects regarding artificial intelligence and neural networks. Also, special thanks to my partners and former partners from Exodus Sistemas, who have helped me in my challenges in programming and IT infrastructure. Finally, I'd like to thank my friend Alan Souza, who wrote this book with me, for having extended to me this authorship.

Alan M.F. Souza is computer engineer from Instituto de Estudos Superiores da Amazônia (IESAM). He holds a post-graduate degree in project management software and a master's degree in industrial processes (applied computing) from Universidade Federal do Pará (UFPA). He has been working with neural networks since 2009 and has worked with IT Brazilian companies developing in Java, PHP, SQL, and other programming languages since 2006. He is passionate about programming and computational intelligence. Currently, he is a professor at Universidade da Amazônia (UNAMA) and a PhD candidate at UFPA.

> Since I was a kid, I thought about writing a book. So, this book is a dream come true and the result of hard work. I'd like to thank God for giving me this opportunity. I'd also like to thank my father, Célio, my mother, Socorro, my sister, Alyne, and my amazing wife, Tayná, for understanding my absences and worries at various moments. I am grateful to all the members of my family and friends for always supporting me in difficult times and wishing for my success. I'd like to thank all the professors who passed through my life, especially Prof. Roberto Limão for introducing me the very first neural network concept. I must register my gratitude to Fábio Soares for this great partnership and friendship. Finally, I must appreciate the tireless team at Packt Publishing for the invitation and for helping us in the production process as a whole.

About the Reviewer

Saeed Afzal, also known as Smac Afzal, is a professional software engineer and technology enthusiast based in Pakistan. He specializes in solution architecture and the implementation of scalable high-performance applications.

He is passionate about providing automation solutions for different business needs on the Web. His current research and work includes the futuristic implementation of a next-generation web development framework, which reduces development time and cost and delivers productive websites with many necessary and killer features by default. He is hopeful of launching his upcoming technology in 2016.

He has also worked on the book *Cloud Bees Development* by Packt Publishing.

You can found out more about his skills and experience at http://sirsmac.com. He can be contacted at sirsmac@gmail.com.

> I would like to thank the Allah Almighty, my parents, and my wife, Dr. H. Zara Saeed, for all their encouragement.

www.PacktPub.com

Support files, eBooks, discount offers, and more

For support files and downloads related to your book, please visit www.PacktPub.com.

Did you know that Packt offers eBook versions of every book published, with PDF and ePub files available? You can upgrade to the eBook version at www.PacktPub.com and as a print book customer, you are entitled to a discount on the eBook copy. Get in touch with us at service@packtpub.com for more details.

At www.PacktPub.com, you can also read a collection of free technical articles, sign up for a range of free newsletters and receive exclusive discounts and offers on Packt books and eBooks.

PACKTLIB

https://www2.packtpub.com/books/subscription/packtlib

Do you need instant solutions to your IT questions? PacktLib is Packt's online digital book library. Here, you can search, access, and read Packt's entire library of books.

Why subscribe?

- Fully searchable across every book published by Packt
- Copy and paste, print, and bookmark content
- On demand and accessible via a web browser

Free access for Packt account holders

If you have an account with Packt at www.PacktPub.com, you can use this to access PacktLib today and view 9 entirely free books. Simply use your login credentials for immediate access.

Table of Contents

Preface	**vii**
Chapter 1: Getting Started with Neural Networks	**1**
Discovering neural networks	**2**
Why artificial neural network?	**2**
How neural networks are arranged	**4**
The very basic element – artificial neuron	5
Giving life to neurons – activation function	5
The fundamental values – weights	6
An important parameter – bias	7
The parts forming the whole – layers	7
Learning about neural network architectures	**8**
Monolayer networks	8
Multilayer networks	9
Feedforward networks	9
Feedback networks	10
From ignorance to knowledge – learning process	**10**
Let the implementations begin! Neural networks in practice	**11**
Summary	**18**
Chapter 2: How Neural Networks Learn	**19**
Learning ability in neural networks	**19**
How learning helps to solve problems	20
Learning paradigms	**20**
Supervised learning	20
Unsupervised learning	21
Systematic structuring – learning algorithm	**22**
Two stages of learning – training and testing	23
The details – learning parameters	24
Error measurement and cost function	25

Examples of learning algorithms	**26**
Perceptron	26
Delta rule	27
Coding of the neural network learning	**27**
Learning parameter implementation	27
Learning procedure	29
Class definitions	30
Two practical examples	**37**
Perceptron (warning system)	37
ADALINE (traffic forecast)	41
Summary	**46**
Chapter 3: Handling Perceptrons	**47**
Studying the perceptron neural network	**48**
Applications and limitations of perceptrons	48
Linear separation	48
Classical XOR case	50
Popular multilayer perceptrons (MLPs)	**52**
MLP properties	52
MLP weights	53
Recurrent MLP	54
MLP structure in an OOP paradigm	55
Interesting MLP applications	**56**
Classification in MLPs	56
Regression in MLPs	58
Learning process in MLPs	**60**
Simple and very powerful learning algorithm – Backpropagation	61
Elaborate and potent learning algorithm – Levenberg–Marquardt	63
Hands-on MLP implementation!	**65**
Backpropagation in action	68
Exploring the code	68
Levenberg–Marquardt implementation	**72**
Practical application – types of university enrolments	**75**
Summary	**78**
Chapter 4: Self-Organizing Maps	**79**
Neural networks' unsupervised way of learning	**80**
Some unsupervised learning algorithms	**80**
Competitive learning or winner takes all	82

Kohonen self-organizing maps (SOMs)	**84**
One-Dimensional SOM	85
Two-Dimensional SOM	86
Step-by-step of SOM learning	88
How to use SOMs	89
Coding of the Kohonen algorithm	**90**
Exploring the Kohonen class	92
Kohonen implementation (clustering animals)	95
Summary	**98**
Chapter 5: Forecasting Weather	**99**
Neural networks for prediction problems	**100**
No data, no neural net – selecting data	**101**
Knowing the problem – weather variables	102
Choosing input and output variables	103
Removing insignificant behaviors – Data filtering	103
Adjusting values – data preprocessing	**104**
Equalizing data – normalization	105
Java implementation for weather prediction	**107**
Plotting charts	107
Handling data files	108
Building a neural network for weather prediction	109
Empirical design of neural networks	**112**
Choosing training and test datasets	112
Designing experiments	113
Results and simulations	113
Summary	**116**
Chapter 6: Classifying Disease Diagnosis	**117**
What are classification problems, and how can neural networks be applied to them?	**118**
A special type of activation function – Logistic regression	**119**
Multiple classes versus binary classes	120
Comparing the expected versus produced results – the confusion matrix	121
Classification measures – sensitivity and specificity	122
Applying neural networks for classification	**123**
Disease diagnosis with neural networks	**126**
Using ANN to diagnose breast cancer	126
Applying NN for an early diagnosis of diabetes	131
Summary	**134**

Table of Contents

Chapter 7: Clustering Customer Profiles — 135
Clustering task — 136
Cluster analysis — 137
Cluster evaluation and validation — 138
External validation — 138
Applied unsupervised learning — 139
Neural network of radial basis functions — 139
Kohonen neural network — 140
Types of data — 141
Customer profiling — 142
Preprocessing data — 142
Implementation in Java — 143
Card credit analysis for customer profiling — 143
Summary — 149

Chapter 8: Pattern Recognition (OCR Case) — 151
What is pattern recognition all about? — 152
Definition of classes among tons of data — 152
What if the undefined classes are undefined? — 153
External validation — 154
How to apply neural networks in pattern recognition — 154
Preprocessing the data — 155
The OCR problem — 156
Simplifying the task – digit recognition — 156
Approach to digit representation — 157
Let the coding begin! — 157
Generating data — 158
Building the neural network — 160
Testing and redesigning – trial and error — 161
Results — 163
Summary — 166

Chapter 9: Neural Network Optimization and Adaptation — 167
Common issues in neural network implementations — 168
Input selection — 168
Data correlation — 169
Dimensionality reduction — 170
Data filtering — 171
Structure selection — 171

Online retraining	**172**
Stochastic online learning	174
Implementation	174
Application	176
Adaptive neural networks	**179**
Adaptive resonance theory	179
Implementation	180
Summary	**182**
Appendix A: Setting up the NetBeans Environment	**183**
Download and install NetBeans	**183**
Setting up the NetBeans environment	**188**
Importing a project	**191**
Programming and running code with NetBeans	**194**
Debugging with NetBeans	**195**
Appendix B: Setting Up the Eclipse Environment	**199**
Download and install Eclipse	**199**
Setting up the Eclipse environment	**204**
Importing a project	**205**
Programming and running code with the Eclipse IDE	**210**
Debugging with the Eclipse IDE	**211**
Appendix C: References	**213**
Chapter 1 – Getting Started with Neural Networks	213
Chapter 2 – How Neural Networks Learn	213
Chapter 3 – Working with Perceptrons	213
Chapter 4 – Self-Organizing Maps	214
Chapter 5 – Forecasting the Weather	214
Chapter 6 – Disease Diagnosis	214
Chapter 7 – Clustering Customer Profiles	215
Chapter 8 – Pattern Recognition (the OCR Case)	215
Chapter 9 – Neural Network Optimization and Adaptation	215
Index	**217**

Preface

The life of a programmer can be described as a continual never-ending learning pathway. A programmer always faces challenges regarding new technology or new approaches. Generally, during our lives, although we become used to repeated things, we are always subjected to learn something new. The process of learning is one of the most interesting topics in science, and there are a number of attempts to describe or reproduce the human learning process.

The writing of this book was guided by the challenge of facing new content and then mastering it. While the name neural networks may appear strange or even give an idea that this book is about neurology, we strived to simplify these nuances by focusing on your reasons for deciding to purchase this book. We intended to build a framework that shows you that neural networks are actually simple and easy to understand, and absolutely no prior knowledge on this topic is required to fully understand the concepts we present here.

So, we encourage you to explore the content of this book to the fullest, beholding the power of neural networks when confronting big problems but always with the point of view of a beginner. Every concept addressed in this book is explained in easy language, and also with a technical background. Our mission in this book is to give you an insight into intelligent applications that can be written using a simple language.

Finally, we would like to thank all those who directly or indirectly have contributed to this book and supported us from the very beginning, right from the Federal University of Pará, which is the university that we graduated from, to the data and component providers INMET (Brazilian Institute of Meteorology), Proben1, and JFreeCharts. We want to give special thanks to our advisor Prof. Roberto Limão, who introduced us to the subject of neural networks and coauthored many papers with us in this field. We also acknowledge the work performed by several authors cited in the references, which gave us a broader vision on neural networks and insights on how to adapt them to the Java language in a didactic way.

Preface

We welcome you to have a very pleasurable reading experience and you are encouraged to download the source code and follow the examples presented in this book.

What this book covers

Chapter 1, Getting Started with Neural Networks, is an introductory foundation on the neural networks and what they are designed for. You will be presented with the basic concepts involved in this book. A brief review of the Java programming language is provided. As in all subsequent chapters, an implementation of a neural network in Java code is also provided.

Chapter 2, How Neural Networks Learn, covers the learning process of neural networks and shows how data is used to that end. The complete structure and design of a learning algorithm is presented here.

Chapter 3, Handling Perceptrons, covers the use of perceptrons, which are one of the most commonly used neural network architectures. We present a neural network structure containing layers of neurons and show how they can learn by data in basic problems.

Chapter 4, Self-Organizing Maps, shows an unsupervised neural network architecture (the Self-Organising Map), which is applied to finding patterns or clusters in records.

Chapter 5, Forecasting Weather, is the first practical chapter showing an interesting application of neural networks in forecasting values, namely weather data.

Chapter 6, Classifying Disease Diagnostics, covers another useful task neural networks are very good at—classification. In this chapter, you will be presented with a very didactic but interesting application for disease diagnosis.

Chapter 7, Clustering Customer Profiles, talks about how neural networks are able to find patterns in data, and a common application is to group customers that share the same properties of buying.

Chapter 8, Pattern Recognition (OCR Case), talks about a very interesting and amazing capability of recognizing patterns, including optical character recognition, and this chapter explores how this can be done with neural networks in the Java language.

Chapter 9, Neural Network Optimization and Adaptation, shows advancements regarding how to optimize and add adaptability to neural networks, thereby strengthening their power.

What you need for this book

You'll need Netbeans (www.netbeans.org) or Eclipse (www.eclipse.org). Both are free and available for download at the previously mentioned websites.

Who this book is for

This book is targeted at both developers and enthusiasts who have a basic or even no Java programming knowledge. No previous knowledge of neural networks is required, this book will teach from scratch. Even if you are familiar with neural networks and/or other machine learning techniques but have little or no experience with Java, this book will take you to the level at which you will be able to develop useful applications. Of course, if you know basic programming concepts, you will benefit most from this book, but no prior experience is required.

Conventions

In this book, you will find a number of text styles that distinguish between different kinds of information. Here are some examples of these styles and an explanation of their meaning.

Code words in text, database table names, folder names, filenames, file extensions, pathnames, dummy URLs, user input, and Twitter handles are shown as follows: "In Java projects, the calculation of these values is done through the Classification class."

A block of code is set as follows:

```
Data cardDataInput      = new Data("data", "card_inputs_training.csv");
Data cardDataInputTestRNA    = new Data("data", "card_inputs_test.csv");
Data cardDataOutputTestRNA   = new Data("data", "card_output_test.csv");
```

New terms and **important words** are shown in bold.

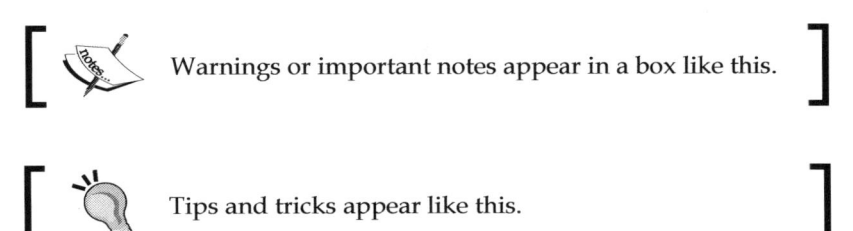

> Warnings or important notes appear in a box like this.

> Tips and tricks appear like this.

Reader feedback

Feedback from our readers is always welcome. Let us know what you think about this book—what you liked or disliked. Reader feedback is important for us as it helps us develop titles that you will really get the most out of.

To send us general feedback, simply e-mail feedback@packtpub.com, and mention the book's title in the subject of your message.

If there is a topic that you have expertise in and you are interested in either writing or contributing to a book, see our author guide at www.packtpub.com/authors.

Customer support

Now that you are the proud owner of a Packt book, we have a number of things to help you to get the most from your purchase.

Downloading the example code

You can download the example code files from your account at http://www.packtpub.com for all the Packt Publishing books you have purchased. If you purchased this book elsewhere, you can visit http://www.packtpub.com/support and register to have the files e-mailed directly to you.

Errata

Although we have taken every care to ensure the accuracy of our content, mistakes do happen. If you find a mistake in one of our books—maybe a mistake in the text or the code—we would be grateful if you could report this to us. By doing so, you can save other readers from frustration and help us improve subsequent versions of this book. If you find any errata, please report them by visiting http://www.packtpub.com/submit-errata, selecting your book, clicking on the **Errata Submission Form** link, and entering the details of your errata. Once your errata are verified, your submission will be accepted and the errata will be uploaded to our website or added to any list of existing errata under the Errata section of that title.

To view the previously submitted errata, go to https://www.packtpub.com/books/content/support and enter the name of the book in the search field. The required information will appear under the **Errata** section.

Piracy

Piracy of copyrighted material on the Internet is an ongoing problem across all media. At Packt, we take the protection of our copyright and licenses very seriously. If you come across any illegal copies of our works in any form on the Internet, please provide us with the location address or website name immediately so that we can pursue a remedy.

Please contact us at copyright@packtpub.com with a link to the suspected pirated material.

We appreciate your help in protecting our authors and our ability to bring you valuable content.

Questions

If you have a problem with any aspect of this book, you can contact us at questions@packtpub.com, and we will do our best to address the problem.

1
Getting Started with Neural Networks

In this chapter, we will introduce **neural networks** and what they are designed for. This chapter serves as a foundation layer for the subsequent chapters, while it presents the basic concepts for neural networks. In this chapter, we will cover the following:

- Artificial Neurons
- Weights and Biases
- Activation Functions
- Layers of Neurons
- Neural Network Implementation in Java

Discovering neural networks

First, the term "neural networks" may create a snapshot of a brain in our minds, particularly for those who have just been introduced to it. In fact, that's right, we consider the brain to be a big and natural neural network. However, what if we talk about **artificial neural networks (ANNs)**? Well, here comes an opposite word to natural, and the first thing now that comes into our head is an image of an artificial brain or a robot, given the term "**artificial**." In this case, we also deal with creating a structure similar to and inspired by the human brain; therefore, this can be called artificial intelligence. So, the reader who doesn't have any previous experience with ANN now may be thinking that this book teaches how to build intelligent systems, including an artificial brain, capable of emulating the human mind using Java codes, isn't it? Of course, we will not cover the creation of artificial thinking machines such as those from the Matrix trilogy movies; however, this book will discuss several incredible capabilities that these structures can do. We will provide the reader with Java codes for defining and creating basic neural network structures, taking advantage of the entire Java programming language framework.

Why artificial neural network?

We cannot begin talking about neural networks without understanding their origins, including the term as well. We use the terms **neural networks (NN)** and ANN interchangeably in this book, although NNs are more general, covering the natural neural networks as well. So, what actually is an ANN? Let's explore a little of the history of this term.

In the 1940s, the neurophysiologist Warren McCulloch and the mathematician Walter Pits designed the first mathematical implementation of an artificial neuron combining the neuroscience foundations with mathematical operations. At that time, many studies were being carried out on understanding the human brain and how and if it could be simulated, but within the field of neuroscience. The idea of McCulloch and Pits was a real novelty because it added the math component. Further, considering that the brain is composed of billions of neurons, each one interconnected with another million, resulting in some trillions of connections, we are talking about a giant network structure. However, each neuron unit is very simple, acting as a mere processor capable to sum and propagate signals.

On the basis of this fact, McCulloch and Pits designed a simple model for a single neuron, initially to simulate the human vision. The available calculators or computers at that time were very rare but capable of dealing with mathematical operations quite well; on the other hand, even today tasks such as vision and sound recognition are not easily programmed without the use of special frameworks, as opposed to the mathematical operations and functions. Nevertheless, the human brain can perform these latter tasks more efficiently than the first ones, and this fact really instigates scientists and researchers.

So, an ANN is supposed to be a structure to perform tasks such as pattern recognition, learning from data, and forecasting trends, just like an expert can do on the basis of knowledge, as opposed to the conventional algorithmic approach that requires a set of steps to be performed to achieve a defined goal. An ANN instead has the capability to learn how to solve some task by itself, because of its highly interconnected network structure.

Tasks Quickly Solvable by Humans	Tasks Quickly Solvable by Computers
Classification of images	Complex calculation
Voice recognition	Grammatical error correction
Face identification	Signal processing
Forecast events on the basis of experience	Operating system management

Getting Started with Neural Networks

How neural networks are arranged

It can be said that the ANN is a nature-inspired structure, so it does have similarities with the human brain. As shown in the following figure, a natural neuron is composed of a nucleus, dendrites, and axon. The axon extends itself into several branches to form synapses with other neurons' dendrites.

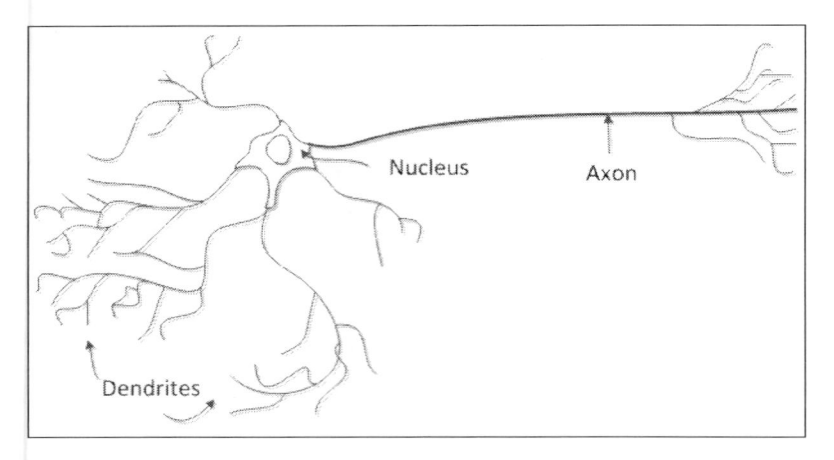

So, the artificial neuron has a similar structure. It contains a nucleus (processing unit), several dendrites (analogous to inputs), and one axon (analogous to output), as shown in the following figure:

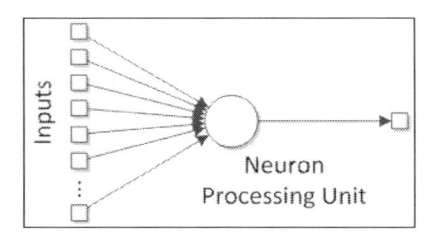

The links between neurons form the so-called neural network, analogous to the synapses in the natural structure.

The very basic element – artificial neuron

Natural neurons have proven to be signal processors since they receive micro signals in the dendrites that can trigger a signal in the axon depending on their strength or magnitude. We can then think of a neuron as having a signal collector in the inputs and an activation unit in the output that can trigger a signal that will be forwarded to other neurons. So, we can define the artificial neuron structure as shown in the following figure:

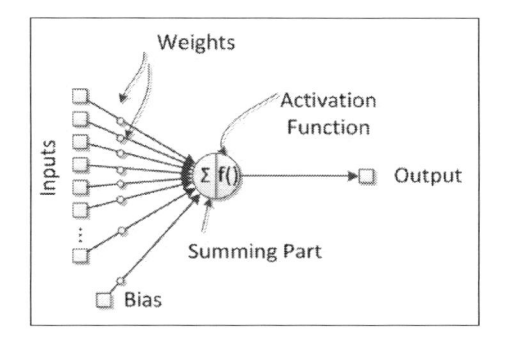

[In natural neurons, there is a threshold potential that when reached, fires the axon and propagates the signal to the other neurons. This firing behavior is emulated with activation functions, which have proven to be useful in representing nonlinear behaviors in the neurons.]

Giving life to neurons – activation function

The neuron's output is given by an activation function. This component adds nonlinearity to neural network processing, which is needed because the natural neuron has nonlinear behaviors. An activation function is usually bounded between two values at the output, therefore being a nonlinear function, but in some special cases, it can be a linear function.

The four most used activation functions are as follows:

- Sigmoid
- Hyperbolic tangent
- Hard limiting threshold
- Purely linear

The equations and charts associated with these functions are shown in the following table:

Function	Equation	Chart
Sigmoid	$f(x) = \dfrac{1}{1+e^{-x}}$	
Hyperbolic tangent	$f(x) = \dfrac{1-e^{-x}}{1+e^{-x}}$	
Hard limiting threshold	$f(x) = \begin{cases} 0 \text{ if } x < 0 \\ 1 \text{ if } x \geq 1 \end{cases}$	
Linear	$f(x) = x$	

The fundamental values – weights

In neural networks, weights represent the connections between neurons and have the capability to amplify or attenuate neuron signals, for example, multiply the signals, thus modifying them. So, by modifying the neural network signals, neural weights have the power to influence a neuron's output, therefore a neuron's activation will be dependent on the inputs and on the weights. Provided that the inputs come from other neurons or from the external world, the weights are considered to be a neural network's established connections between its neurons. Thus, since the weights are internal to the neural network and influence its outputs, we can consider them as neural network knowledge, provided that changing the weights will change the neural network's capabilities and therefore actions.

An important parameter – bias

The artificial neuron can have an independent component that adds an extra signal to the activation function. This component is called **bias**.

Just like the inputs, biases also have an associated weight. This feature helps in the neural network knowledge representation as a more purely nonlinear system.

The parts forming the whole – layers

Natural neurons are organized in layers, each one providing a specific level of processing; for example, the input layer receives direct stimuli from the outside world, and the output layers fire actions that will have a direct influence on the outside world. Between these layers, there are a number of hidden layers, in the sense that they do not interact directly with the outside world. In the artificial neural networks, all neurons in a layer share the same inputs and activation function, as shown in the following figure:

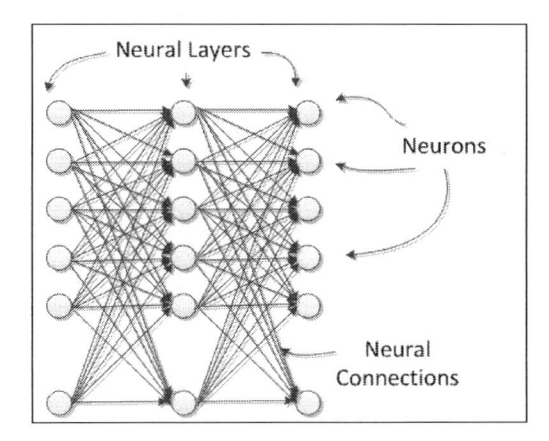

Neural networks can be composed of several linked layers, forming the so-called multilayer networks. The neural layers can be basically divided into three classes:

- Input layer
- Hidden layer
- Output layer

In practice, an additional neural layer adds another level of abstraction of the outside stimuli, thereby enhancing the neural network's capacity to represent more complex knowledge.

> Every neural network has at least an input/output layer irrespective of the number of layers. In the case of a multilayer network, the layers between the input and the output are called hidden.

Learning about neural network architectures

Basically, a neural network can have different layouts, depending on how the neurons or neuron layers are connected to each other. Every neural network architecture is designed for a specific end. Neural networks can be applied to a number of problems, and depending on the nature of the problem, the neural network should be designed in order to address this problem more efficiently.

Basically, there are two modalities of architectures for neural networks:

- Neuron connections
    - Monolayer networks
    - Multilayer networks

- Signal flow
    - Feedforward networks
    - Feedback networks

Monolayer networks

In this architecture, all neurons are laid out in the same level, forming one single layer, as shown in the following figure:

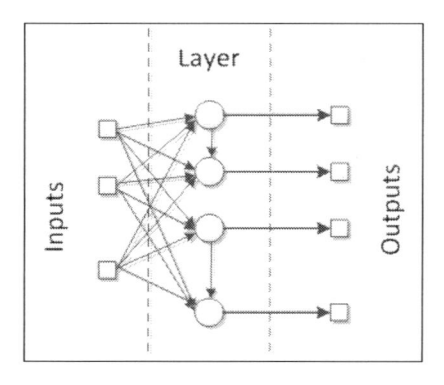

The neural network receives the input signals and feeds them into the neurons, which in turn produce the output signals. The neurons can be highly connected to each other with or without recurrence. Examples of these architectures are the single-layer perceptron, Adaline, self-organizing map, Elman, and Hopfield neural networks.

Multilayer networks

In this category, neurons are divided into multiple layers, each layer corresponding to a parallel layout of neurons that shares the same input data, as shown in the following figure:

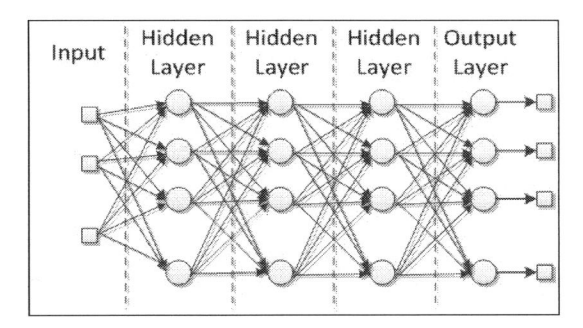

Radial basis functions and multilayer perceptrons are good examples of this architecture. Such networks are really useful for approximating real data to a function specially designed to represent that data. Moreover, because they have multiple layers of processing, these networks are adapted to learn from nonlinear data, being able to separate it or determine more easily the knowledge that reproduces or recognizes this data.

Feedforward networks

The flow of the signals in neural networks can be either in only one direction or in recurrence. In the first case, we call the neural network architecture feedforward, since the input signals are fed into the input layer; then, after being processed, they are forwarded to the next layer, just as shown in the figure in the multilayer section. Multilayer perceptrons and radial basis functions are also good examples of feedforward networks.

Feedback networks

When the neural network has some kind of internal recurrence, it means that the signals are fed back in a neuron or layer that has already received and processed that signal, the network is of the type feedback. See the following figure of feedback networks:

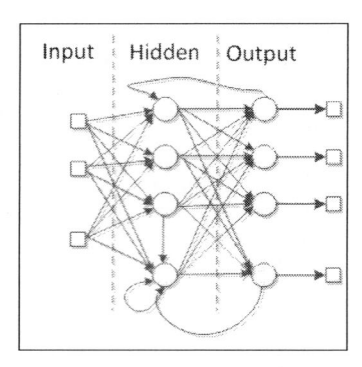

The special reason to add recurrence in the network is the production of a dynamic behavior, particularly when the network addresses problems involving time series or pattern recognition, that require an internal memory to reinforce the learning process. However, such networks are particularly difficult to train, eventually failing to learn. Most of the feedback networks are single layer, such as Elman and Hopfield networks, but it is possible to build a recurrent multilayer network, such as echo and recurrent multilayer perceptron networks.

From ignorance to knowledge – learning process

Neural networks learn by adjusting the connections between the neurons, namely the weights. As mentioned in the neural structure section, weights represent the neural network knowledge. Different weights cause the network to produce different results for the same inputs. So, a neural network can improve its results by adapting its weights according to a learning rule. The general schema of learning is depicted in the following figure:

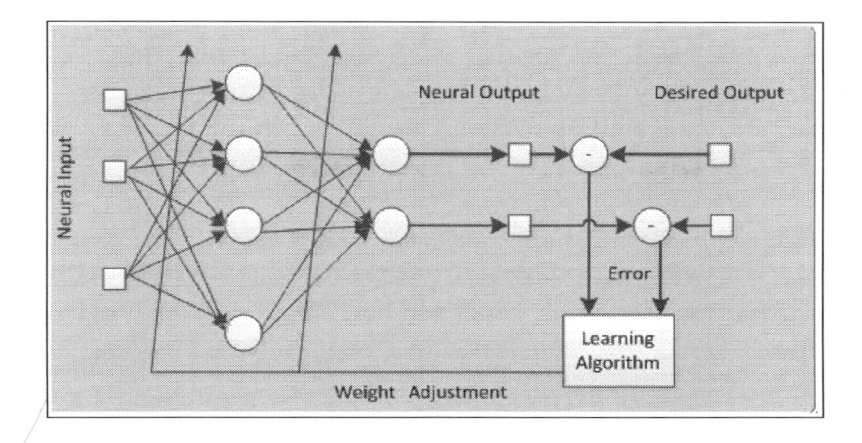

The process depicted in the preceding figure is called **supervised learning** because there is a desired output, but neural networks can learn only by the input data, without any desired output (supervision). In *Chapter 2, How Neural Networks Learn*, we are going to dive deeper into the neural network learning process.

Let the implementations begin! Neural networks in practice

In this book, we will cover the entire process of implementing a neural network by using the Java programming language. Java is an object-oriented programming language that was created in the 1990s by a small group of engineers from Sun Microsystems, later acquired by Oracle in the 2010s. Nowadays, Java is present in many devices that are part of our daily life.

In an object-oriented language, such as Java, we deal with classes and objects. A class is a blueprint of something in the real world, and an object is an instance of this blueprint, something like a car (class referring to all and any car) and my car (object referring to a specific car—mine). Java classes are usually composed of attributes and methods (or functions), that include **objects-oriented programming** (**OOP**) concepts. We are going to briefly review all of these concepts without diving deeper into them, since the goal of this book is just to design and create neural networks from a practical point of view. Four concepts are relevant and need to be considered in this process:

- **Abstraction**: The transcription of a real-world problem or rule into a computer programming domain, considering only its relevant features and dismissing the details that often hinder development.

- **Encapsulation**: Analogous to a product encapsulation by which some relevant features are disclosed openly (public methods), while others are kept hidden within their domain (private or protected), therefore avoiding misuse or excess of information.
- **Inheritance**: In the real world, multiple classes of objects share attributes and methods in a hierarchical manner; for example, a vehicle can be a superclass for car and truck. So, in OOP, this concept allows one class to inherit all features from another one, thereby avoiding the rewriting of code.
- **Polymorphism**: Almost the same as inheritance, but with the difference that methods with the same signature present different behaviors on different classes.

Using the neural network concepts presented in this chapter and the OOP concepts, we are now going to design the very first class set that implements a neural network. As can be seen, a neural network consists of layers, neurons, weights, activation functions, and biases, and there are basically three types of layers: input, hidden, and output. Each layer may have one or more neurons. Each neuron is connected either to a neural input/output or to another neuron, and these connections are known as weights.

It is important to highlight that a neural network may have many hidden layers or none, as the number of neurons in each layer may vary. However, the input and output layers have the same number of neurons as the number of neural inputs/outputs, respectively.

So, let's start implementing. Initially, we are going to define six classes, detailed as follows:

Class name: Neuron	
Attributes	
`private ArrayList<Double> listOfWeightIn`	An `ArrayList` variable of real numbers that represents the list of input weights
`private ArrayList<Double> listOfWeightOut`	An `ArrayList` variable of real numbers that represents the list of output weights
Methods	
`public double initNeuron()`	Initializes `listOfWeightIn` and `listOfWeightOut` function with a pseudo random real number
	Parameters: None
	Returns: A pseudo random real number

`public void setListOfWeightIn(ArrayList<Double> listOfWeightIn)`	Sets the `listOfWeightIn` function with a list of real numbers list	
	Parameters: The list of real numbers to be stored in the class object	
	Returns: None	
`public void setListOfWeightOut(ArrayList<Double> listOfWeightOut)`	Sets the `listOfWeightOut` function with a list of real numbers list	
	Parameters: The list of real numbers to be stored in the class object	
	Returns: None	
`public ArrayList<Double> getListOfWeightIn()`	Returns the input weights a list of neurons	
	Parameters: None	
	Returns: The list of real numbers stored in the `listOfWeightIn` variable	
`public ArrayList<Double> getListOfWeightOut()`	Returns the output weights a list of neurons	
	Parameters: None	
	Returns: The list of real numbers stored in the `listOfWeightOut` variable	

Class implementation with Java: file Neuron.java

Class Name: Layer

Note: This class is abstract and cannot be instantiated.

Attributes

`private ArrayList<Neuron> listOfNeurons`	An `ArrayList` variable of objects of the Neuron class
`private int numberOfNeuronsInLayer`	Integer number to store the quantity of neurons that are part of the layer

Methods

`public ArrayList<Neuron> getListOfNeurons()`	Returns the list of neurons by layer
	Parameters: None
	Returns: An `ArrayList` variable of objects by the `Neuron` class
`public void setListOfNeurons(ArrayList<Neuron> listOfNeurons)`	Sets the `listOfNeurons` function with an `ArrayList` variable of objects of the `Neuron` class
	Parameters: The list of objects of the `Neuron` class to be stored
	Returns: None

`public int getNumberOfNeuronsInLayer()`	Returns the number of neurons by layer
	Parameters: None
	Returns: The number of neurons by layer
`public void setNumberOfNeuronsInLayer(int numberOfNeuronsInLayer)`	Sets the number of neurons in a layer
	Parameters: The number of neurons in a layer
	Returns: None

Class implementation with Java: file Layer.java

Class name: InputLayer

Note: This class inherits attributes and methods from the Layer class.

Attributes

None

Methods

`public initLayer(InputLayer inputLayer)`	Initializes the input layer with pseudo random real numbers
	Parameters: An object of the `InputLayer` class
	Returns: None
`public void printLayer(InputLayer inputLayer)`	Prints the input weights of the layer
	Parameters: An object of the `InputLayer` class
	Returns: None

Class implementation with Java: file InputLayer.java

Class name: HiddenLayer

Note: This class inherits attributes and methods from the Layer class.

Attributes

None

Methods

`public ArrayList<HiddenLayer> initLayer(HiddenLayer hiddenLayer, ArrayList<HiddenLayer> listOfHiddenLayer, InputLayer inputLayer, OutputLayer outputLayer)`	Initializes the hidden layer(s) with pseudo random real numbers
	Parameters: An object of the `HiddenLayer` class, a list of objects of the `HiddenLayer` class, an object of the `InputLayer` class, an object of the `OutputLayer` class
	Returns: None
`public void printLayer(ArrayList<HiddenLayer> listOfHiddenLayer)`	Prints the weights of the layer(s)
	Parameters: A list of objects of the `HiddenLayer` class
	Returns: None

Chapter 1

Class implementation with Java: file HiddenLayer.java	
Class name: OutputLayer	
Note: This class inherits attributes and methods from the Layer class.	
Attributes	
None	
Methods	
`public OutputLayer initLayer(OutputLayer outputLayer)`	Initializes the output layer with pseudo random real numbers
	Parameters: An object of the `OutputLayer` class
	Returns: None
`public void printLayer(OutputLayer outputLayer)`	Prints the weights of the layer
	Parameters: An object of the `OutputLayer` class
	Returns: None
Class implementation with Java: file OutputLayer.java	
Class name: NeuralNet	
Note: The values of the neural net topology are fixed in this class (two neurons in the input layer, two hidden layers with three neurons each, and one neuron in the output layer). Reminder: It's the first version.	
Attributes	
`private InputLayer inputLayer;`	An object of the `InputLayer` class
`private HiddenLayer hiddenLayer;`	An object of the `HiddenLayer` class
`private ArrayList<HiddenLayer> listOfHiddenLayer;`	An `ArrayList` variable of objects of the `HiddenLayer` class. It is possible to have more than one hidden layer
`private OutputLayer outputLayer;`	An object of the `OutputLayer` class
`private int numberOfHiddenLayers;`	Integer number to store the quantity of layers that are part of the hidden layer

	Methods
`public void initNet()`	Initializes the neural net as a whole. Layers are built, and each list of the weights of neurons is built randomly
	Parameters: None
	Returns: None
`public void printNet()`	Prints the neural net as a whole. Each input and output weight of each layer is shown
	Parameters: None
	Returns: None
Class implementation with Java: file NeuralNet.java	

One advantage of OOP languages is the ease to document the program in **Unified Modeling Language (UML)**. UML class diagrams present classes, attributes, methods, and relationships between classes in a very simple and straightforward manner, thus helping the programmer and/or stakeholders to understand the project as a whole. The following figure represents the very first version of the project's class diagram:

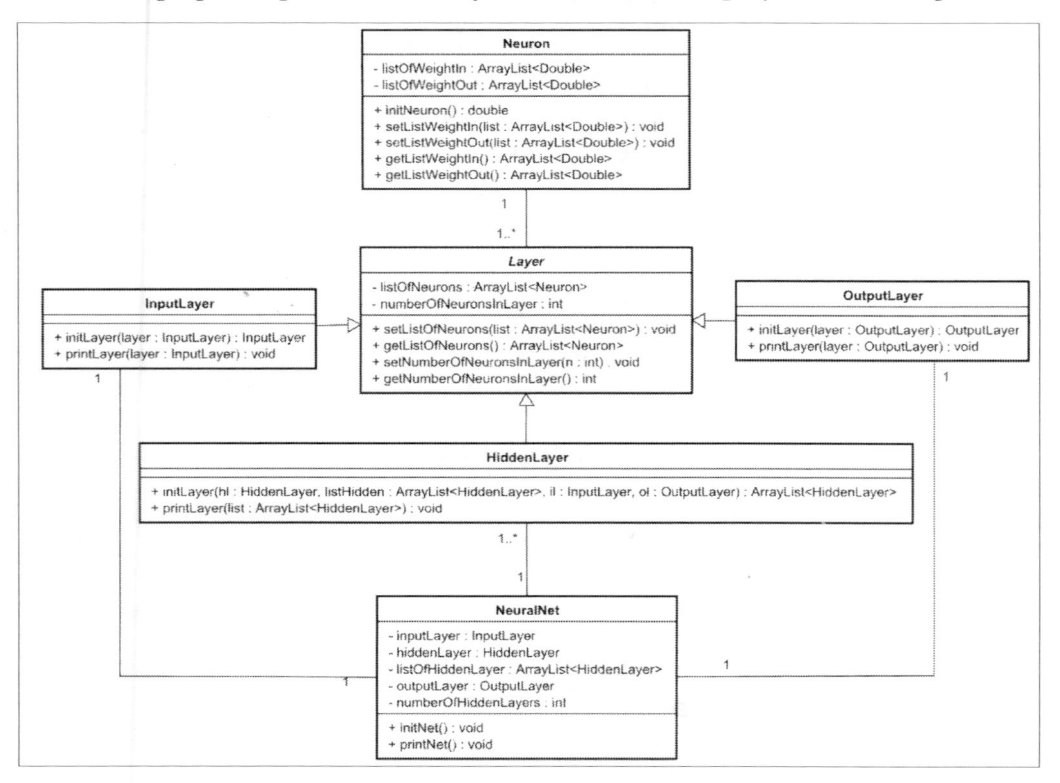

Neuron
- listOfWeightIn : ArrayList<Double>
- listOfWeightOut : ArrayList<Double>
+ initNeuron() : double
+ setListWeightIn(list : ArrayList<Double>) : void
+ setListWeightOut(list : ArrayList<Double>) : void
+ getListWeightIn() : ArrayList<Double>
+ getListWeightOut() : ArrayList<Double>

Layer
- listOfNeurons : ArrayList<Neuron>
- numberOfNeuronsInLayer : int
+ setListOfNeurons(list : ArrayList<Neuron>) : void
+ getListOfNeurons() : ArrayList<Neuron>
+ setNumberOfNeuronsInLayer(n : int) : void
+ getNumberOfNeuronsInLayer() : int

InputLayer
+ initLayer(layer : InputLayer) : InputLayer
+ printLayer(layer : InputLayer) : void

OutputLayer
+ initLayer(layer : OutputLayer) : OutputLayer
+ printLayer(layer : OutputLayer) : void

HiddenLayer
+ initLayer(hl : HiddenLayer, listHidden : ArrayList<HiddenLayer>, il : InputLayer, ol : OutputLayer) : ArrayList<HiddenLayer>
+ printLayer(list : ArrayList<HiddenLayer>) : void

NeuralNet
- inputLayer : InputLayer
- hiddenLayer : HiddenLayer
- listOfHiddenLayer : ArrayList<HiddenLayer>
- outputLayer : OutputLayer
- numberOfHiddenLayers : int
+ initNet() : void
+ printNet() : void

Now, let's apply these classes and get some results. The code shown next has a test class, a main method with an object of the `NeuralNet` class called n. When this method is called (by executing the class), it calls the `initNet()` and `printNet()` methods from the object n, generating the following result shown in the figure right after the code. It represents a neural network with two neurons in the input layer, three in the hidden layer, and one in the output layer:

```
public class NeuralNetTest {
   public static void main(String[] args) {
      NeuralNet n = new NeuralNet();
      n.initNet();
      n.printNet();

   }
}
```

It's relevant to remember that each time that the code runs, it generates new pseudo random weight values. So, when you run the code, the other values will appear in Console:

```
### INPUT LAYER ###
Neuron #1:
Input Weights:
[0.14807775975598858]
Neuron #2:
Input Weights:
[0.8727293470608676]

### HIDDEN LAYER ###
Hidden Layer #1
Neuron #1
Input Weights:
[0.05866233407910926, 0.3346175321226982]
Output Weights:
[0.753834856960778, 0.5991166717101689, 0.9640865431238916]
Neuron #2
Input Weights:
[0.7785881890303767, 0.7510078286193399]
Output Weights:
[0.4515976004418254, 0.5314541172397611, 0.5199533089338912]
Neuron #3
Input Weights:
[0.24697896006780296, 0.5222732600968314]
Output Weights:
[0.9080810264397966, 0.9287579381151893, 0.10676994160077102]

### OUTPUT LAYER ###
Neuron #1:
Output Weights:
[0.1576552703295493]
```

Summary

In this chapter, we've seen an introduction to the neural networks, what they are, what they are used for, and their basic concepts. We've also seen a very basic implementation of a neural network in the Java programming language, wherein we applied the theoretical neural network concepts in practice, by coding each of the neural network elements. It's important to understand the basic concepts before we move on to advanced concepts. The same applies to the code implemented with Java.

In the next chapter, we will delve into the learning process of a neural network and explore the different types of leaning with simple examples.

2
How Neural Networks Learn

In this chapter, we will show the learning process that neural networks perform in order to learn from data. We present the concepts of training, test, and validation, and show how to implement them in Java. We also show some methods for evaluating a neural network's performance in learning as well as learning algorithms' parameters. In summary, the following are the concepts addressed in this chapter:

- Learning process
- Learning algorithm
- Types of learning
    ○ Supervised
    ○ Unsupervised
- Training, test, and validation
- Error measurements
- Generalization

Learning ability in neural networks

What is really amazing about neural networks is their capacity to learn from the environment, just like brain-gifted beings are able to. We, as humans, experience the learning process through observations and repetitions, until some task or concept is completely mastered. From the physiological point of view, the learning process in the human brain is a reconfiguration of the neural connections between the nodes (neurons), which results in a new thinking structure.

While the connectionist nature of neural networks distributes the learning process all over the entire structure, this feature makes this structure flexible enough to learn a wide variety of knowledge. As opposed to ordinary digital computers that can execute only those tasks that they are programmed to, neural systems are able to improve and perform new activities according to some satisfaction criteria. In other words, neural networks don't need to be programmed; they learn the program by themselves.

How learning helps to solve problems

Considering that every task that requires solving solve may have a huge number of theoretically possible solutions, the learning process seeks to find an optimal solution that can produce a satisfying result. The use of structures like artificial neural networks (ANNs) is encouraged because of their ability to acquire knowledge of any type, strictly by receiving input stimuli, that is, data relevant to the task/problem. First, the ANN will produce a random result and an error, and based on this error, the ANN parameters will be adjusted.

> We can then think of the ANN parameters (weights) as the components of a solution. Let's imagine that one single solution represents a single point in the solution hyperspace. Each single solution produces an error measure, which informs how far away that solution is from the optimal one. For each iteration, the learning algorithm seeks a solution that can yield a smaller error and therefore, be closer to the optimal one.

Learning paradigms

There are basically two types of learning for neural networks, namely supervised and unsupervised. The learning in the human mind, for example, also works in this way. We can learn from observations without any kind of target pattern (unsupervised), or we can have a teacher who shows us the right pattern to follow (supervised). The difference between these two paradigms relies mainly on the relevance of a target pattern and varies from problem to problem.

Supervised learning

This category of learning deals in pairs of X's and Y's, and the objective is to map them in a function $f: X \rightarrow Y$. Here, the Y data is the supervisor, the target desired outputs, and the X data is the source-independent data that generates the Y data. It is analogous to a teacher who is teaching somebody a certain task to be performed, as shown in the following figure:

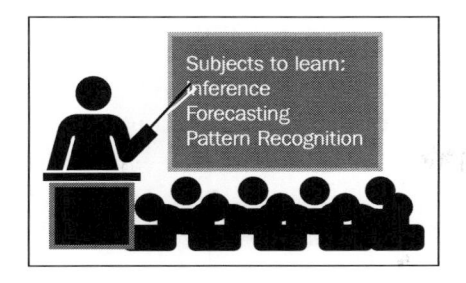

One particular feature of this learning paradigm is that there is a direct error reference, which is just the comparison between the target and the current actual result. The network parameters are fed into a cost function, which quantifies the mismatch between the desired and the actual outputs.

> A cost function is just a measurement to be minimized in an optimization problem. That means that one seeks to find the parameters that drive the cost function to the lowest possible value.
> The cost function will be covered in detail further in this chapter.

Supervised learning is very suitable for tasks that already provide a pattern, a goal to be reached. Some examples are as follows: classification of images, speech recognition, function approximation, and forecasting. Note that the neural network should be provided previous knowledge of both input-independent values (X) and the output classification-dependent values (Y). The presence of a dependent output value is a necessary condition for the learning to be supervised.

Unsupervised learning

As illustrated in the following figure, in unsupervised learning, we deal only with data without any labeling or classification; instead, our neural structure tries to draw inferences and extract knowledge by taking into account only the input data X.

This is analogous to self-learning, when someone learns by him/herself taking into account his/her experience and a set of supporting criteria. In unsupervised learning, we don't have a defined desired pattern to be applied on each observation, but the neural structure can produce one by itself without any supervising need.

> Here, the cost function plays an important role. It will strongly affect all the neural properties as well as the relation between the input data.

Examples of tasks that unsupervised learning can be applied to are as follows: clustering, data compression, statistical modeling, and language modeling. This learning paradigm will be covered in more detail in *Chapter 4, Self-Organizing Maps*.

Systematic structuring – learning algorithm

So far, we have theoretically defined the learning process and how it is carried out. However, in practice, we must dive a little bit deeper into the mathematical logic, the learning algorithm itself. A learning algorithm is a procedure that drives the learning process of neural networks and is strongly determined by the neural network architecture. From the mathematical point of view, one wishes to find the optimal weights W that can drive the cost function $C(X,[Y])$ to the lowest possible value.

In general, this process is carried out in the fashion presented in the following flowchart:

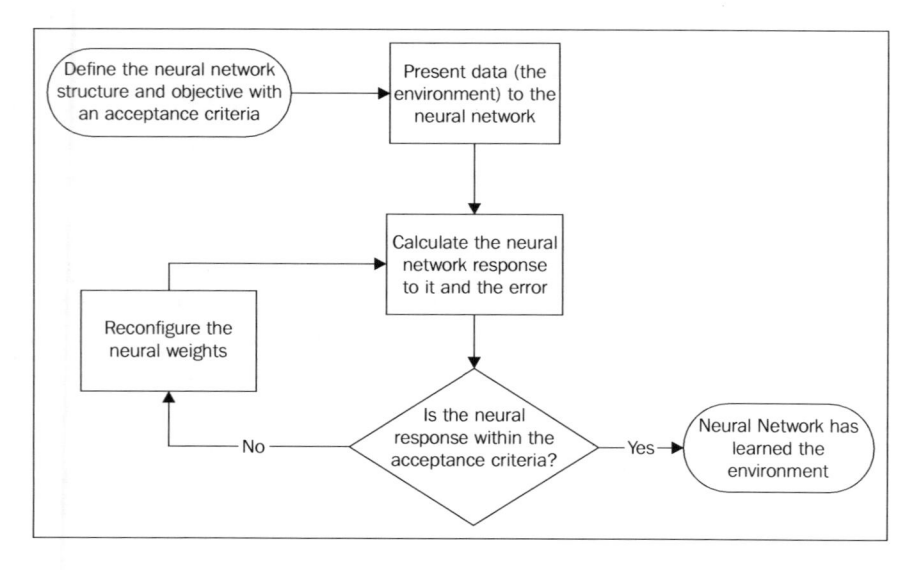

Just like any program that we wish to write, we should have defined our goal, so in here, we are talking about a neural network to learn some knowledge. We should present this knowledge (or environment) to the ANN and check its response, which naturally will make no sense. The network response is then compared to the expected result, and this is fed to a cost function C. This cost function will determine how the weights W can be updated. The learning algorithm then computes the ΔW term, which means the variation of the values of the weights to be added. The weights are updated as in the equation.

$$W(k+1) = W(k) + \Delta W$$

Where k refers to the kth iteration and $W(k)$ refers to the neural weights at the kth iteration, and subsequently, $k+1$ refers to the next iteration.

As the learning process is run, the neural network must give results closer and closer to the expectation, until finally, it reaches the acceptation criteria. The learning process is then considered to be finished.

Two stages of learning – training and testing

Well, we might ask now whether the neural network has already learned from the data, but how can we attest it has effectively learnt the data? The answer is just like in the exams that students are subjected to; we need to check the network response after training. But wait! Do you think it is likely that a teacher would put in an exam the same questions he/she has presented in the classes? There is no sense in evaluating somebody's learning with examples that are already known or a suspecting teacher would conclude the student might have memorized the content, instead of having learnt it.

Okay, let's now explain this part. What we are talking about here is testing. The learning process that we have covered is called training. After training a neural network, we should test it whether it has really learnt. For testing, we must present to the neural network another fraction of data from the same environment that it has learnt from. This is necessary because, just like the student, the neural network could respond properly with only the data points that it had been exposed to; this is called overtraining. To check whether the neural network has not passed on overtraining, we must check its response to other data points.

How Neural Networks Learn

The following figure illustrates the overtraining problem. Imagine that our network is designed to approximate some function *f(x)* whose definition is unknown. The neural network was fed with some data from that function and produced the following result shown in the figure on the left. However, when expanding to a wider domain, we note that the neural response does not follow the data.

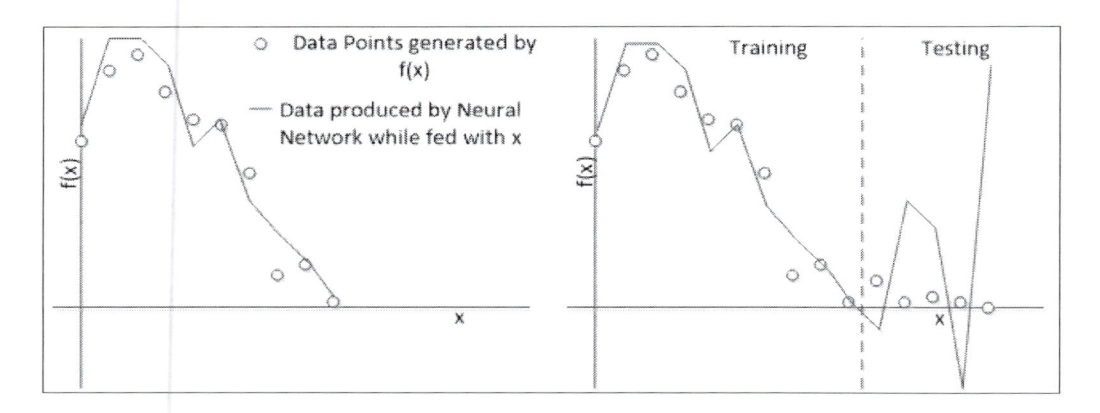

In this case, we see that the neural network failed to learn the whole environment (the function *f(x)*). This happens because of a number of reasons:

- The neural network didn't receive enough information from the environment
- The data from the environment is nondeterministic
- The training and testing datasets are poorly defined
- The neural network has learnt a lot from the training data and forgets about the testing data

In this book, we will cover this process to prevent this and other issues that may arise during training.

The details – learning parameters

The learning process may be, and is recommended to be, controlled. One important parameter is the learning rate, often represented by the Greek letter η. This parameter dictates how strongly the neural weights would vary in the weights' hyperspace. Let's imagine a simple neural network with two inputs and one neuron, therefore one output. So, we've got two weights *w1* and *w2*. Now suppose that we want to train this network and imagine whether we could evaluate the error for each pair of weights. Suppose that we found a surface like the one in the following figure:

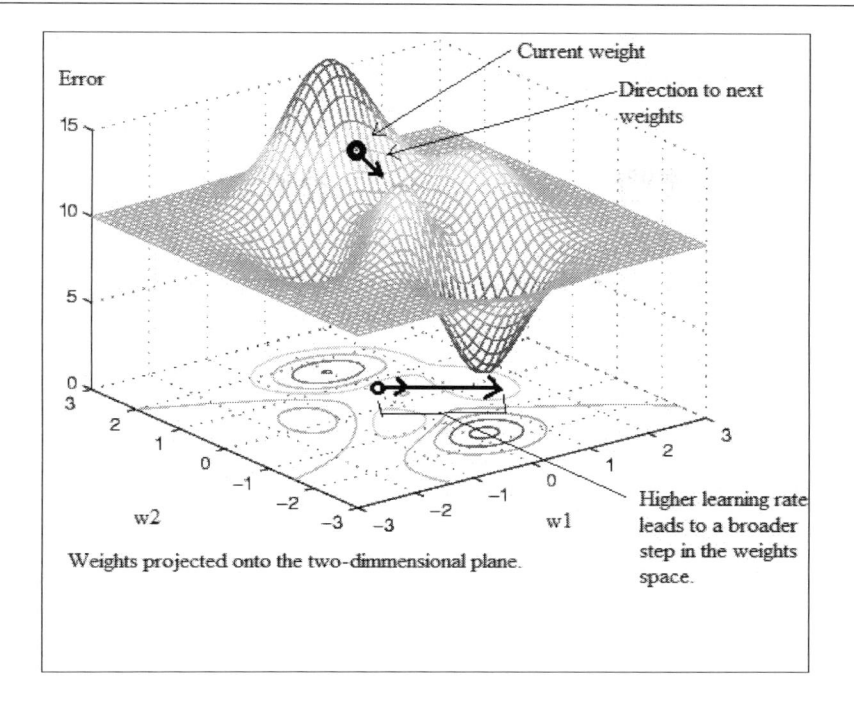

Weights projected onto the two-dimensional plane.

Higher learning rate leads to a broader step in the weights space.

The learning rate is responsible for regulating how far the weights are going to move on the surface. This may speed up the learning process but can also lead to a set of weights worse than the previous one.

Another important parameter is the condition for stopping. Usually, the training stops when the general mean error is reached, but there are cases in which the network fails to learn and there is little or no change in the weights' values. In the latter case, the maximum number of iterations, or epochs, is the condition for stopping.

Error measurement and cost function

This is extremely important for the success of the training in the supervised learning. Let's suppose that we present for the network a set of N records containing pairs of X and T variables, whereas X are the input-independent values and T are the target values dependent on X. Let's consider the neural network as a mathematical function $ANN()$ that produces Y on the output when being fed with the X values.

$$y = ANN(x)$$

For each x value given to the *ANN*, it will produce a y value that when compared to the t value gives an error e.

$$e = y - t$$

However, this is a mere individual error measurement per data point. We should take into account a general measurement, covering all the N data pairs because we want the network to learn all the data points and the same weights must be able to produce the data covering the entire training set. That's the role of the cost function C.

$$C(X,T,W) = \frac{1}{N} \sum_{i=1}^{n=N} [ANN(x[i]) - t[i]]^2$$

Where X are the inputs, T are the target outputs, W are the weights, $x[i]$ is the input at the ith instant, and $t[i]$ is the target output for the ith instant. The result of this function is an overall measurement of the error between the target outputs and the neural outputs, and this should be minimized.

Examples of learning algorithms

Let's now merge the theoretical content presented so far together into simple examples of learning algorithms. In this chapter, we are going to explore two neural architectures: **perceptron** and **adaline**. Both are very simple, containing only one layer.

Perceptron

The perceptrons learn by taking into account only the error between the target and the output, and the learning rate. The update rule is as follows:

$$\Delta w_i = \eta(t[k] - y[k])x_i[k]$$

Where w_i is the weight connecting the ith input to the neuron, $t[k]$ is the target output for the kth sample, $y[k]$ is the result of the neural network for the kth sample, $x_i[k]$ is the ith input for the kth sample, and η is the learning rate. It can be seen that this rule is very simplistic and does not consider the perceptron nonlinearities present in the activation function; it just goes in the opposite direction of the error in the naïve hope that this would take the network close to the objective.

Delta rule

A better algorithm based on the gradient descent method was developed to consider nonlinearity as well as its derivative. What this algorithm has in addition to the perceptron rule is the derivative of the activation function *g(h)*, with *h* being the weighted sum of all the neuron inputs before passing them to the activation function. So, the update rule is as follows:

$$\Delta w_i = \eta(t[k] - y[k])x_i[k]g'(h_i[k])$$

Coding of the neural network learning

Now, it is time to develop a neural network using OOP concepts and explain the related theory. The project presented in the previous chapter was adapted to implement the perceptron and adaline rules, as well as the Delta rule.

The `NeuralNet` class presented in the previous chapter has been updated to include the training dataset (input and target output), learning parameters, and activation function settings. The `InputLayer` function was also updated to include one method. We added to the project the `Adaline`, `Perceptron`, and `Training` classes. Details on the implementation of each class can be found in the codes. However, now, let's make the connection between the neural learning and the Java implementation of the Training class.

Learning parameter implementation

The `Training` class should be used for training neural networks. In this chapter, we are going to use this class to train `Perceptron` and `Adaline` classes. Also, the activation functions that are foreseen to be used in the neural networks in this chapter should be considered. So, now, let's define two enumeration sets that will handle these settings:

```
public enum TrainingTypesENUM {
   PERCEPTRON, ADALINE;
}

public enum ActivationFncENUM {
   STEP, LINEAR, SIGLOG, HYPERTAN;
}
```

In addition to these parameters, we need to define the condition for stopping, the error, the MSE error, and the number of epochs, as shown in the following code:

```
private int epochs;
private double error;
private double mse;
```

The learning rate has already been defined in the `NeuralNet` class and will be used here.

Finally, we need a method to update the weights of a given neuron. So, let's take a look at the `CalcNewWeight` method:

```
private double calcNewWeight(TrainingTypesENUM trainType,
    double inputWeightOld, NeuralNet n, double error,
    double trainSample, double netValue) {
  switch (trainType) {
  case PERCEPTRON:
    return inputWeightOld + n.getLearningRate() * error *
trainSample;
  case ADALINE:
    return inputWeightOld + n.getLearningRate() * error *
trainSample
        * derivativeActivationFnc(n.getActivationFnc(), netValue);
  default:
    throw new IllegalArgumentException(trainType
        + " does not exist in TrainingTypesENUM");
  }
}
```

We see in this method a switch clause that selects the update procedure according to the training type (`Adaline` or `Perceptron`). We can also see the `inputWeightOld` (the old weights), `n` (neural network under training), `error` (difference between target and neural output), `trainsample` (input to the weight), and `netValue` (weighted sum before processing by activation function) parameters. The learning rate is retrieved by calling the `getLearningRate()` function of the `NeuralNet` class.

One interesting detail is the derivative of the activation function that is called for the `Adaline` training type, which is the `Delta` rule. All the activation functions are implemented as methods inside the `Training` class, and their respective derivatives are implemented as well. The `derivativeActivationFnc` method helps to call the derivative corresponding to the activation function passed in the argument.

Learning procedure

Two special methods are implemented in the `Training` class: one for training the neural network and the other for training the neurons of some layer. Although this won't be necessary in this chapter, it is always good to have a code prepared for future examples or updates. Let's take a quick look at the implementation of the method train:

```java
public NeuralNet train(NeuralNet n) {

    ArrayList<Double> inputWeightIn = new ArrayList<Double>();

    int rows = n.getTrainSet().length;
    int cols = n.getTrainSet()[0].length;

    while (this.getEpochs() < n.getMaxEpochs()) {

      double estimatedOutput = 0.0;
      double realOutput = 0.0;

      for (int i = 0; i < rows; i++) {

        double netValue = 0.0;

        for (int j = 0; j < cols; j++) {
          inputWeightIn = n.getInputLayer().getListOfNeurons().get(j)
              .getListOfWeightIn();
          double inputWeight = inputWeightIn.get(0);
          netValue = netValue + inputWeight * n.getTrainSet()[i][j];
        }

        estimatedOutput = this.activationFnc(n.getActivationFnc(),
            netValue);
        realOutput = n.getRealOutputSet()[i];

        this.setError(realOutput - estimatedOutput);

        if (Math.abs(this.getError()) > n.getTargetError()) {
          // fix weights
          InputLayer inputLayer = new InputLayer();
          inputLayer.setListOfNeurons(this.teachNeuronsOfLayer(cols,
              i, n, netValue));
          n.setInputLayer(inputLayer);
        }
```

[29]

```
        }

        this.setMse(Math.pow(realOutput - estimatedOutput, 2.0));
        n.getListOfMSE().add(this.getMse());

        this.setEpochs(this.getEpochs() + 1);

    }

    n.setTrainingError(this.getError());

    return n;
}
```

This method receives a neural network in the parameter and produces another neural network with trained weights. Further, we see a `while` clause that loops while the number of epochs does not reach the maximum set out in the `Training` class. Inside this loop, there is a `for` clause that iterates over all the training samples that are presented to the network and so begins the process of calculating the neural output for the input in the current iteration.

When it gets the real output of the network, it compares it to the estimated output and calculates the error. This error is checked, and if it is higher than the minimum error, then it starts the update procedure by calling the `teachNeuronsOfLayer` method in the following line:

```
inputLayer.setListOfNeurons(this.teachNeuronsOfLayer(cols,
        i, n, netValue));
```

The implementation of this method is found in the codes attached with this chapter.

Then, this process is repeated iteratively until all the neural samples are passed to the neural network, and then, until the maximum number of epochs is reached.

Class definitions

The following table shows all the fields and methods for all the classes covered in this chapter:

Class name: Training	
Note: This class is abstract and cannot be instantiated.	
Attributes	
`private int epochs`	Integer number to store the training cycle, known as **epoch**

`private double error`	Real number to store the error between estimated output and real output
`private double mse`	Real number to store the mean square error (MSE)
Enums	
Note: enum helps to control different types	

`public enum TrainingTypesENUM {`
`    PERCEPTRON, ADALINE;`
`}`
	Enumeration to store types of training supported by project (`Perceptron` and `Adaline`)

`public enum ActivationFncENUM {`
`    STEP, LINEAR, SIGLOG,`
`HYPERTAN;`
`}`
	Enumeration to store types of activation functions supported by project (step, linear, sigmoid logistics, and hyperbolic tangent)

Methods	
`public NeuralNet train(NeuralNet n)`	Trains the neural network
	Parameters: `NeuralNet` object (neural net untrained)
	Returns: `NeuralNet` object (neural net trained)
`public ArrayList<Neuron> teachNeuronsOfLayer(int numberOfInputNeurons, int line, NeuralNet n, double netValue)`	Teaches neurons of the layer, calculating and changing its weights
	Parameters: Number of input neurons, samples line, `NeuralNet` object, neural net output
	Returns: `ArrayList` of objects by the `Neuron` class
`private double calcNewWeight(TrainingTypesENUM trainType, double inputWeightOld, NeuralNet n, double error, double trainSample, double netValue)`	Calculates the new weight of a neuron
	Parameters: Train type enum value, old input weight value, `NeuralNet` object, error value, training sample value, output net value
	Returns: Real number represents a new weight value
`public double activationFnc (ActivationFncENUM fnc, double value)`	Decides which activation function to use and calls the method of computing it
	Parameters: Activation function enum value, real number value
	Returns: Calculated value of the activation function

How Neural Networks Learn

`public double derivativeActivationFnc ( ActivationFncENUM fnc, double value)`	Decides which activation function to use and calls the method of computing the derivative value
	Parameters: Activation function enum value, real number value
	Returns: Calculated value of the derivative of the activation function
`private double fncStep (double v)`	Computes step function
	Parameters: Real number value
	Returns: Real number value
`private double fncLinear (double v)`	Computes linear function
	Parameters: Real number value
	Returns: Real number value
`private double fncSigLog (double v)`	Computes sigmoid logistics function
	Parameters: Real number value
	Returns: Real number value
`private double fncHyperTan (double v)`	Computes hyperbolic tangent function
	Parameters: Real number value
	Returns: Real number value
`private double derivativeFncLinear (double v)`	Computes the derivative of the linear function
	Parameters: Real number value
	Returns: Real number value
`private double derivativeFncSigLog (double v)`	Computes the derivative of the sigmoid logistics function
	Parameters: Real number value
	Returns: Real number value
`private double derivativeFncHyperTan (double v)`	Computes the derivative of the hyperbolic tangent function
	Parameters: Real number value
	Returns: Real number value
`public void printTrainedNetResult (NeuralNet trainedNet)`	Prints trained neural net and shows its results
	Parameters: `NeuralNet` object
	Returns: None
`public int getEpochs()`	Returns the number of epochs of the training
`public void setEpochs (int epochs)`	Sets the number of epochs of the training
`public double getError()`	Returns the training error (comparison between estimated and real values)

`public void setError (double error)`	Sets the training error
`public double getMse()`	Returns the MSE
`public void setMse (double mse)`	Sets the MSE
	**Class implementation with Java: file Training.java**

	**Class name: Perceptron**
	**Note**: This class inherits attributes and methods from the `Training` class
	**Attributes**
None	
	**Method**
`public NeuralNet train(NeuralNet n)`	Trains the neural network using the perceptron algorithm
	Parameters: `NeuralNet` object (neural net untrained)
	Returns: `NeuralNet` object (neural net trained via Perceptron)
	**Class implementation with Java: file Perceptron.java**

	**Class name: Adaline**
	**Note**: This class inherits attributes and methods from the `Training` class.
	**Attributes**
None	
	**Method**
`public NeuralNet train(NeuralNet n)`	Trains the neural network using the adaline algorithm
	Parameters: `NeuralNet` object (neural net untrained)
	Returns: `NeuralNet` object (neural net trained via adaline)
	**Class implementation with Java: file Adaline.java**

	**Class name: InputLayer**
	**Note**: This class already existed in the previous version and has been updated as follows:
	**Attributes**
None	
	**Method**
`public void setNumberOfNeuronsInLayer( int numberOfNeuronsInLayer)`	Sets the number of neurons in the input layer. It increased by one because of the bias

	**Class implementation with Java: file InputLayer.java**
	**Class name: NeuralNet**
	**Note**: This class already existed in the previous version and has been updated as follows:
	**Attributes**
`private double[][] trainSet`	Matrix to store the training set of input data
`private double[] realOutputSet`	Vector to store the training set of output data
`private int maxEpochs`	Integer number to store the maximum number of epochs that neural net will train
`private double learningRate`	Real number to store the learning rate
`private double targetError`	Real number to store the target error
`private double trainingError`	Real number to store the training error
`private TrainingTypesENUM trainType`	Enum value of the training type that will be used to train the neural net
`private ActivationFncENUM activationFnc`	Enum value of the activation function that will be used in training
`private ArrayList<Double> listOfMSE = new ArrayList<Double>()`	`ArrayList` of real numbers to store the MSE error of each epoch
	**Methods**
`public NeuralNet trainNet (NeuralNet n)`	Trains the neural network
	Parameters: `NeuralNet` object (neural net untrained)
	Returns: `NeuralNet` object (neural net trained)
`public void printTrainedNetResult ( NeuralNet n)`	Prints the trained neural net and shows its results
	Parameters: `NeuralNet` object
	Returns: None
`public double[][] getTrainSet()`	Returns the matrix of the training set of input data
`public void setTrainSet(double[][] trainSet)`	Sets the matrix of the training set of input data
`public double[] getRealOutputSet()`	Returns the vector training set of output data

`public void setRealOutputSet(double[] realOutputSet)`	Sets the vector training set of output data
`public int getMaxEpochs()`	Returns the maximum number of epochs that the neural net will train
`public void setMaxEpochs(int maxEpochs)`	Sets the maximum number of epochs that the neural net will train
`public double getTargetError()`	Returns the target error
`public void setTargetError(double targetError)`	Sets the target error
`public double getLearningRate()`	Returns the learning rate used in training
`public void setLearningRate(double learningRate)`	Sets the learning rate used in training
`public double getTrainingError()`	Returns the training error
`public void setTrainingError(double trainingError)`	Sets the training error
`public ActivationFncENUM getActivationFnc()`	Returns the enum value of the activation function that will be used in training
`public void setActivationFnc(ActivationFncENUM activationFnc)`	Sets the enum value of the activation function that will be used in training
`public TrainingTypesENUM getTrainType()`	Returns the enum value of the training type that will be used to train the neural net
`public void setTrainType(TrainingTypesENUM trainType)`	Sets the enum value of the training type that will be used to train the neural net
`public ArrayList<Double> getListOfMSE()`	Returns the list of real numbers that stores the MSE error of each epoch
`public void setListOfMSE(ArrayList<Double> listOfMSE)`	Sets the list of real numbers that stores the MSE error of each epoch
Class implementation with Java: file NeuralNet.java	

How Neural Networks Learn

The updated class diagram is shown in the following figure. Attributes and methods already explained in the previous chapter were omitted. Further, configuration methods of new attributes (setters and getters) were also omitted.

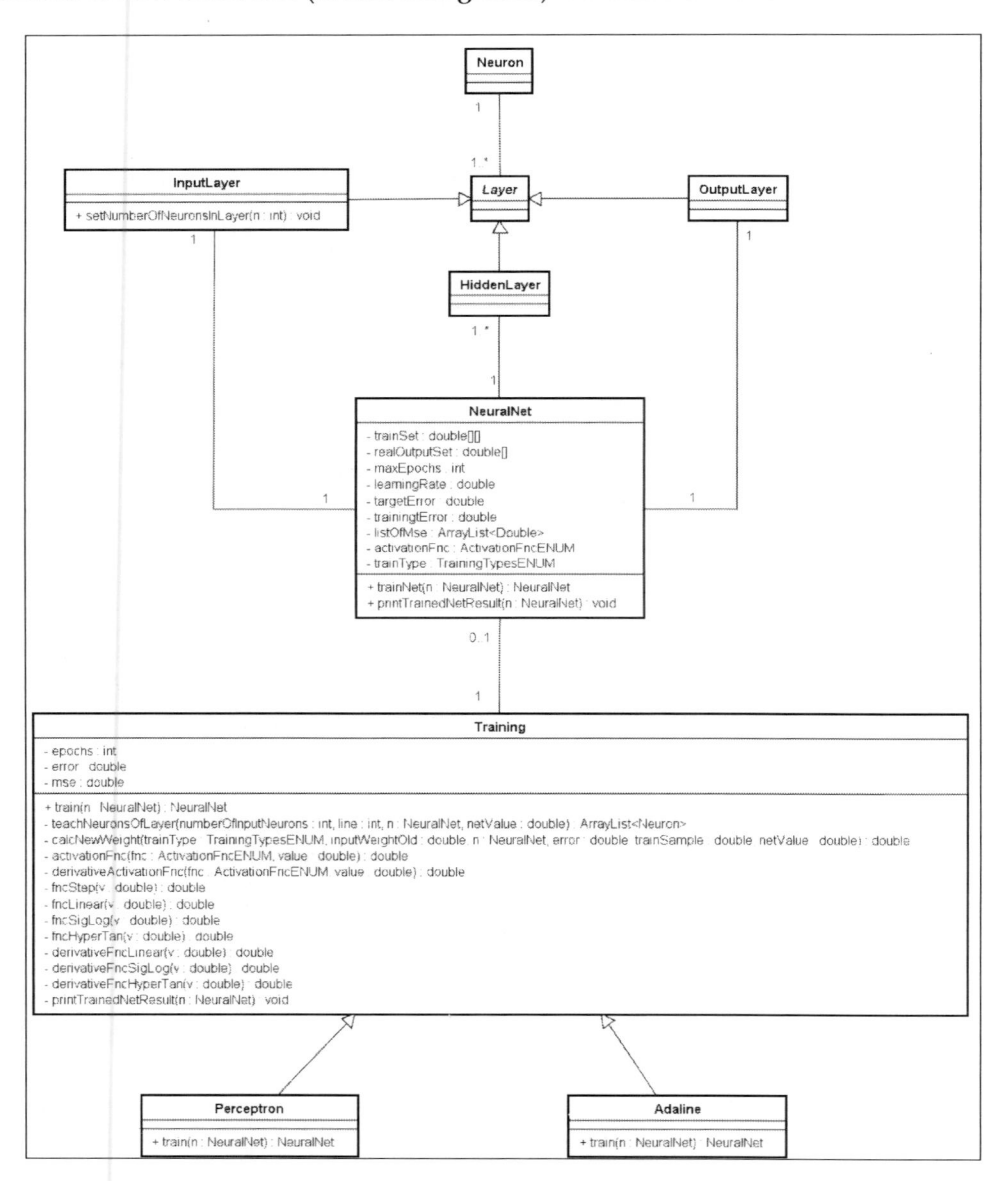

[36]

Two practical examples

Now, let's take a look at two examples of applications of these simple neural network architectures.

Perceptron (warning system)

To facilitate understanding about perceptron, let's consider a basic warning system. It is based in **AND** logic. There are two sensors, and the rules of warning are as follows:

- If both or one of them is disabled, the warning is trigged
- If both are enabled, the warning is not trigged

The following figure shows the basic warning system:

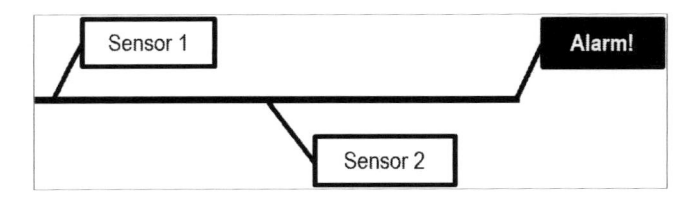

To encode the problem, inputs are represented as follows. **0** means disabled, and **1** means enabled. Output is represented as follows. **0** means enabled, and **1** means disabled. The following table summarizes this:

Sample	Sensor 1	Sensor 2	Alarm
1	0	0	0
2	0	1	0
3	1	0	0
4	1	1	1

How Neural Networks Learn

The *Basic warning system* figure illustrates how neurons and layers must be organized to solve this problem. It is the architecture of the neural net:

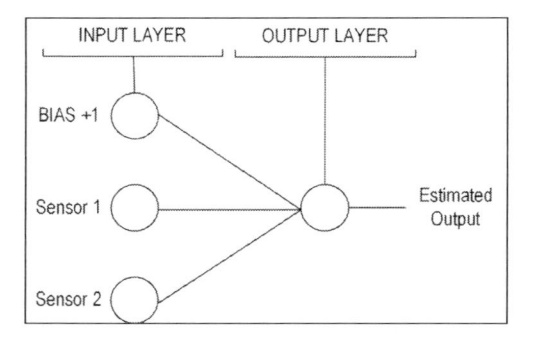

Now, let's use the class previously cited. Two methods have been created in the test class: `testPerceptron()` and `testAdaline()`. Let's analyze the first one:

```java
private void testPerceptron() {
   NeuralNet testNet = new NeuralNet();

   testNet = testNet.initNet(2, 0, 0, 1);

   System.out.println("---------PERCEPTRON INIT NET---------");

   testNet.printNet(testNet);

   NeuralNet trainedNet = new NeuralNet();

   // first column has BIAS
   testNet.setTrainSet(new double[][] { { 1.0, 0.0, 0.0 },
      { 1.0, 0.0, 1.0 }, { 1.0, 1.0, 0.0 }, { 1.0, 1.0, 1.0 } });
   testNet.setRealOutputSet(new double[] { 0.0, 0.0, 0.0, 1.0 });
   testNet.setMaxEpochs(10);
   testNet.setTargetError(0.002);
   testNet.setLearningRate(1.0);
   testNet.setTrainType(TrainingTypesENUM.PERCEPTRON);
   testNet.setActivationFnc(ActivationFncENUM.STEP);

   trainedNet = testNet.trainNet(testNet);

   System.out.println();
   System.out.println("---------PERCEPTRON TRAINED NET---------");
```

```
        testNet.printNet(trainedNet);

        System.out.println();
        System.out.println("---------PERCEPTRON PRINT RESULT---------");

        testNet.printTrainedNetResult(trainedNet);

    }
```

First, an object of the `NeuralNet` class is created. After that, this object is used to initialize the neural net with two neurons in the input layer, none in the hidden layer, and one neuron in the output layer. Then, a message and the untrained neural net are shown on the screen. Another object of the `NeuralNet` class is created and represents the trained neural net. After that, the `testNet` object is set with the training input dataset (the first column has bias values), training output dataset, maximum number of epochs, target error, learning rate, training type (perceptron), and activation function (step). Then, the `trainNet` method is called to train the neural net. To finalize, the perceptron-trained net results are printed. These results are shown in the following screenshot:

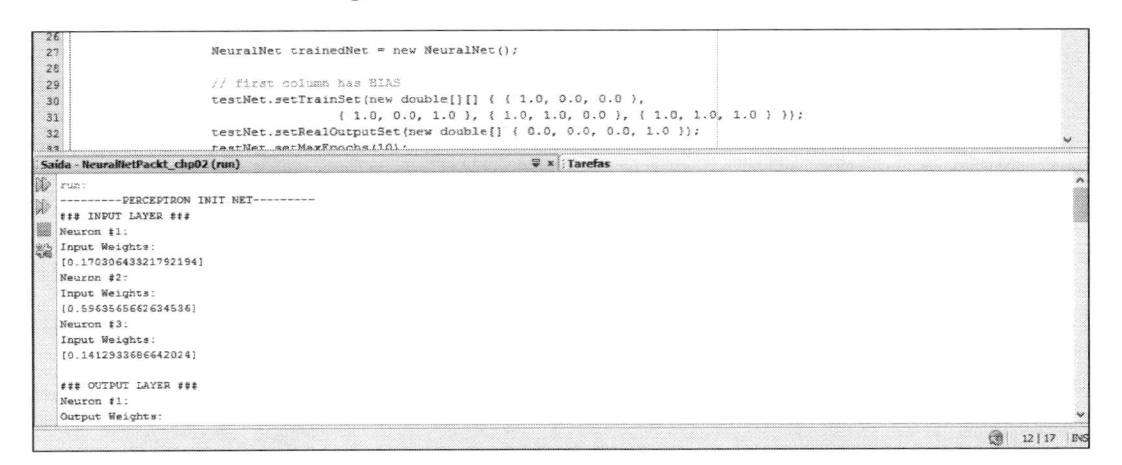

```
---------PERCEPTRON INIT NET---------
### INPUT LAYER ###
Neuron #1:
Input Weights:
[0.179227246819473]
Neuron #2:
Input Weights:
[0.927776315380873]
Neuron #3:
Input Weights:
```

```
[0.7639255282026901]

### OUTPUT LAYER ###
Neuron #1:
Output Weights:
[0.7352957201253741]

---------PERCEPTRON TRAINED NET---------
### INPUT LAYER ###
Neuron #1:
Input Weights:
[-2.820772753180527]
Neuron #2:
Input Weights:
[1.9277763153808731]
Neuron #3:
Input Weights:
[1.76392552820269]

### OUTPUT LAYER ###
Neuron #1:
Output Weights:
[0.7352957201253741]

---------PERCEPTRON PRINT RESULT---------
1.0  0.0  0.0    NET OUTPUT: 0.0    REAL OUTPUT: 0.0    ERROR: 0.0
1.0  0.0  1.0    NET OUTPUT: 0.0    REAL OUTPUT: 0.0    ERROR: 0.0
1.0  1.0  0.0    NET OUTPUT: 0.0    REAL OUTPUT: 0.0    ERROR: 0.0
1.0  1.0  1.0    NET OUTPUT: 1.0    REAL OUTPUT: 1.0    ERROR: 0.0
```

According to the results, it is possible to check whether the weights changed and conclude that the neural net learned how to classify when an alarm should be enabled or not. Reminder: The acquired knowledge belongs inside the weights `[-2.820772753180527]`, `[1.9277763153808731]`, and `[1.76392552820269]`. Besides, as the neurons are initialized with pseudo-random values, each time this code is run, the results change.

ADALINE (traffic forecast)

To demonstrate the adaline algorithm, let us imagine that a small part of a city has an avenue and three streets lead to this avenue. In this avenue, there are many accidents and heavy traffic. Assume that the government traffic department has decided to develop a forecasting and warning system. This system aims to anticipate traffic jams, warning drivers and taking the necessary measures to reduce the incurred losses, as demonstrated in the following figure:

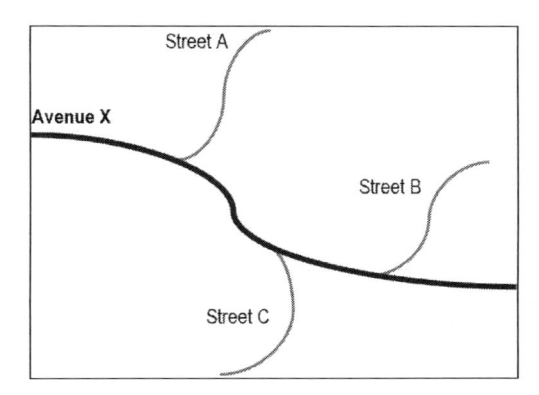

To develop the system, information is collected for every street and avenue for a week: the number of cars that travel on these routes per minute, as shown in the following table:

Sample	Street A (cars/minute)	Street B (cars/minute)	Street C (cars/minute)	Avenue (cars/minute)
1	0.98	0.94	0.95	0.80
2	0.60	0.60	0.85	0.59
3	0.35	0.15	0.15	0.23
4	0.25	0.30	0.98	0.45
5	0.75	0.85	0.91	0.74
6	0.43	0.57	0.87	0.63
7	0.05	0.06	0.01	0.10

How Neural Networks Learn

Then, the architecture of a neural net to solve this problem is designed as shown in the following figure:

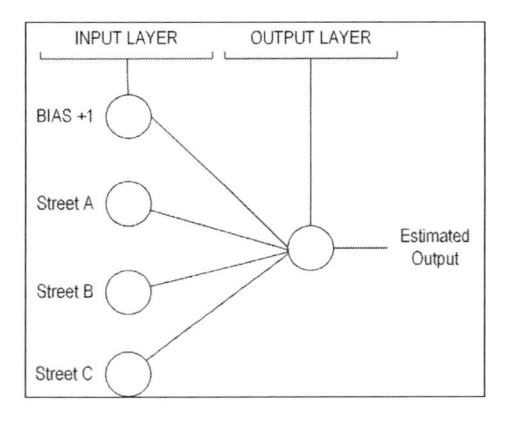

Figure: Neural network architecture with INPUT LAYER (BIAS +1, Street A, Street B, Street C) connected to OUTPUT LAYER producing Estimated Output.

Next, let's analyze the second test method named `testAdaline()`. It is as follows:

```
private void testAdaline() {

    NeuralNet testNet = new NeuralNet();

    testNet = testNet.initNet(3, 0, 0, 1);

    System.out.println("---------ADALINE INIT NET---------");

    testNet.printNet(testNet);

    NeuralNet trainedNet = new NeuralNet();

    // first column has BIAS

    testNet.setTrainSet(new double[][] { { 1.0, 0.98, 0.94, 0.95 },
        { 1.0, 0.60, 0.60, 0.85 }, { 1.0, 0.35, 0.15, 0.15 },
        { 1.0, 0.25, 0.30, 0.98 }, { 1.0, 0.75, 0.85, 0.91 },
        { 1.0, 0.43, 0.57, 0.87 }, { 1.0, 0.05, 0.06, 0.01 } });
    testNet.setRealOutputSet(new double[] { 0.80, 0.59, 0.23, 0.45,
 0.74, 0.63, 0.10 });
    testNet.setMaxEpochs(10);
    testNet.setTargetError(0.0001);
    testNet.setLearningRate(0.5);
    testNet.setTrainType(TrainingTypesENUM.ADALINE);
    testNet.setActivationFnc(ActivationFncENUM.LINEAR);

    trainedNet = new NeuralNet();
    trainedNet = testNet.trainNet(testNet);

    System.out.println();
```

```
        System.out.println("---------ADALINE TRAINED NET---------");

        testNet.printNet(trainedNet);

        System.out.println();
        System.out.println("---------ADALINE PRINT RESULT---------");

        testNet.printTrainedNetResult(trainedNet);

        System.out.println();
        System.out.println("---------ADALINE MSE BY EPOCH---------");
        System.out.println( Arrays.deepToString( trainedNet.getListOfMSE().
    toArray() ).replace(" ", "\n") );

    }
```

The adaline test logic is very similar to perceptron's. The parameters that differ are as follows. Three neurons in the input layer, training dataset, output dataset, training type sets such as adaline, and activation function sets such as Linear. To finalize, adaline-trained net results and the adaline MSE list are printed. These results are shown in the following figure:

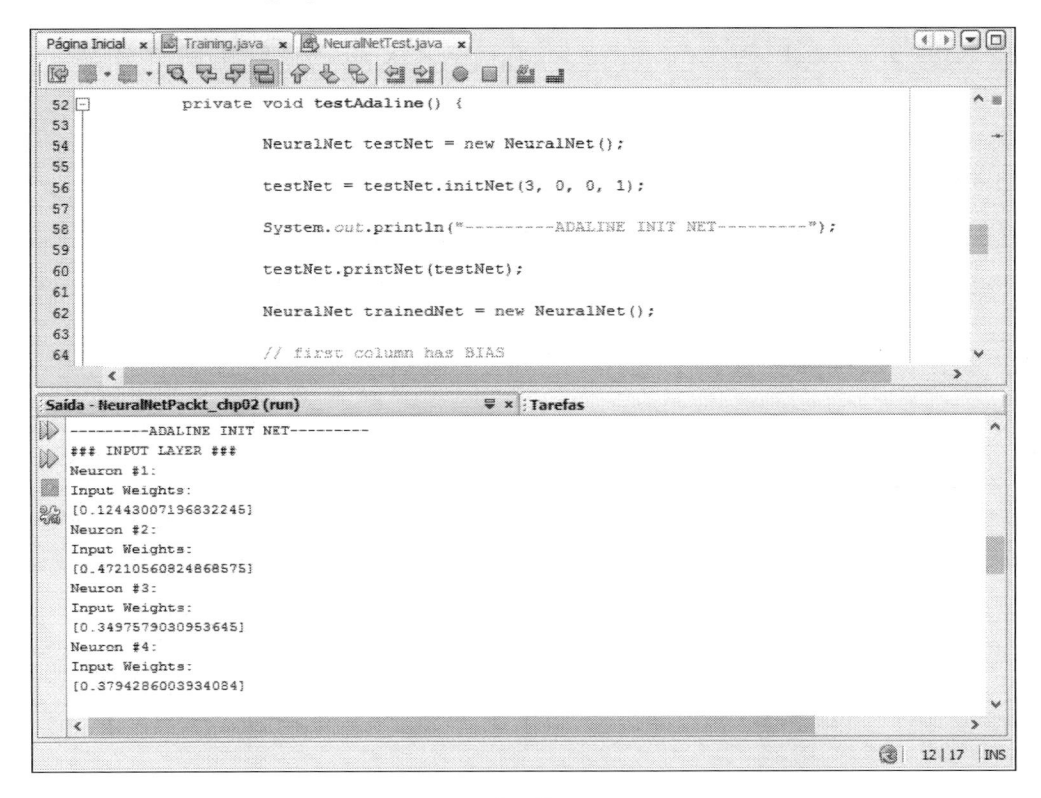

[43]

How Neural Networks Learn

```
The complete results are displayed via following code:
---------ADALINE INIT NET---------
### INPUT LAYER ###
Neuron #1:
Input Weights:
[0.39748670958336774]
Neuron #2:
Input Weights:
[0.0018141925587737973]
Neuron #3:
Input Weights:
[0.3705005221910509]
Neuron #4:
Input Weights:
[0.20624007274978795]

### OUTPUT LAYER ###
Neuron #1:
Output Weights:
[0.16125863508860827]

---------ADALINE TRAINED NET---------
### INPUT LAYER ###
Neuron #1:
Input Weights:
[0.08239521813153253]
Neuron #2:
Input Weights:
[0.08060471820877586]
Neuron #3:
Input Weights:
[0.4793193652720801]
Neuron #4:
Input Weights:
[0.259894055603035]

### OUTPUT LAYER ###
Neuron #1:
Output Weights:
[0.16125863508860827]

---------ADALINE PRINT RESULT---------
1.0    0.98   0.94   0.95   NET OUTPUT: 0.85884   REAL OUTPUT: 0.8
ERROR: 0.05884739815477136
1.0    0.6    0.6    0.85   NET OUTPUT: 0.63925   REAL OUTPUT: 0.59
ERROR: 0.04925961548262592
1.0    0.35   0.15   0.15   NET OUTPUT: 0.22148   REAL OUTPUT: 0.23 ERROR:
```

[44]

```
-0.008511117364128656
1.0    0.25   0.3    0.98   NET OUTPUT: 0.50103   REAL OUTPUT: 0.45
ERROR: 0.05103838175632486
1.0    0.75   0.85   0.91   NET OUTPUT: 0.78677   REAL OUTPUT: 0.74
ERROR: 0.046773807868144446
1.0    0.43   0.57   0.87   NET OUTPUT: 0.61637   REAL OUTPUT: 0.63
ERROR: -0.013624886458967755
1.0    0.05   0.06   0.01   NET OUTPUT: 0.11778   REAL OUTPUT: 0.1   ERROR:
0.017783556514326462

---------ADALINE MSE BY EPOCH---------
[0.04647154331286084,
0.018478851884998992,
0.008340477769290564,
0.004405551259806042,
0.0027480838150394362,
0.0019914963464723553,
0.0016222114177244264,
0.00143318844904685,
0.0013337070214879325,
0.001280852868781586]
```

One more time, according to the abovementioned results, it is possible to conclude that the neural net learned to predict traffic jams in a specific area. This can be proven by changing weights and by the MSE list. Look at the graphic plotted using the MSE data in the following figure. It is easy to note that the MSE decreases as the number of epochs increases.

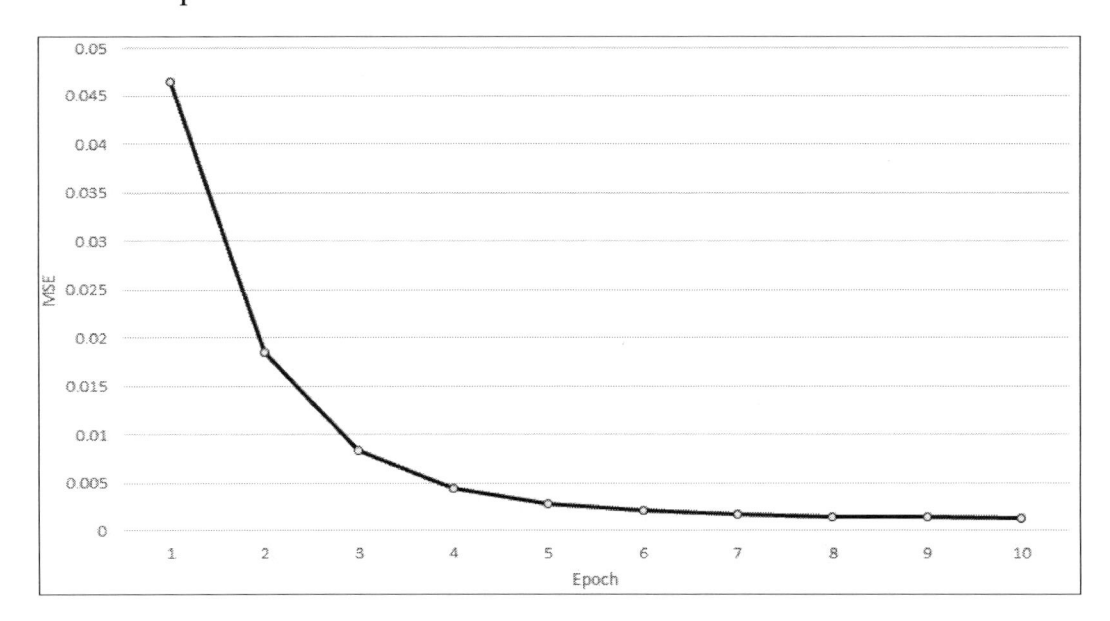

Summary

This chapter presented the reader with the entire learning process of neural networks. We presented the very basic foundations of learning, inspired by human learning itself. To illustrate this process in practice, we have implemented two learning algorithms in Java and applied them in two examples. With this, the reader can gain a basic but useful understanding of how neural networks learn and even how one can systematically describe the learning process. This will be the foundation for the next chapter, which will present more complex examples.

3
Handling Perceptrons

In this chapter, we are going to explore one of the most popular and basic types of neural network architecture: the perceptrons. This chapter also presents their extended generalized version, the so-called multilayer perceptrons, as well as their features, learning algorithms, and parameters. Also, the reader will learn how to implement them in Java and how to use them for solving some basic problems:

- Perceptrons
    - Applications and limitations
- Multilayer perceptrons
    - Classification
    - Regression
- Backpropagation algorithm
- Java implementation
- Practical problems

Studying the perceptron neural network

Perceptron is the most simple neural network architecture. Projected by Frank Rosenblatt in 1957, it has just one layer of neurons, receiving a set of inputs and producing a set of outputs. This was one of the first representations of neural networks to gain attention, particularly because of its simplicity. The structure of a single neuron is shown as follows:

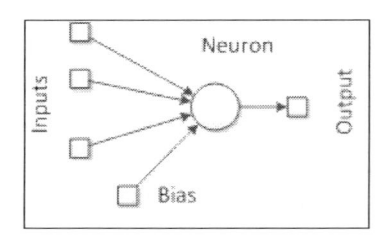

Applications and limitations of perceptrons

However, scientists did not take long to conclude that a perceptron neural network could only be applied to simple tasks because of its simplicity. At that time, neural networks were being used for simple classification problems, but perceptrons usually failed when faced with more complex datasets. Let's review the first example of *Chapter 2*, *How Neural Networks Learn*, (AND) to better understand this issue.

Linear separation

The example consists of an AND function that takes two inputs x1 and x2. This function can be plotted in a two-dimensional chart as follows:

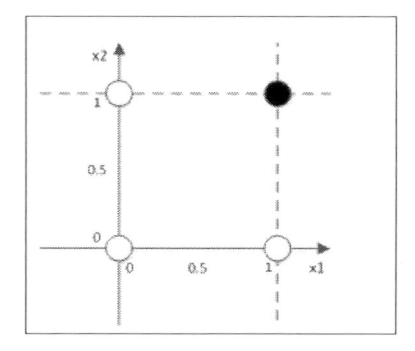

Now, let's examine how the neural network evolves in the training by using the perceptron rule, considering a pair of two weights **w1** and **w2**, initially **0.5**, and a bias value of **0.5**. Assume that the learning rate η equals **0.2**.

Epoch	x1	x2	w1	w2	b	y	t	E	Δw1	Δw2	Δb
1	0	0	0,5	0,5	0,5	0,5	0	-0,5	0	0	-0,1
1	0	1	0,5	0,5	0,4	0,9	0	-0,9	0	-0,18	-0,18
1	1	0	0,5	0,32	0,22	0,72	0	-0,72	-0,144	0	-0,144
1	1	1	0,356	0,32	0,076	0,752	1	0,248	0,0496	0,0496	0,0496
2	0	0	0,406	0,370	0,126	0,126	0	-0,126	0,000	0,000	-0,025
2	0	1	0,406	0,370	0,100	0,470	0	-0,470	0,000	-0,094	-0,094
2	1	0	0,406	0,276	0,006	0,412	0	-0,412	-0,082	0,000	-0,082
2	1	1	0,323	0,276	-0,076	0,523	1	0,477	0,095	0,095	0,095
...	...										
89	0	0	0,625	0,562	-0,312	-0,312	0	0,312	0	0	0,062
89	0	1	0,625	0,562	-0,25	0,313	0	-0,313	0	-0,063	-0,063
89	1	0	0,625	0,500	-0,312	0,313	0	-0,313	-0,063	0	-0,063
89	1	1	0,562	0,500	-0,375	0,687	1	0,313	0,063	0,063	0,063

After **89** epochs, we find the network to produce values close to the desired output. Since in this example, the outputs are binary (zero or one), we can assume that any value produced by the network that is below **0.5** is considered to be **0** and any value above **0.5** is considered to be **1**. So, we can draw a function $Y = x_1 w_1 + x_2 w_2 + b = 0.5$, with the final weights and bias found by the learning algorithm $w1 = 0.562$, $w2 = 0.5$, and $b = -0.375$, defining the linear boundary as shown in the following chart:

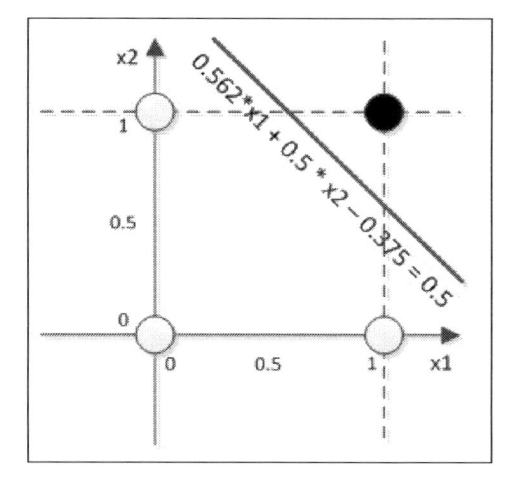

This boundary is a definition of all classifications given by the network. You can see that the boundary is linear, given that the function is linear. Thus, the perceptron network is really suitable for problems whose patterns are linearly separable.

Classical XOR case

Let's analyze the XOR case, whose chart can be seen in the following figure:

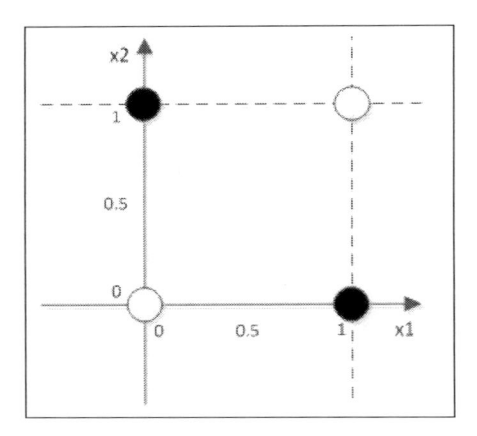

We see that in two dimensions, it is impossible to draw a line to separate the two patterns. What would happen if we tried to train a single-layer perceptron to learn this function? Suppose that we tried; let's see what happened through the following table:

Epoch	x1	x2	w1	w2	b	y	t	E	Δw1	Δw2	Δb
1	0	0	0,5	0,5	0,5	0,5	0	-0,5	0	0	-0,1
1	0	1	0,5	0,5	0,4	0,9	1	0,1	0	0,02	0,02
1	1	0	0,5	0,52	0,42	0,92	1	0,08	0,016	0	0,016
1	1	1	0,516	0,52	0,436	1,472	0	-1,472	-0,294	-0,294	-0,294
2	0	0	0,222	0,226	0,142	0,142	0	-0,142	0,000	0,000	-0,028
2	0	1	0,222	0,226	0,113	0,339	1	0,661	0,000	0,132	0,132
2	1	0	0,222	0,358	0,246	0,467	1	0,533	0,107	0,000	0,107
2	1	1	0,328	0,358	0,352	1,038	0	-1,038	-0,208	-0,208	-0,208
...	...										
127	0	0	-0,250	-0,125	0,625	0,625	0	-0,625	0,000	0,000	-0,125
127	0	1	-0,250	-0,125	0,500	0,375	1	0,625	0,000	0,125	0,125
127	1	0	-0,250	0,000	0,625	0,375	1	0,625	0,125	0,000	0,125
127	1	1	-0,125	0,000	0,750	0,625	0	-0,625	-0,125	-0,125	-0,125

The perceptron just could not find any pair of weights that would drive the error below **0.625**. This can be explained mathematically as we have already perceived from the chart that this function cannot be linearly separable in two dimensions. So, what if we add another dimension? Let's see the previous XOR chart in three dimensions:

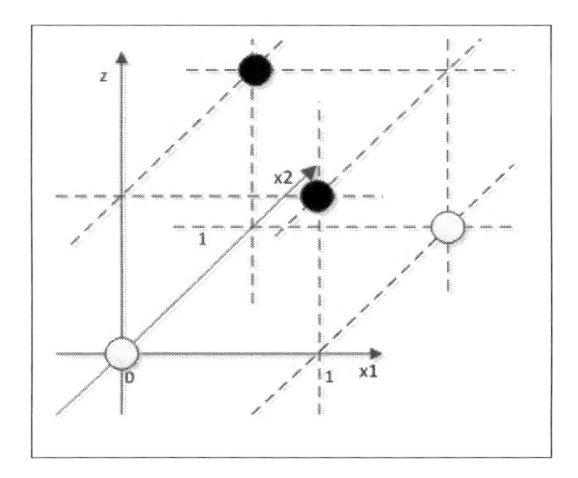

In three dimensions, it is possible to draw a plane that would separate the patterns, provided that this additional dimension could properly transform the input data. Okay, but now, there is an additional problem: How can we derive this additional dimension since we have only two input variables? One obvious but "workaround" answer would be adding a third variable as a derivation from the two original ones. With this third variable a (derivation), our neural network would probably get the following shape:

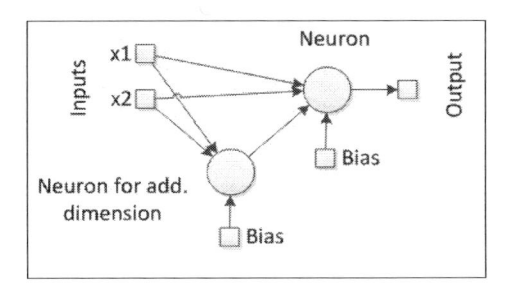

Okay, now, the perceptron has three inputs, one of them being a composition of the other two. This also leads to a new question: How should this composition be processed? We can see that this component can act as a neuron, thereby giving the neural network a nested architecture. If so, there would be another new question: How would the weights of this new neuron be trained, since the error is on the output neuron?

Popular multilayer perceptrons (MLPs)

As we can see, one simple example, in which the patterns are not linearly separable, has led us to more and more issues related to the use of the perceptron architecture. This need has led to the application of multilayer perceptrons. In *Chapter 1*, *Getting Started with Neural Networks*, we dealt with the fact that the natural neural network is structured in layers as well, and each layer captures pieces of information from a specific environment. In artificial neural networks, layers of neurons act in this way, by extracting and abstracting information from the data, transforming it into another dimension or shape.

In the XOR example, we found the solution to be the addition of the third component that would make a linear separation possible. However, there remained a few questions regarding how that third component would be computed. Now, let's consider the same solution as a two-layer perceptron, shown as follows:

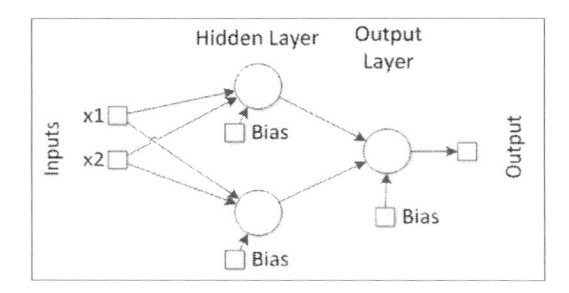

Now, we have three neurons instead of just one, but in the output, the information transferred by the previous layer is transformed into another dimension or shape, whereby it would be theoretically possible to establish a linear boundary on the data points. However, the question of finding the weights for the first layer remains unanswered, or can we apply the same training rule to neurons other than the output? We are going to deal with this issue in the generalized delta rule section.

MLP properties

Multilayer perceptrons can have any number of layers and any number of neurons in each layer. The activation functions may be different on any layer. An MLP network is usually composed of at least two layers, one for the output and the other for the "hidden" layer.

> There are also some references that consider the input layer as the nodes that collect input data. Therefore, for these cases, the MLP is considered to have at least three layers. For the purposes of this book, let's consider the input layer as a special type of layer that has no weights, and as the effective layers, that is, those enabled to be trained, we'll consider the hidden and output layers.

A hidden layer is so-called because it actually "hides" its outputs from the external world. Hidden layers can be connected in series in any number, thus forming a deep neural network. However, the more layers a neural network has, the slower both the training and running would be, and according to mathematical foundations, a neural network with one or two hidden layers at most can learn as well as deep neural networks with dozens of hidden layers.

> It is recommended that the activation functions be nonlinear in the hidden layers, particularly if in the output layer the activation function is linear. According to linear algebra, having a linear activation function in all layers is equivalent to having only one output layer, provided that the additional variables introduced by the layers would be mere linear combinations of the previous ones or the inputs. Usually, activation functions such as hyperbolic tangent or sigmoid are used because they are derivable.

MLP weights

In an MLP feedforward network, a certain neuron i receives data from a neuron j of the previous layer and forwards its output to a neuron k of the next layer, as can be seen in the following schema:

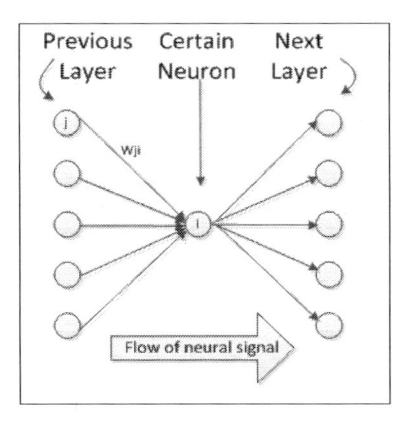

MLPs in theory may be partially or fully connected. Partially means that not all neurons from one layer are connected to each neuron of the next layer, and fully connected means that all neurons from one layer are connected to all neurons of the next layer. The following figure shows both the partially and fully connected layers:

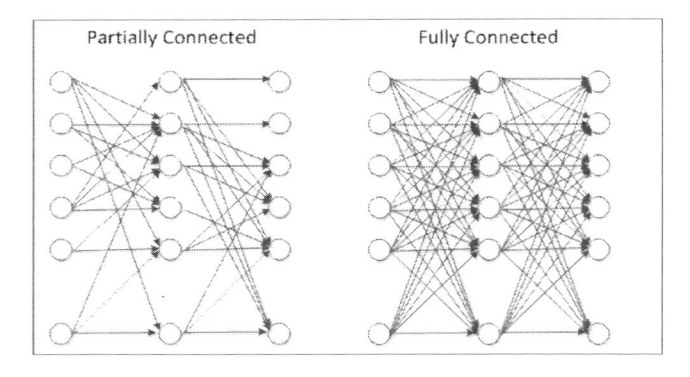

For mathematical simplicity, let's work only on fully connected MLPs, which can be described mathematically by the equation:

$$y_o = f_o\left(\sum_{i=1}^{n_{h_l}} w_i f_i\left(\sum_{j=1}^{n_{h_{l-1}}} w_{ij} f_j\left(\sum_{k=1}^{n_{h_{l-2}}} w_{jk} f_k(\cdots) + b_j\right) + b_i\right) + b_o\right)$$

Where y_o is the network output (if we have multiple outputs, we can replace y_0 by Y, representing a vector), f_o is the activation function of the output, l is the number of hidden layers, n_{hi} is the number of neurons in the hidden layer i, w_i is the weight connecting the ith neuron of the last hidden layer to the output, f_i is the activation function of the neuron i, and b_i is the bias of the neuron i. It can be seen that this equation gets larger, as the number of layers increase. In the last summing operation, there will be the inputs x_i.

Recurrent MLP

Neural networks can be both feedforward and feedback (recurrent). So, it is possible that some neurons or layers forward signals to a previous layer. This behavior allows the neural network to maintain state on some data sequence, and this feature is particularly exploited when dealing with time series or handwriting recognition. For training purposes, a recurrent MLP network can have feedback connections only in the output layer. In order to give it a more fully recurrent nature, one can connect multiple recurrent MLPs in cascade.

Although recurrent networks are very suitable for some problems, they are usually harder to train, and eventually, the computer may run out of memory while executing them. In addition, there are recurrent network architectures better than MLPs such as the Elman, Hopfield, echo state, and bi-directional RNN. However, we are not going to dive deep into these architectures, because this book focuses on the simplest applications for those who have minimal experience in programming. However, a good reference is the book of Haykin [2008], whose specifications can be found at the end of this book on recurrent networks for those who are interested in it.

MLP structure in an OOP paradigm

Bringing these concepts into the OOP point of view, we can review the classes already designed so far already designed, resulting in the following diagram:

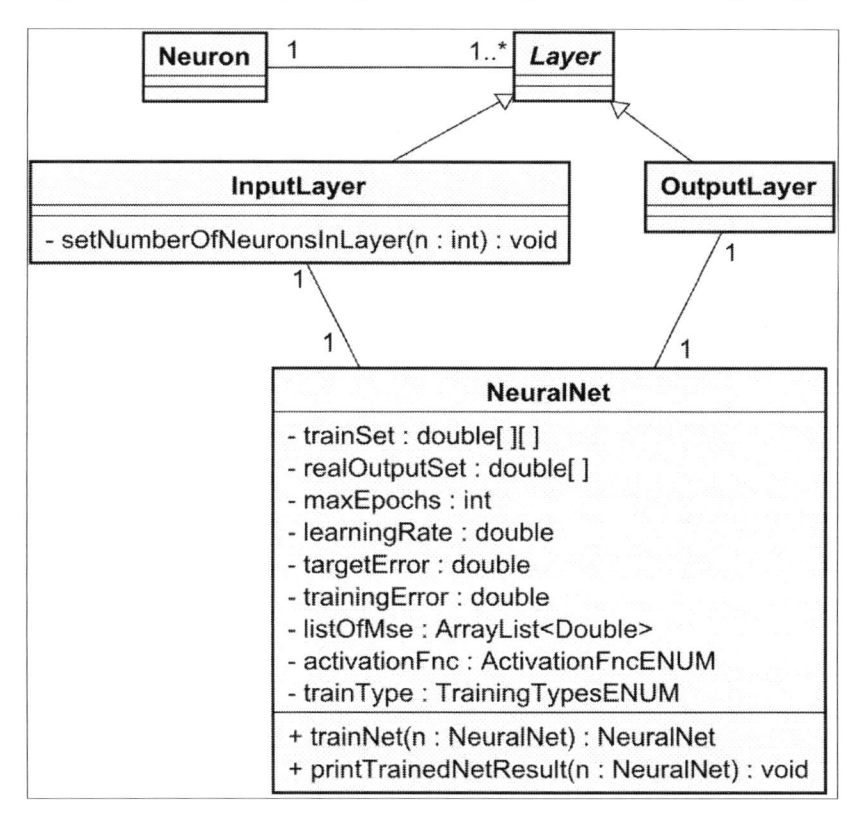

```
          Neuron  1            1..*  Layer
                                       △
                                       |
           ┌───────────────────────────┴──────────┐
      InputLayer                              OutputLayer
   - setNumberOfNeuronsInLayer(n : int) : void
                      1                           1
                      |                           |
                      1                           1
                           NeuralNet
                  - trainSet : double[ ][ ]
                  - realOutputSet : double[ ]
                  - maxEpochs : int
                  - learningRate : double
                  - targetError : double
                  - trainingError : double
                  - listOfMse : ArrayList<Double>
                  - activationFnc : ActivationFncENUM
                  - trainType : TrainingTypesENUM
                  + trainNet(n : NeuralNet) : NeuralNet
                  + printTrainedNetResult(n : NeuralNet) : void
```

Handling Perceptrons

One can see that the neural network structure is hierarchical. A neural network is composed of layers that are composed of neurons. In the MLP architecture, there are three types of layers: input, hidden, and output. So, suppose that in Java, we would like to define a neural network consisting of three inputs, one output, and one hidden layer containing five neurons. The resulting code would be as follows:

```
NeuralNet n = NeuralNet();
InputLayer input = new InputLayer();
input.setNumberOfNeuronsInLayer(3);
HiddenLayer hidden = new HiddenLayer();
hidden.setNumberOfNeuronsInLayer(5);
OutputLayer output = new OutputLayer();
output.setNumberOfNeuronsInLayer(1);
////...
n.setInputLayer(input);
n.setHiddenLayer(hidden);
n.setOutputLayer(output);
```

Interesting MLP applications

The two broader classes of problems that MLPs are suitable for are as follows: **classification** and **regression**. Classification means that given a dataset composed of records, each record should be labeled or classified. Regression means that given a set of inputs and outputs, one must find a function that maps the inputs to the outputs. Both types of problems belong to the category of supervised learning.

Classification in MLPs

Given a list of classes and a dataset, one wishes to classify them, according to a historical dataset containing records and their respective classes. The following table shows an example of this dataset, considering the subjects' average grades between 0 and 10.

Student ID	\multicolumn{8}{c}{Subjects}	Profession
	English	Math	Physics	Chemistry	Geography	History	Literature	Biology	
89543	7.82	8.82	8.35	7.45	6.55	6.39	5.90	7.03	Electrical engineer
93201	8.33	6.75	8.01	6.98	7.95	7.76	6.98	6.84	Marketing professional
95481	7.76	7.17	8.39	8.64	8.22	7.86	7.07	9.06	Doctor
94105	8.25	7.54	7.34	7.65	8.65	8.10	8.40	7.44	Lawyer
96305	8.05	6.75	6.54	7.20	7.96	7.54	8.01	7.86	School principal

Chapter 3

Student ID	Subjects								Profession
	English	Math	Physics	Chemistry	Geography	History	Literature	Biology	
92904	6.95	8.85	9.10	7.54	7.50	6.65	5.86	6.76	Programmer
...	...	...							

One example is the prediction of profession based on academic grades. Let's consider a dataset of former students who are now working. We compile a dataset containing each student's average grade on each subject and his/her current profession. Note that the output would be the name of professions, which neural networks are not able to give directly. Instead, we need to make one column (one output) for each known profession. If that student chose a certain profession, the column corresponding to that profession would have the value one; otherwise, it would be zero. The following chart shows a view of how this matrix would look like:

$$\overbrace{\begin{matrix}7.82 & \cdots & 7.03\\ \vdots & \ddots & \vdots\\ 5.66 & \cdots & 6.22\end{matrix}}^{\text{Subject Grades}} \overbrace{\begin{matrix}1 & \cdots & 0\\ \vdots & \ddots & \vdots\\ 0 & \cdots & 1\end{matrix}}^{\text{Professions}}$$

Now, we want to predict which profession a student will be likely to choose on the basis of his/her grades. To this end, we structure a neural network containing the number of academic subjects as the input and the number of known professions as the output, and an arbitrary number of hidden neurons in the hidden layer. A neural net schema for this problem is presented in the following figure:

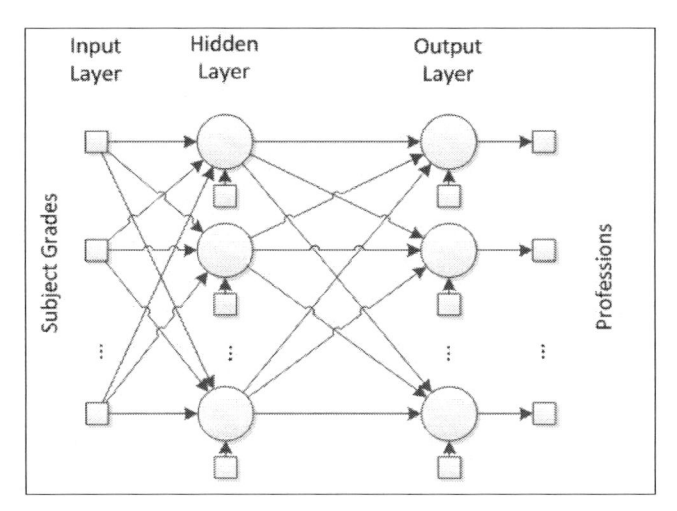

[57]

For the classification problem, there is usually only one class for each data point. So, in the output layer, the neurons are fired to produce either zero or one; it is better to use activation functions that are output bounded between these two values. However, we must consider a case in which more than one neuron would fire, giving two classes for a record. There are a number of mechanisms to prevent this case, such as the softmax function or the winner-takes-all algorithm, for example. These mechanisms are going to be detailed in the practical application in *Chapter 6, Classifying Disease Diagnosis*.

After being trained, the neural network has learnt what the most probable profession for a given student will be, given his/her grades.

Regression in MLPs

Regression involves finding some function that maps a set of inputs to a set of outputs. The following table shows a dataset containing k records of m independent inputs **X** known to be bound to n dependent outputs.

Input-independent data				Output-dependent data			
X1	X2	...	XM	T1	T2	...	TN
x1[0]	x2[0]	...	xm[0]	t1[0]	t2[0]	...	tn[0]
x1[1]	x2[1]	...	xm[1]	t1[1]	t2[1]	...	tn[1]
...	...	...	...	...	...	...	...
x1[k]	x2[k]	...	xm[k]	t1[k]	t2[k]	...	tn[k]

The preceding table can be compiled in the matrix format:

$$[X \quad T]$$

Where

$$X_{k,m} = \begin{bmatrix} x_1[0] & x_2[0] & \ldots & x_m[0] \\ x_1[1] & x_2[1] & \ldots & x_m[1] \\ \vdots & \vdots & \ddots & \vdots \\ x_1[k] & x_2[k] & \ldots & x_m[k] \end{bmatrix}$$

$$T_{k,n} = \begin{bmatrix} t_1[0] & t_2[0] & \ldots & t_n[0] \\ t_1[1] & t_2[1] & \ldots & t_n[1] \\ \vdots & \vdots & \ddots & \vdots \\ t_1[k] & t_2[k] & \ldots & t_n[k] \end{bmatrix}$$

Unlike the classification, the output values are numerical instead of labels or classes. There is also a historical database containing records of some behavior that we would like the neural network to learn. One example is the prediction of bus ticket prices between two cities. In this example, we collect information from a list of cities and the current ticket prices of a bus departing from one city and arriving in another. We structure the city features as well as the distance and/or time between them as the input and the bus ticket price as the output. The following figure illustrates this road net between the cities, represented as letters:

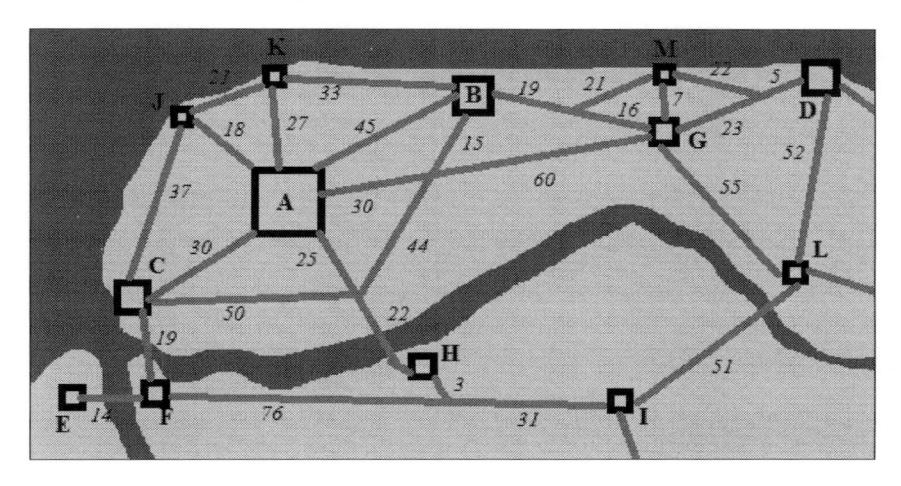

The following table shows a list of records taken from the cities mentioned in the preceding image and the structure to be fed into the neural network:

Features of city of origin			Features of city of destination			Features of the route			Ticket fare
Population	GDP	Routes	Population	GDP	Routes	Distance	Time	Stops	
500,000	4.5	6	45,000	1.5	5	90	1,5	0	15
120,000	2.6	4	500,000	4.5	6	30	0,8	0	10
30,000	0.8	3	65,000	3.0	3	103	1,6	1	20
35,000	1.4	3	45,000	1.5	5	7	0.4	0	5
...									
120,000	2.6	4	12,000	0.3	3	37	0.6	0	7

Having structured the dataset, we define an MLP network containing the exact number of features (multiplied by 2 in the case of two cities) plus the route features in the input, one output, and an arbitrary number of neurons in the hidden layer. In the case presented in the preceding table, there would be nine inputs. Since the output is numerical, there is no need to bound the output layer, so it is better to choose the linear function as the activation function in the output layer.

This neural network would give an estimate price for a route between two cities, which currently is not served by any bus transportation company.

Learning process in MLPs

The multilayer perceptron network learns on the basis of the delta rule, which is also inspired by the gradient descent optimization method. The gradient method is broadly applied to find the minima or maxima of a given function. An example of evolution of a gradient based search method is shown in the following figure:

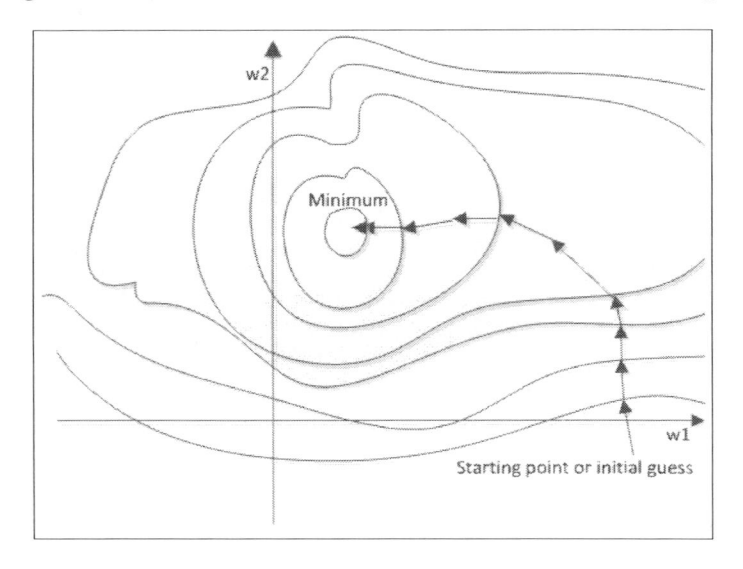

This method is applied at "walking," the direction where the function's output is higher or lower, depending on the criteria. This concept is explored in the delta rule.

$$\Delta w_i = \eta(t[k] - y[k])x_i[k]g'(h_i[k])$$

The function that the delta rule wants to minimize is the error between the neural network output and the target output, and the parameters to be found are the neural weights. This is an enhanced learning algorithm compared to the perceptron rule, because it takes into account the activation function derivative $g'(h)$, which in mathematical terms indicates the direction where the function is decreasing the most.

Simple and very powerful learning algorithm – Backpropagation

Although the delta rule works well for the neural networks having only output and input layers, for the MLP networks, the pure delta rule cannot be applied because of the hidden layer neurons. To overcome this issue, in the 1980s, Rummelhart et al. proposed a new algorithm, also inspired by a gradient method called backpropagation.

This algorithm is indeed a generalization of the delta rule for MLPs. The benefits of having additional layers to abstract more data from the environment have motivated the development of a training algorithm that can properly adjust the weights of the hidden layer. On the basis of the gradient method, the error from the output would be (back)propagated to the previous layers, thereby making the weight update using the same equation as the delta rule, possible. The algorithm runs according to the flowchart in the figure:

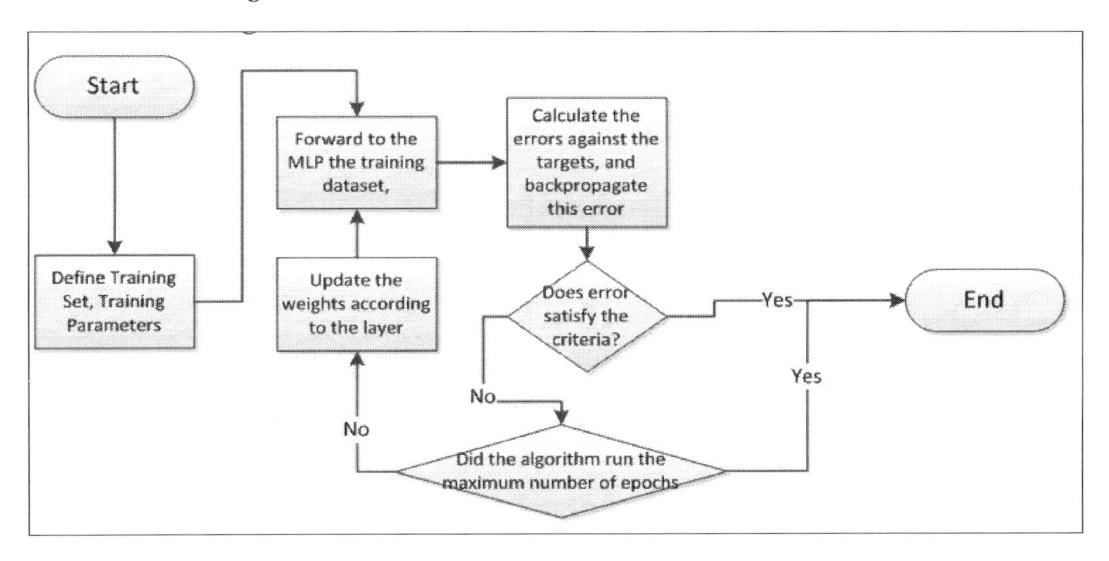

The second step is the backpropagation itself. What it does is find the weight variation according to the gradient, which is the base for the delta rule.

$$\frac{\partial E}{\partial w_{ji}} = \frac{\partial E}{\partial o_i}\frac{\partial o_i}{\partial h_i}\frac{\partial h_i}{\partial w_{ji}} = (t-y)f'(h_i)x_j$$

Where E is the error, w_{ji} is the weight between the neurons i and j, o_i is the output of the ith neuron, h_i is the weighted sum of that neuron's inputs before passing to the activation function. Remember that $o_i = f(h_i)$, where f is the activation function.

Updating in the hidden layers is a bit more complicated as we consider the error as a function of all the neurons between the weight to be updated and the output. To facilitate this process, we should compute the sensibility or the backpropagation error:

$$\delta_i = \frac{\partial E}{\partial o_i} \frac{\partial o_i}{\partial h_i}$$

Further, the weight update is as follows:

$$\Delta w_{ji} = -\eta \frac{\partial E}{\partial w_{ji}} = -\eta \delta_i x_j$$

The calculation of the backpropagation error varies for the output and for the hidden layers as follows:

- Backpropagation for the output layer

$$\delta_i = (o_i - t_i) f'(h_i)$$

  ○ Where o_i is the ith output, t_i is the desired i^{th} output, $f'(h_i)$ is the derivative of the output activation function, and h_i is the weighted sum of the ith neuron inputs.

- Backpropagation for the hidden layer

$$\delta_i = \sum_l \delta_l w_{il} f'(h_i)$$

  ○ Where l is a neuron of the layer ahead, w_{il} is the weight that connects the current neuron to the lth neuron of the layer immediately ahead.

For the sake of simplicity, we do not demonstrate fully how the backpropagation equation was developed. Anyway, if the reader is interested in the details, we recommend the references [Haykin, 2008; Rumelhart et al., 1986], which the reader can consult for further information.

This is how backpropagation works, enabling MLP networks to learn.

Elaborate and potent learning algorithm – Levenberg–Marquardt

The backpropagation algorithm, like all gradient-based methods, presents usually slow convergence, particularly when it falls in a zig-zag situation and when the weights are changed to almost the same value every two iterations. This drawback was studied in problems like curve-fitting interpolations by Kenneth Levenberg in 1944 and later by Donald Marquart in 1963, who developed a method for finding coefficients based on the Gauss–Newton algorithm and the gradient descent algorithm, so from there comes the name of the algorithm.

The algorithm deals with some optimization terms that are beyond the scope of this book, but in the references section, the reader will find good resources to learn more about these concepts, so we will present this method in a simpler way. Let's suppose that we have a list of inputs x's and outputs t's:

$$\begin{bmatrix} x_1[0] & x_2[0] & \cdots & x_m[0] & t_1[0] & t_2[0] & \cdots & t_n[0] \\ x_1[1] & x_2[1] & \cdots & x_m[1] & t_1[1] & t_2[1] & \cdots & t_n[1] \\ \vdots & \vdots & \ddots & \vdots & \vdots & \vdots & \ddots & \vdots \\ x_1[k] & x_2[k] & \cdots & x_m[k] & t_1[k] & t_2[k] & \cdots & t_n[k] \end{bmatrix}$$

We have seen that a neural network has the property to map inputs to outputs just like a nonlinear function f with coefficients W (weights and bias):

$$Y = f(X, W)$$

The nonlinear function will produce values different from the outputs T because we marked the variable Y in the equation. The Levenberg–Marquardt algorithm works over a Jacobian matrix, which is a matrix of all partial derivatives with respect to each weight and bias for each data row. So, the Jacobian matrix has the following format:

$$J = \begin{bmatrix} \dfrac{\partial f(X[1], W)}{W_1} & \cdots & \dfrac{\partial f(X[1], W)}{W_p} \\ \vdots & \ddots & \vdots \\ \dfrac{\partial f(X[k], W)}{W_1} & \cdots & \dfrac{\partial f(X[k], W)}{W_p} \end{bmatrix}$$

Where k is the total number of data points and p is the total number of weights and bias. In the Jacobian matrix, all weights and bias are stored serially in a single row. The elements of the Jacobian matrix are calculated from the gradients:

$$\frac{\partial E}{\partial w_{ji}} = (t-y)\frac{\partial f(x_i, W)}{\partial w_{ji}} \Rightarrow \frac{\partial f(x_i, W)}{\partial w_{ji}} = \frac{\partial E}{\partial w_{ji}}(t-y)^{-1}$$

The partial derivative of the error E in relation to each weight is calculated in the backpropagation algorithm, so this algorithm is going to run the backpropagation step as well.

In every optimization problem, one wishes to minimize the total error:

$$E(W) = \sum [Y_i - f(X_i, W)]^2$$

Where W (weights and bias in the NN case) are the variables to optimize. The optimization algorithm updates W by adding ΔW. By applying some algebra, we can extend the last equation as follows:

$$E(W + \Delta W) = \sum [Y_i - f(X_i, W) - J_i \Delta W]^2$$

Converting to the vector and notation, we obtain:

$$E(W + \Delta W) = \|Y - f(X, W) - J\Delta W\|^2$$

Finally, by setting the error E to zero, we get the Levenberg–Marquardt equation after some manipulation:

$$\Delta W = (J^T J + \lambda I)^{-1} J^T (Y - f(X, W))$$

Which is the weight update rule. As can be seen, it involves matrix operations such as transposition and inversion. The Greek letter λ is the damping factor, an equivalent of the learning rate.

Hands-on MLP implementation!

Now, let's implement all the theory that we've discussed so far. Here, we use the classes that define the ANN structures `NeuralNet`, `Layer`, `Neuron`, and so on. Now, we add `HiddenLayer` and `OutputLayer` functions, which are inherited from the `Layer` class, to implement multilayer neural networks.

We also implement the two learning algorithms that we've presented in this chapter: Backpropagation and Levenberg-Marquardt. In the `Training` class, we add two new terms to the enum Training types: `BACKPROPAGATION` and `LEVENBERG_MARQUARDT`.

In order to make the execution of the Levenberg-Marquardt algorithm possible, we add a new package called `edu.packt.neuralnet.util` and two more classes, namely `Matrix` and `IdentityMatrix`. These classes implement matrix operations, which are applied in the Levenberg-Marquardt algorithm. However, we are not going to detail these classes now; we're just going to use the basic operations of matrix.

The following table shows a list of relevant attributes and methods of the classes used in this chapter:

Class name: Training	
Note: This class is abstract and cannot be instantiated.	
Enums	
Note: Enum helps to control different types.	

`public enum TrainingTypesENUM {`
`    PERCEPTRON, ADALINE,`
`BACKPROPAGATION;`
`}`
	Enumeration to store types of training supported by project (Backpropagation was added)

Class name: Backpropagation	
Note: This class inherits attributes and methods from the Training class.	
Attributes	
None	
Method	
`public NeuralNet train (NeuralNet n)`	Trains the neural network using the backpropagation algorithm. This method overrides the method from the Training class
	Parameters: `NeuralNet` object (neural net untrained)
	Returns: `NeuralNet` object (neural net trained via backpropagation)

`private NeuralNet forward (NeuralNet n, int row)`	Performs the propagation of the signal from the first layer to the hidden layer and to the output layer
	Parameters: `NeuralNet` object, line number of training set
	Returns: `NeuralNet` object
`private NeuralNet backpropagation (NeuralNet n, int row)`	Performs the retro-propagation of the signal from the output layer to the hidden layer and to the first layer. In this method, the weights are adjusted
	Parameters: `NeuralNet` object, line number of training set.
	Returns: `NeuralNet` object.

Class implementation with Java: file Backpropagation.java

Class name: LevenbergMarquardt

Note: This class inherits attributes and methods from the backpropagation class.

Attributes	
`private double dampingFactor`	The damping factor, which also works as the learning rate
`private Matrix jacobian`	The Jacobian matrix used in the Levenberg–Marquardt algorithm

Method	
`public NeuralNet train (NeuralNet n)`	Trains the neural network using the Levenberg–Marquardt algorithm. This method overrides the method from the backpropagation class
	Parameters: `NeuralNet` object (neural net untrained)
	Returns: `NeuralNet` object (neural net trained via backpropagation)
`public void buildJacobianMatrix (NeuralNet n, int row)`	Calculate the gradients for each weight and bias of the neural network for the corresponding row of the training dataset and saves them in the corresponding row in the Jacobian matrix
	Parameters: `NeuralNet` object (neural net untrained), row (the ith data point)
	Returns: Nothing

Class name: NeuralNet	
Note: This class already existed in previous version and has been updated as follows:	
Attributes	
`private double[][] realMatrixOutputSet`	Matrix to store the training set of the output data (matrix format)
`private double errorMean`	Real number to store the mean of the error between two or more neurons
`private ActivationFncENUM activationFncOutputLayer`	Enum value of the activation function that will be used in the output layer of the net
Methods	
Note: The getters and setters methods of these attributes were created too.	
Class implementation with Java: file NeuralNet.java	

The class diagram changes are shown in the following figure. Attributes and methods already explained in the previous chapters and their configuration methods (getters and setters) were omitted.

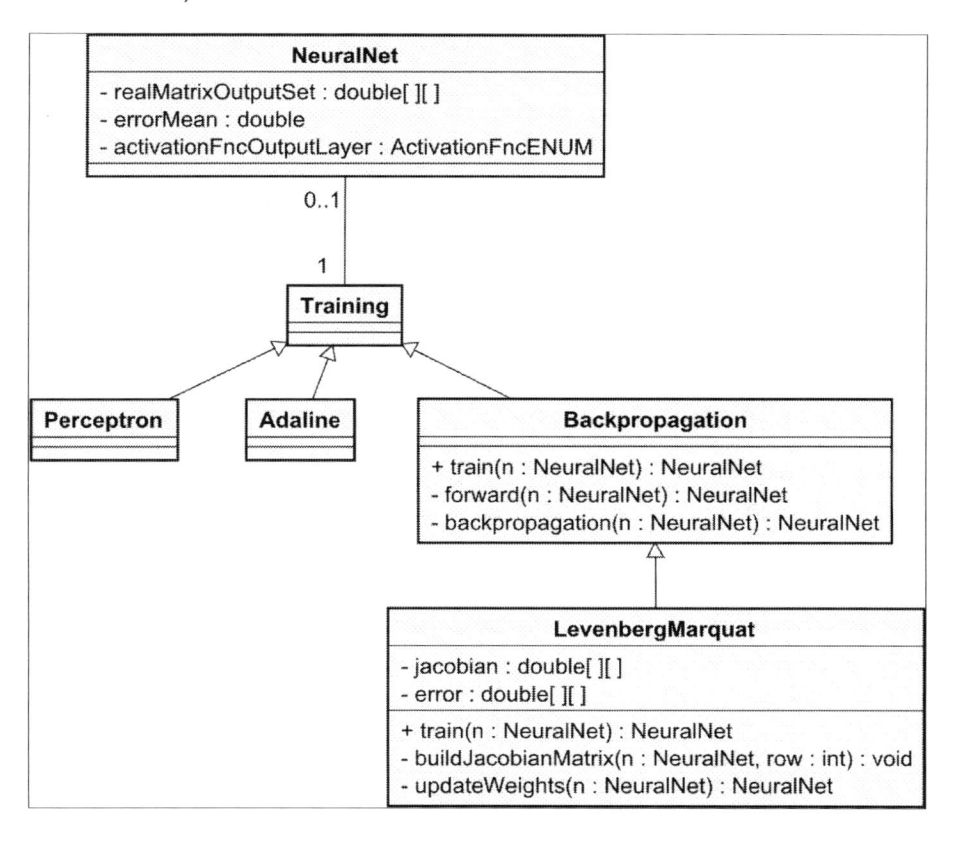

```
┌─────────────────────────────────────────────────────────┐
│                       NeuralNet                          │
├─────────────────────────────────────────────────────────┤
│ - realMatrixOutputSet : double[ ][ ]                     │
│ - errorMean : double                                     │
│ - activationFncOutputLayer : ActivationFncENUM           │
└─────────────────────────────────────────────────────────┘
                           │ 0..1
                           │
                           │ 1
                  ┌────────────────┐
                  │    Training    │
                  └────────────────┘
                    △     △     △
         ┌──────────┘     │     └──────────────┐
  ┌────────────┐   ┌────────────┐      ┌──────────────────────────────────────────────┐
  │ Perceptron │   │  Adaline   │      │              Backpropagation                 │
  └────────────┘   └────────────┘      ├──────────────────────────────────────────────┤
                                        │ + train(n : NeuralNet) : NeuralNet           │
                                        │ - forward(n : NeuralNet) : NeuralNet         │
                                        │ - backpropagation(n : NeuralNet) : NeuralNet │
                                        └──────────────────────────────────────────────┘
                                                               △
                                        ┌──────────────────────────────────────────────────┐
                                        │                LevenbergMarquat                  │
                                        ├──────────────────────────────────────────────────┤
                                        │ - jacobian : double[ ][ ]                        │
                                        │ - error : double[ ][ ]                           │
                                        ├──────────────────────────────────────────────────┤
                                        │ + train(n : NeuralNet) : NeuralNet               │
                                        │ - buildJacobianMatrix(n : NeuralNet, row : int) : void │
                                        │ - updateWeights(n : NeuralNet) : NeuralNet       │
                                        └──────────────────────────────────────────────────┘
```

Backpropagation in action

We have seen in the flowchart that the backpropagation algorithm has two phases:

- Forward the neural signals
- Backpropagate the error

So, the backpropagation class will have two special methods for each of these phases: `forward()` and `backpropagation()`. The `train()` method of the backpropagation class will call these two latter functions.

Exploring the code

Let's analyze the methods forward, backpropagation, and train. The train method calls forward and backpropagation.

```java
public NeuralNet train(NeuralNet n) {

    int epoch = 0;
    setMse(1.0);

    while(getMse() > n.getTargetError()) {

      if ( epoch >= n.getMaxEpochs() ) break;

      int rows = n.getTrainSet().length;
      double sumErrors = 0.0;

      for (int rows_i = 0; rows_i < rows; rows_i++) {

        n = forward(n, rows_i);
        n = backpropagation(n, rows_i);
        sumErrors = sumErrors + n.getErrorMean();

      }

      setMse( sumErrors / rows );

      System.out.println( getMse() );

      epoch++;

    }

    System.out.println("Number of epochs: "+epoch);

    return n;

}
```

First, this code gets the training parameters and sets the MSE (which stands for mean square error), which will be the stop condition. The first loop handles this stop condition in case the MSE falls below the target. Also, inside this loop, there is a break in case the number of epochs currently executed reaches the maximum.

The second loop will go over every data point in the training dataset, repeating for each data point the training process, first calling the forward function and then the backpropagation function, which will be detailed ahead in this section. The errors are summed up. After going over all the data points in the training set, this method sets the current MSE, prints it on the screen, and increases the number of epochs.

Now, let's analyze the forward and backpropagation functions. Since they are quite long, we are going to explore the most important parts.

The forward function executes the neural computation from the input to the output layers. For simplicity, this implementation will handle only one hidden layer and one output layer, provided that this simple architecture is proved to work quite well when compared to multiple hidden layer networks. The function receives as a parameter the neural network and the row of the dataset to be forwarded.

```
private NeuralNet forward(NeuralNet n, int row)
```

It initializes some parameters such as sum error and the estimated and real outputs. There is basically one major loop containing two minor loops, one for the hidden layer and the other for the output layer.

```
for (HiddenLayer hiddenLayer : listOfHiddenLayer) {

   int numberOfNeuronsInLayer = hiddenLayer.
getNumberOfNeuronsInLayer();

   for (Neuron neuron : hiddenLayer.getListOfNeurons()) {

      for (int layer_j = 0; layer_j < numberOfNeuronsInLayer - 1; layer_j++) {

      }

      for (int outLayer_i = 0; outLayer_i < n.getOutputLayer().
getNumberOfNeuronsInLayer(); outLayer_i++){
```

Handling Perceptrons

```
    }

    double errorMean = sumError / n.getOutputLayer()
        .getNumberOfNeuronsInLayer();
    n.setErrorMean(errorMean);

    n.getListOfHiddenLayer().get(hiddenLayer_i)
        .setListOfNeurons(hiddenLayer.getListOfNeurons());

  }
}
```

After computing the outputs for the hidden and output layers, this function finally calculates the error, which will be used for backpropagation. The computation for the hidden layer and the output layer is detailed in the source codes attached to this chapter.

The backpropagation function also receives as parameters the neural network and the row indicating the data point to be trained.

```
private NeuralNet backpropagation(NeuralNet n, int row)
```

For an easier understanding, this function is divided into six parts:

1. Initialize training parameters and retrieve neural network layers (hidden and output).
2. Calculate the sensibility for the output layer.
3. Calculate the sensibility for the hidden layer.
4. Update the weights of the output layer.
5. Update the weights of the hidden layer.
6. Update the neural layers in the neural network.

Let's focus on parts 2 to 5. The sensibility for the output layer is quite simple. Looking at the line computing the sensibility parameter shows us the delta rule.

```
//sensibility output layer
for (Neuron neuron : outputLayer) {
  error = neuron.getError();
  netValue = neuron.getOutputValue();
  sensibility = derivativeActivationFnc(
      n.getActivationFncOutputLayer(), netValue ) * error;

  neuron.setSensibility(sensibility);
}
```

Chapter 3

For the hidden layer, there is a need to sum up the weights and the sensibilities of the output layer. The local variable called tempSensibility handles this sum, after being used in the calculation of the sensibility. It can be seen that this parameter is calculated inside a loop that runs over all neurons contained in that layer.

```
for (Neuron neuron : hiddenLayer) {

  sensibility = 0.0;

  if(neuron.getListOfWeightIn().size() > 0) { //exclude bias
    ArrayList<Double> listOfWeightsOut = new ArrayList<Double>();

    listOfWeightsOut = neuron.getListOfWeightOut();

    double tempSensibility = 0.0;

    int weight_i = 0;
    for (Double weight : listOfWeightsOut) {
      tempSensibility = tempSensibility + (weight *
          outputLayer.get(weight_i)
          .getSensibility());
      weight_i++;
    }

    sensibility = derivativeActivationFnc (
      n.getActivationFnc(), neuron.getOutputValue() ) *
      tempSensibility;

    neuron.setSensibility(sensibility);

  }
}
```

The weight updating in the output layer is as simple as its respective sensibility. There is a loop inside this part to walk over all the hidden layer neurons connected to each output neuron. The local variable called newWeight is in charge of receiving the new value for the respective weight.

```
//fix weights (teach) [output layer to hidden layer]
for (int outLayer_i = 0; outLayer_i < n.getOutputLayer().
getNumberOfNeuronsInLayer(); outLayer_i++) {
    for (Neuron neuron : hiddenLayer) {
      double newWeight = neuron.getListOfWeightOut()
          .get( outLayer_i ) + ( n.getLearningRate() *
              outputLayer.get( outLayer_i )
```

```
            .getSensibility() *
            neuron.getOutputValue() );

      neuron.getListOfWeightOut().set(outLayer_i,
          newWeight);
    }
  }
```

For the hidden layer, it is the sensibility parameters that are used, according to the equations shown in the backpropagation section. There is also an inside loop to walk over all the neural inputs.

```
  //fix weights (teach) [hidden layer to input layer]
  for (Neuron neuron : hiddenLayer) {

    ArrayList<Double> hiddenLayerInputWeights = new
ArrayList<Double>();
    hiddenLayerInputWeights = neuron.getListOfWeightIn();

    if(hiddenLayerInputWeights.size() > 0) { //exclude bias

      int hidden_i = 0;
      double newWeight = 0.0;
      for (int i = 0; i < n.getInputLayer().
getNumberOfNeuronsInLayer(); i++) {

      newWeight = hiddenLayerInputWeights.get(hidden_i) +
          ( n.getLearningRate() *
            neuron.getSensibility() *
            n.getTrainSet()[row][i]   );

      neuron.getListOfWeightIn().set(hidden_i, newWeight);

      hidden_i++;
      }
    }
  }
```

Levenberg–Marquardt implementation

The Levenberg–Marquardt algorithm uses many features of the backpropagation algorithm; that's why we inherited this class from backpropagation. Basically, the train function is the same, except for the following piece of code:

```
    for (int rows_i = 0; rows_i < rows; rows_i++) {
      n = forward(n, rows_i);
```

```
        buildJacobianMatrix(n, rows_i);
        sumErrors = sumErrors + n.getErrorMean();
    }
    n=updateWeights(n);
```

The loop, where it goes over the training dataset, calls the `buildJacobianMatrix` method for each data row. This method calls the original version from the inherited backpropagation method in order to compute the gradients.

As seen in the LMA theory explained earlier, the row of a Jacobian matrix contains all weights and the bias in a serial sequence. So, the corresponding columns of the weights in the Jacobian matrix can be detailed as in the following table:

Layer	Weight or bias	Position
Hidden	j^{th} weight of the ith neuron	`(i * (numberOfInputs)) + j`
Output	Bias of the ith neuron	`((numberOfInputs) * (numberOfHiddenNeurons - 1)) + (i * (numberOfHiddenNeurons) + numberOfHiddenNeurons)`

Since the `buildJacobianMatrix` method is a bit similar to backpropagation, we are going to highlight the Jacobian row construction. For the weights in the hidden layer, the following line of code is called:

```
    jacobian.setValue( row, ( i * ( numberOfInputs ) ) + j,
        ( neuron.getSensibility() *
        n.getTrainSet()[row][j] ) / nb.getErrorMean() );
```

We can see the sensibility of the hidden neuron being used in the gradient. Now, for the output layer, we use the following:

```
    jacobian.setValue( row,
        ( numberOfInputs + 1 ) * ( numberOfHiddenNeurons ) +
        ( i * ( numberOfHiddenNeurons + 1 ) ) + j,
        ( output.getSensibility() * neuron.getOutputValue() ) /
           n.getErrorMean() );
```

In this piece of code, the neuron object refers to the hidden neuron that precedes the output layer.

One more difference between the backpropagation and the Levenberg–Marquardt algorithm is that the weights here are updated once at an epoch, not on every data point. This is necessary because the Jacobian matrix is built using the entire dataset.

We can see in the train method that after building the Jacobian matrix, the algorithm calls the `updateWeights` method. In this method, the Levenberg–Marquardt matrix equation is solved, and then, the weights are added to the corresponding contribution from the delta matrix.

Solution of the Levenberg–Marquardt matrix equation:

```
Matrix term1 = jacobian.transpose().multiply(jacobian)
    .add(new IdentityMatrix(jacobian.getNumberOfColumns())
    .multiply(damping));
Matrix term2 = jacobian.transpose().multiply(error);
Matrix delta = term1.inverse().multiply(term2);
```

Update of the jth weight of the ith neuron in the hidden layer:

```
newWeight = hiddenLayerInputWeights.get( i ) +
    delta.getValue( ( i * ( numberOfInputs + 1 ) + j ) ,0 );
hidden.getListOfWeightIn().set( i, newWeight );
neuron.getListOfWeightIn().set( hidden_i, newWeight );
```

For the output layer:

```
newWeight = neuron.getListOfWeightOut().get(i) +
    delta.getValue(  ( numberOfInputs + 1 ) *
            ( numberOfHiddenNeurons ) +
            ( i*(numberOfHiddenNeurons+1) )+j , 0);
neuron.getListOfWeightOut().set(i, newWeight);
```

Practical application – types of university enrolments

In Brazil, one of the ways for a person to enter university is taking an exam and if he/she achieves the minimum grade required for the course that he/she is seeking, then he/she can enroll. To demonstrate the backpropagation algorithm, let us consider this scenario. Data showed in the following table was collected from a university database. The second column represents the person's gender (one means female, and zero means male); the third column has grades scaled by **100**, and the last column is formed by two neurons (**1,0** means performed enrollment, and **0,1** means waiver enrollment.

Sample	Gender	Grade	Enrollment status
1	1	0.73	1,0
2	1	0.81	1,0
3	1	0.86	1,0
4	0	0.65	1,0
5	0	0.45	1,0
6	1	0.70	0,1
7	0	0.51	0,1
8	1	0.89	0,1
9	1	0.79	0,1
10	0	0.54	0,1

The following figure displays the architecture of the neural net to solve this problem:

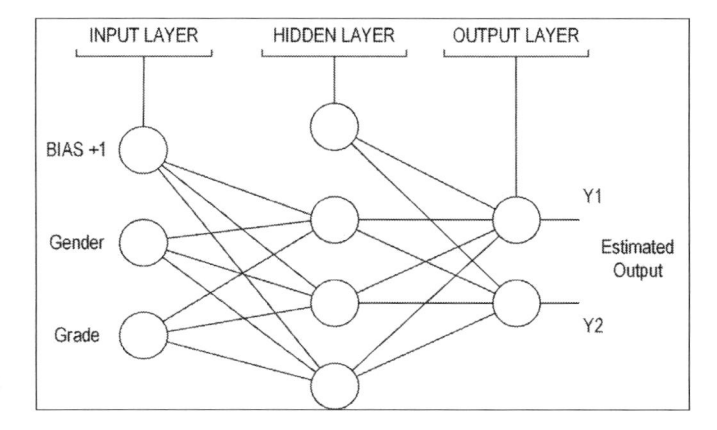

Now, let's analyze the test method named `testBackpropagation()`. It is as follows:

```java
private void testBackpropagation(){
    NeuralNet testNet = new NeuralNet();

    testNet = testNet.initNet(2, 1, 3, 2);

    System.out.println("---BACKPROPAGATION INIT NET---");

    testNet.printNet(testNet);

    NeuralNet trainedNet = new NeuralNet();

    // first column has BIAS
    testNet.setTrainSet(new double[][] { { 1.0, 1.0, 0.73 }, { 1.0, 1.0, 0.81 }, { 1.0, 1.0, 0.86 }, { 1.0, 1.0, 0.95 }, { 1.0, 0.0, 0.45 }, { 1.0, 1.0, 0.70 }, { 1.0, 0.0, 0.51 }, { 1.0, 1.0, 0.89 }, { 1.0, 1.0, 0.79 }, { 1.0, 0.0, 0.54 }     });
    testNet.setRealMatrixOutputSet(new double[][] { {1.0, 0.0}, {1.0, 0.0}, {1.0, 0.0}, {1.0, 0.0}, {1.0, 0.0}, {0.0, 1.0}, {0.0, 1.0}, {0.0, 1.0}, {0.0, 1.0}, {0.0, 1.0}     });
    testNet.setMaxEpochs(1000);
    testNet.setTargetError(0.002);
    testNet.setLearningRate(0.1);
    testNet.setTrainType(TrainingTypesENUM.BACKPROPAGATION);
    testNet.setActivationFnc(ActivationFncENUM.SIGLOG);

    testNet.setActivationFncOutputLayer(
            ActivationFncENUM.LINEAR );

    trainedNet = testNet.trainNet(testNet);

    System.out.println();
    System.out.println("---BACKPROPAGATION TRAINED NET---");

    testNet.printNet(trainedNet);

}
```

The backpropagation test logic is similar to Adaline's and perceptron's. First, an object of the `NeuralNet` class is created and used for initializing the net with two neurons in the input layer, one hidden layer with three neurons, and two neurons in the output layer. The data to train is taken from the preceding table. The maximum number of epochs is large, because the backpropagation algorithm prolongs the learning process. To conclude, the backpropagation-trained net weights and the MSE list are printed. A summary of the results is shown in the following figure:

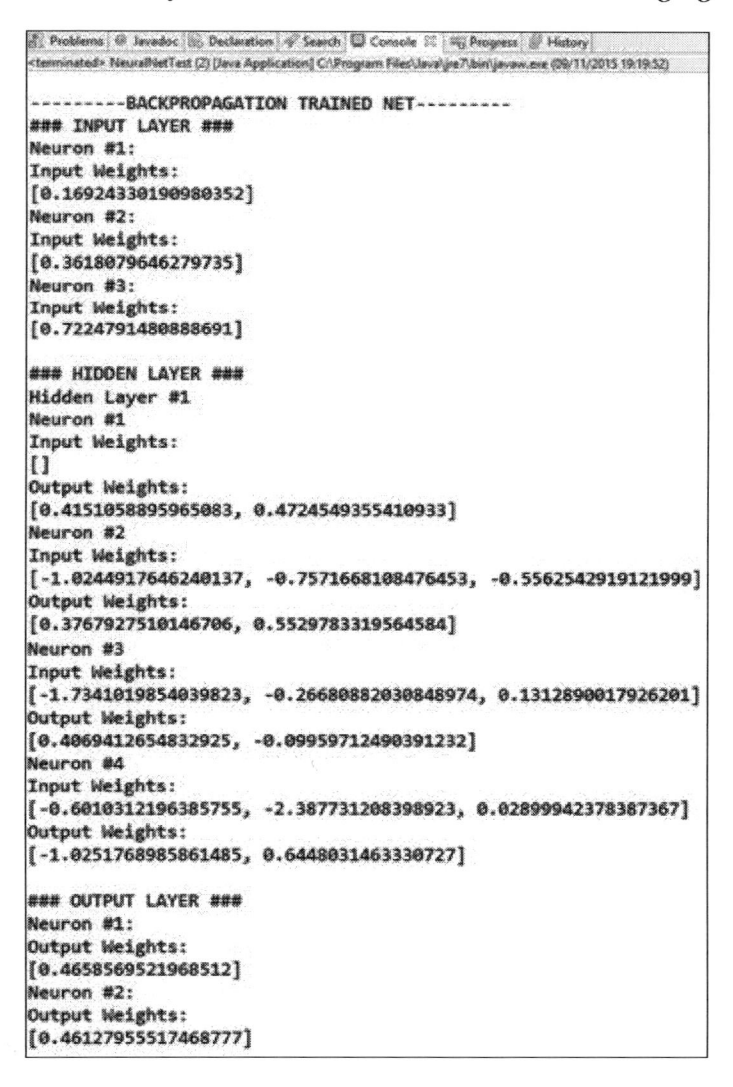

```
----------BACKPROPAGATION TRAINED NET---------
### INPUT LAYER ###
Neuron #1:
Input Weights:
[0.16924330190980352]
Neuron #2:
Input Weights:
[0.3618079646279735]
Neuron #3:
Input Weights:
[0.7224791480888691]

### HIDDEN LAYER ###
Hidden Layer #1
Neuron #1
Input Weights:
[]
Output Weights:
[0.4151058895965083, 0.4724549355410933]
Neuron #2
Input Weights:
[-1.0244917646240137, -0.7571668108476453, -0.5562542919121999]
Output Weights:
[0.3767927510146706, 0.5529783319564584]
Neuron #3
Input Weights:
[-1.7341019854039823, -0.26680882030848974, 0.1312890017926201]
Output Weights:
[0.4069412654832925, -0.09959712490391232]
Neuron #4
Input Weights:
[-0.6010312196385755, -2.387731208398923, 0.02899942378387367]
Output Weights:
[-1.0251768985861485, 0.6448031463330727]

### OUTPUT LAYER ###
Neuron #1:
Output Weights:
[0.4658569521968512]
Neuron #2:
Output Weights:
[0.46127955517468777]
```

Analyzing the graphic by using the MSE of each epoch plotted in the following figure, it is possible to conclude that neural net learned to classify, on the basis of gender and grade, whether a person will or will not enroll at this university.

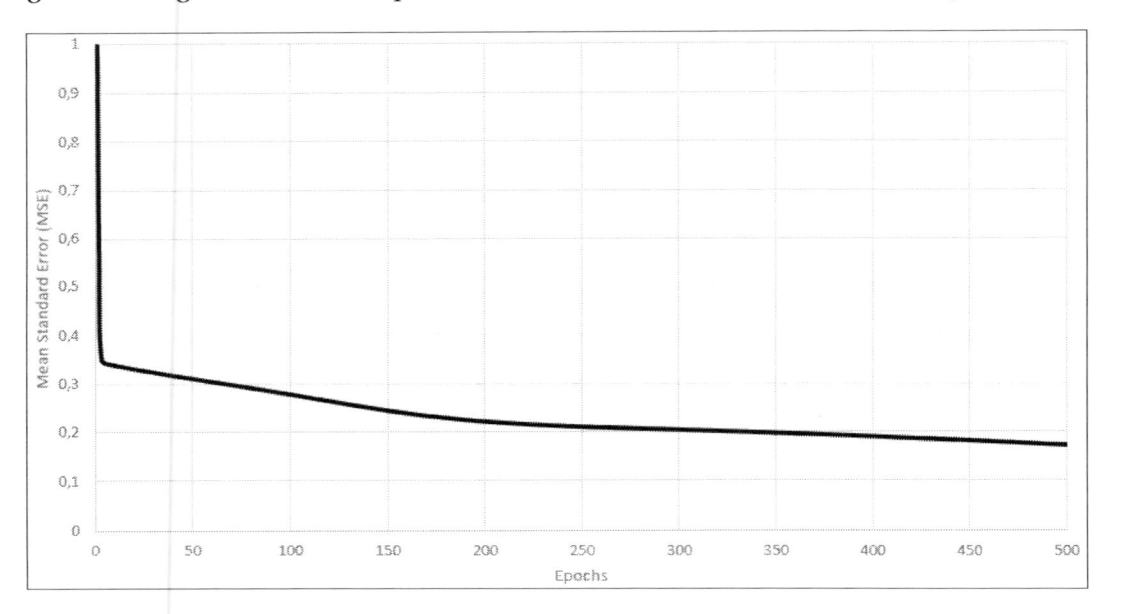

Summary

In this chapter, we've seen how perceptrons can be applied to solve linear separation problems and discussed their limitations with respect to the classification of nonlinear data. To suppress these limitations, we presented multilayer perceptrons (MLPs) and a new training algorithm called backpropagation. We've also seen some classes of problems that MLPs can be applied to, such as classification and regression. It's important to assimilate such concepts to understand their applications in the subsequent approaches. The Java implementation explored the power of the backpropagation algorithm with respect to updating the weights in both the output layer and the hidden layer. One practical application is shown to demonstrate the MLPs with respect to the solutions of the considered problems.

In the next chapter, we will explore the other learning paradigm of neural networks, unsupervised learning, that differs slightly from the learning algorithms that we've seen in this chapter; however, it can produce amazing results.

4
Self-Organizing Maps

In this chapter, we present a neural network architecture that is suitable for unsupervised learning: **Self-Organizing Maps (SOMs)**, also known as **Kohonen network**. A special feature of this type of neural network is that they can categorize records of data without any target output. In this chapter, we are going to explore how this is achieved, as well as an application to attest its capacity. The subtopics of this chapter are as follows:

- Neural networks unsupervised learning
    - Competitive learning
- Kohonen SOMs
    - 1-Dimensional SOMs
    - 2-Dimensional SOMs
- Problems solved with unsupervised learning
- Coding of the Kohonen algorithm
- Practical problems

Neural networks' unsupervised way of learning

We've been acquainted with this type of learning in *Chapter 2*, *How Neural Networks Learn*, and now, we are going to explore the features of this learning paradigm in a detailed fashion. Unsupervised learning algorithms in essence aim at finding patterns within datasets by using only the information presented in the datasets themselves. Here, the unsupervised learning algorithm will adjust the parameters (weights in the case of neural networks) without any error measure, and this is the crucial feature that distinguishes unsupervised from supervised learning. The learning itself is triggered only on the basis of the fact that in neurology, similar stimuli produce similar responses. So, applying this fundamental knowledge to artificial neural networks, we can say that similar data produce similar outputs, and these outputs can be grouped in clusters.

Although this learning may be used in other mathematical fields such as statistics, its core functionality is intended and designed for machine learning problems such as data mining and pattern recognition. Neural networks are a subfield in the machine learning discipline, and provided that their structure allows iterative learning, they serve as a good framework to apply this concept on.

One wishes to apply unsupervised learning algorithms when there is no defined target on the data, as well as there is a need to find hidden patterns amongst the data. Most of the unsupervised learning applications are aimed at clustering tasks, which means that similar data points are clustered together, while different data points from different clusters. Further, one application that unsupervised learning is suitable for is dimensionality reduction, wherein one wants some multidimensional data to be classified or reorganized in a less-dimensional domain. In the references [Duda et. al, 2001; Hinton et. al, 1999; Rummelhart & Zipser, 1985; Kohonen, 1982] the reader may find a useful list of articles that show more examples of applications of unsupervised learning.

Some unsupervised learning algorithms

There are a multitude of unsupervised algorithms, not only for neural networks. Examples are K-means, expectation maximization, methods of moments, and so on. Such algorithms assume the entire dataset as the knowledge to be learned, so one common feature through all the learning algorithms is that they do not have an input–output relationship in the current dataset. However, one wishes to find a different meaning of these data, and that's the goal of any unsupervised learning algorithm.

Bringing this concept into the neural network context, let's take a look at an ANN and how it deals with data in an unsupervised organization.

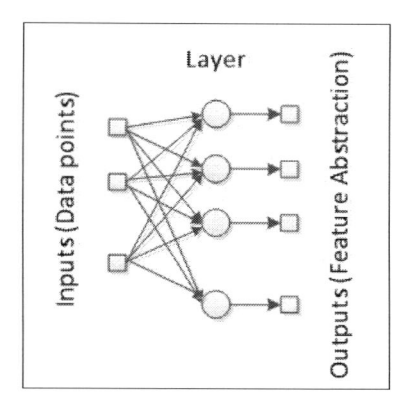

The neural network output is considered to be an abstraction of the original data points. As opposed to the supervised learning paradigm, there is no causality between the input data points or data variables; instead, we want the neural network to derive consequent variables that would be able to give another meaning to the presented data. While in supervised learning algorithms, we usually have a smaller number of outputs, for unsupervised learning, there is a need to produce an abstract data representation that may require a high number of outputs. However, except for classification tasks, their meaning is totally different from the one presented in the case of supervised learning. Usually, each output neuron is responsible for representing a feature or a class present in the input data. In most architectures, not all output neurons need to be activated at a time; usually, only a restricted set of output neurons is fired, meaning that a neuron is able to better represent most of the information being fed as the neural input.

> One advantage of unsupervised learning over supervised learning is that as less computational power is required by the former for the learning of huge datasets, the time consumption increases linearly, while for supervised learning, it increases exponentially.

In this chapter, we are going to explore two unsupervised learning algorithms: competitive learning and Kohonen SOMs.

Competitive learning or winner takes all

As the name implies, competitive learning handles a competition between the output neurons to determine which one is the winner. To facilitate understanding, suppose we want to train a single layer neural network with two inputs and four outputs, as shown in the following figure:

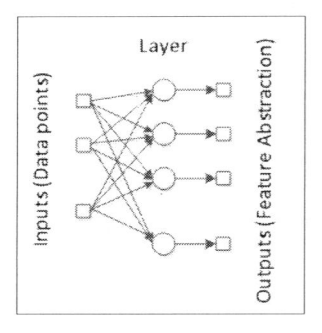

Every output neuron is then connected to these two inputs; hence, for each neuron, there are two weights.

> For this learning, the bias is dropped from the neurons, so the neurons will process only the weighted inputs.

The competition starts after the data have been processed by the neurons. The winner neuron will be the one that produces the greatest output value. One additional difference compared to the supervised learning algorithm is that only the winner neuron may update its weights, while the others remain unchanged. This is the so-called winner-takes-all rule. This intention to bring the neuron "nearer" to the input causes it to win the competition.

Considering that every input neuron i is connected to all output neurons j through a weight wij. In our case, we would have a set of weights:

$$W = \begin{bmatrix} w_{11} & w_{21} \\ w_{12} & w_{22} \\ w_{13} & w_{23} \\ w_{14} & w_{24} \end{bmatrix}$$

Provided that the weights of every neuron have the same dimensionality of the input data, let's consider all the input data points together in a plot with the weights of each neuron.

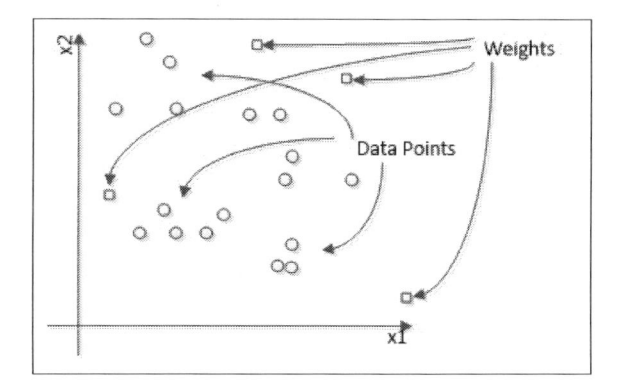

In this chart, let's consider the circles as the data points and the squares as the neuron weights. We can see that some data points are closer to certain weights, while the others are farther but nearer to others. The neural network performs computations related to the distance between the inputs and the weights:

$$o_j(X) = f_j\left(\sum w_{ij} x_i\right)$$

The result of this equation will determine how "strong" a neuron is against its competitors. The winner neuron connections are then adjusted to the neurons according to the following update rule:

$$\Delta w_{ij} = \eta(x_i - w_{ij})$$

Where η denotes the learning rate. After many iterations, the weights are driven so near enough to the data points that triggers the greatest output values on the corresponding neuron, that weight updates are either too small or fall in a zig-zag pattern. Finally, when the network is already trained, the chart takes another shape:

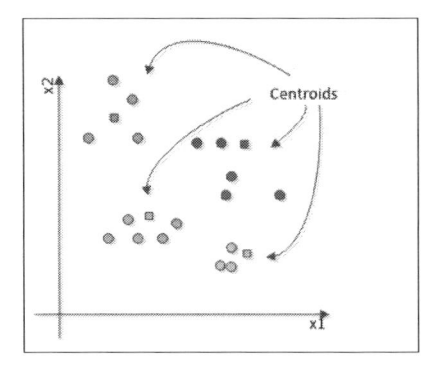

As can be seen, the neurons form centroids that surround the points capable of making the corresponding neuron stronger than its competitors.

> In an unsupervised neural network, the number of outputs is completely arbitrary. Sometimes, only some neurons are able to change their weights, while in other cases, all the neurons may respond differently to the same input, causing the neural network to never learn. For these cases, it is recommended either to review the number of output neurons or to consider another type of unsupervised learning.

There are basically two stopping conditions of competitive learning:

- Predefined number of epochs: This prevents our algorithm from running for a relatively long time without convergence
- Minimum value of weight update: This prevents the algorithm from running longer than necessary

Kohonen self-organizing maps (SOMs)

This network architecture was created by the Finnish professor Teuvo Kohonen at the beginning of the 80s. It consists of one single-layer neural network capable of providing a "visualization" of the data in one or two dimensions.

> Theoretically, a Kohonen network would be able to provide a 3D (or even a higher-dimensional) representation of the data; however, in printed material, such as this book, it is not possible to show 3D charts without overlapping some data. Thus, in this book, we are going to deal only with 1D and 2D Kohonen networks.

The major difference between the Kohonen SOMs and the traditional single-layer competitive neural networks is the concept of neighborhood neurons. While in a neural network, usually, there is no importance of the order in which the neurons are positioned in the output, in an SOM, the neighboring neurons play a relevant role during the learning phase.

An SOM has two modes of functioning: mapping and learning. In the mapping mode, the input data is classified in the most appropriate neuron, while in the learning mode, the input data helps the learning algorithm to build the "map." This map can be interpreted as a lower-dimensional representation from a certain dataset.

In this chapter, we are going to present two types of SOMs: 1D and 2D SOMs.

One-Dimensional SOM

This architecture is similar to the network presented in the last section: competitive learning, with the addition of the neighborhood amongst the output neurons.

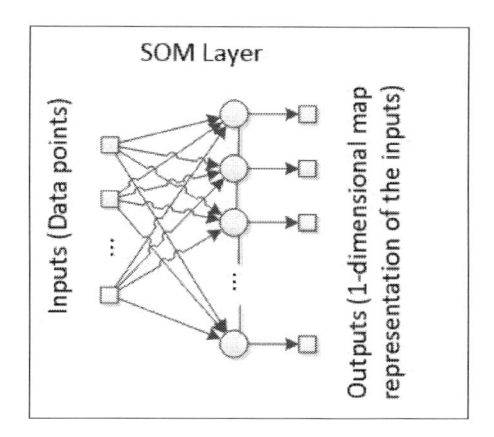

Note that every neuron on the output layer has two neighbors. Similarly, the neuron that fires the greatest value updates its weights, but in an SOM, the neighboring neurons also update their weights at a relatively slow rate.

The effect of the neighborhood extends the activation area to a wider area of the map, provided that all the output neurons observe an organization, a path in the 1D case. The neighborhood function also allows for a better exploration of the properties of the input space, since it forces the neural network to maintain the connections between neurons, therefore resulting in more information in addition to only the clusters that are formed.

In a plot of the input data points with the neural weights, we can see the path formed by the neurons.

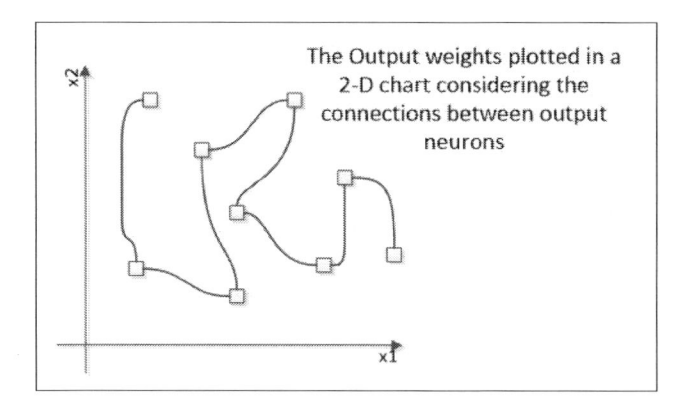

Self-Organizing Maps

In the chart presented here, for the sake of simplicity, we plotted only the output weights to demonstrate how the map is designed in a (in this case) 2D space. After training over many iterations, the neural network converges to the final shape that represents all data points. Provided this structure, a certain set of data may cause the Kohonen network to design another shape in the space. This is a good example of dimensionality reduction, since a multidimensional dataset when presented to the SOM is able to produce a single line (in the 1D SOM) that "summarizes" the entire dataset.

Two-Dimensional SOM

This is the architecture that is most frequently used to demonstrate the power of a Kohonen neural network visually. The output layer is a matrix containing N x N neurons, interconnected like a grid:

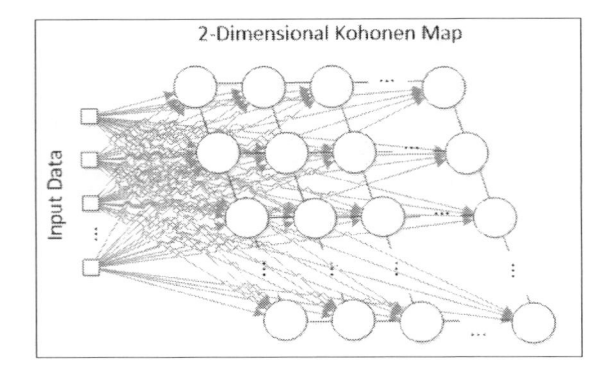

In 2D SOMs, every neuron now will have up to four neighbors, although in some representations, the diagonal neurons may also be considered, thus resulting in up to eight neighbors. Basically, the working principle of 2D SOMs is the same. Let's see an example of how a 3 x 3 SOM plot looks in a 2D chart (considering two input variables):

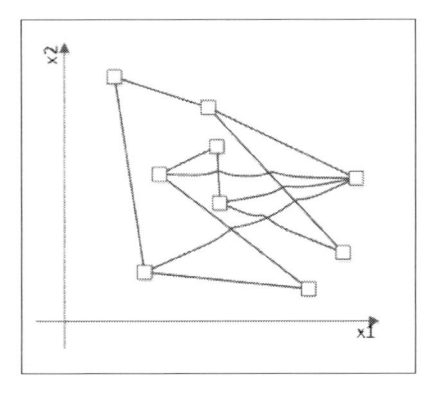

First, the untrained Kohonen network shows a shape that is very strange and screwed up. The shape of the weights will depend solely on the input data that are going to be fed to the SOM. Let's see an example of how the map starts to organize itself.

- Suppose that we have the dense dataset shown in the following plot:

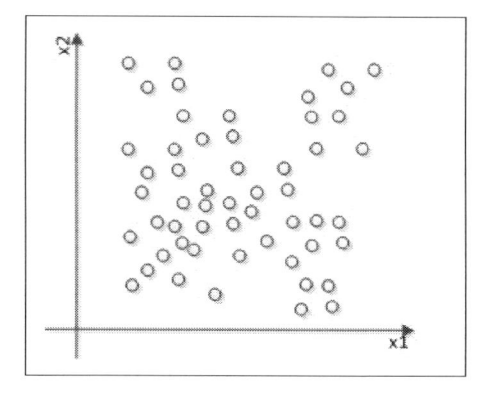

- Upon the application of the SOM, the 2D shape gradually changes, until the network achieve its final configuration:

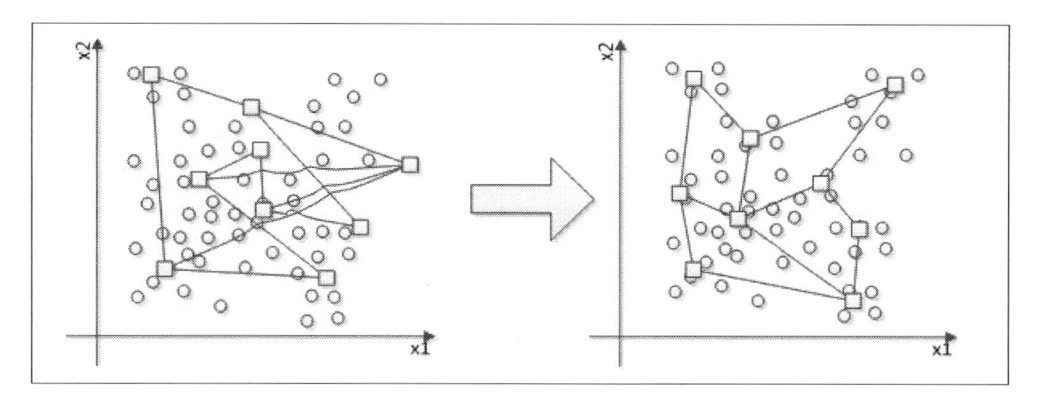

The final shape of a 2-D SOM may not always be a perfect square; instead, it will resemble a shape that could be drawn from the dataset. The neighborhood function is an important component in the learning process because it approximates the neighboring neurons in the plot, and the structure moves to a configuration that is more "organized."

> The grid on a chart is just for didactic purposes. There are other ways of illustrating an SOM diagram, such as the U-matrix and the cluster boundaries.

Self-Organizing Maps

Step-by-step of SOM learning

An SOM aims at classifying the input data by clustering data points that trigger the same response on the output. Initially, the untrained network will produce random outputs, but as more examples are presented, the neural network identifies which neurons are more often activated, and then, their "position" in the SOM output space is changed. This algorithm is based on competitive learning, which means that a winner neuron (also known as **Best Matching Unit, BMU**) will update its weights and its neighboring weights.

The following flowchart illustrates the learning process of an SOM network:

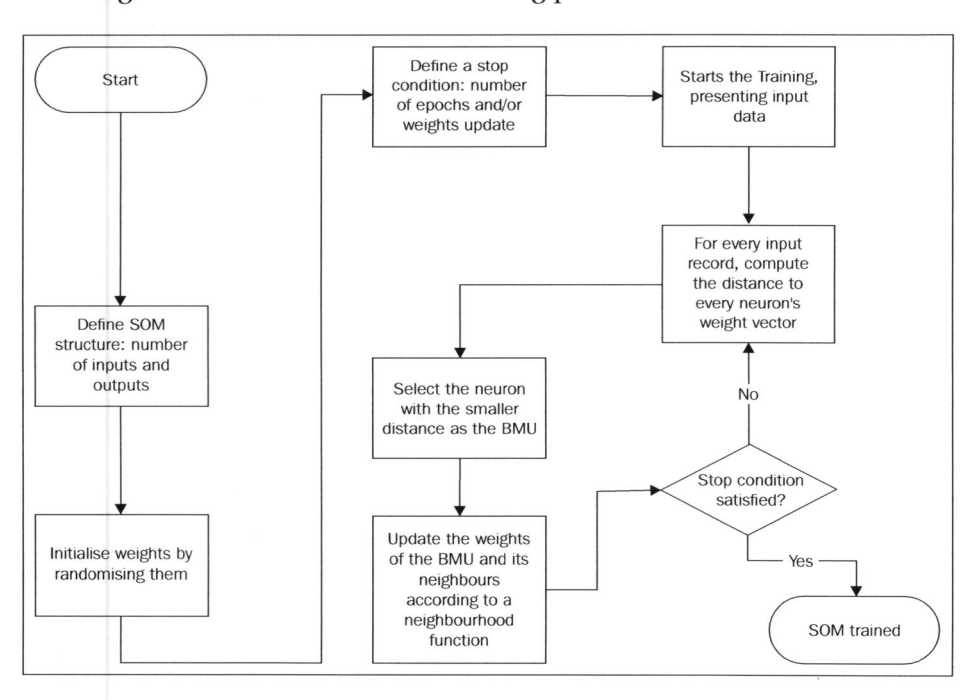

The learning slightly resembles that of the algorithms addressed in *Chapter 2, How Neural Networks Learn* and *Chapter 3, Handling Perceptrons*. The three major differences are the determination of the BMU with the distance, the weight update rule, and the absence of an error measure. The distance implies that nearer points should produce similar outputs; thus, here, the criteria to determine the BMU is the neuron that presents a lower distance to some data point. This Euclidean distance is usually used, and in this book, we will apply it for the sake of simplicity:

$$d(X, W_i) = \sqrt{(X_1 - W_{1i})^2 + (X_2 - W_{2i})^2 + \cdots + (X_n - W_{ni})^2}$$

The weight update rule uses the neighborhood function $\Theta(i,j)$, which states how much a neighboring neuron i is close to neuron j. Remember that in the SOM, the BMU neuron is updated together with its neighboring neurons. The update rule is as follows:

$$\Delta W_{kj} = \Theta(i,j)\alpha(X_k - W_{kj})$$

Where a denotes the learning rate; Θ, the neighborhood function; Xk, the *kth* input; and Wkj, the weight connecting the *kth* input to the *jth* output. Another characteristic of this learning is that both the learning rate and the neighborhood function are dependent on the number of epochs. The neighborhood function is usually Gaussian:

$$\Theta(i,j) = \exp\left(\frac{d(W_i, W_j)^2}{2\sigma^2(t)}\right)$$

Where σ denotes the Gaussian parameter of variance, Wi and Wj represent the weights of neurons i and j, and t denotes the number of epochs.

The learning rate starts at an initial value and then decreases:

$$\alpha(t) = \alpha(0)(1.0 - t/r)$$

Where r represents a parameter of the learning rate.

How to use SOMs

There are many applications of SOMs, most of them in the field of clustering, data abstraction, and dimensionality reduction. However, the clustering applications are the most interesting because of the many possibilities one may apply them to. The real advantage of clustering is that there is no need to worry about the input–output relationship; rather, the problem solver can concentrate on the input data. One example of a clustering application will be explored in *Chapter 7, Clustering Customer Profiles*.

Coding of the Kohonen algorithm

Now, it is time to get hands-on and implement the Kohonen neural network in Java. On the basis of the previous changes in the Java code and because of the application of OOP concepts, it was possible to implement new features without much effort and without rewriting the code already completed in the project. For the sake of simplicity, for now, we will implement only competitive learning and the single-neuron weight updating rule. The changes made are shown in the following table:

Class name: NeuralNet	
Note: This class already exists in the previous version and has been updated as follows:	
Attributes	
`private double[][] validationSet;`	Matrix to store the validation set of input data
Methods	
Note: The getters and setters methods of this attribute were created too.	
Class implementation with Java: file NeuralNet.java	
Interface name: Validation	
Note: In Java, interfaces are structures that may have constant attributes and/or methods signatures that must be implemented inside a class.	
Attributes	
None	
Method	
`public void netValidation(NeuralNet n);`	Performs neural network validation, printing some results on the PC screen
	Parameters: `NeuralNet` object (neural net trained)
	Returns: -
Interface implementation with Java: file Validation.java	
Class name: Kohonen	
Note: This class inherits from `NeuralNet` and implements the `Validation` interface.	
Attributes	
None	
Method	

`public NeuralNet train (NeuralNet n)`	Trains the neural network by applying the Kohonen algorithm. This method overrides the method from the `Training` class
	Parameters: NeuralNet object (neural net untrained)
	Returns: NeuralNet object (neural net trained via Kohonen)
`private NeuralNet initNet (NeuralNet n)`	Initializes `listOfWeightOut` of the list of neurons from the input layer with zero
	Parameters: NeuralNet object without the input layer initialized
	Returns: NeuralNet object with the input layer initialized
`private ArrayList<Double> calcEuclideanDistance (NeuralNet n, double[][] data, int row)`	Calculates the Euclidian distance between the training data and the weights of the neural network
	Parameters: NeuralNet object, training data, and the row of training data
	Returns: List of real values with Euclidian distances
`private NeuralNet fixWinnerWeights (NeuralNet n, int winnerNeuron, int trainSetRow)`	Adjusts weights of the winner neuron (on the basis of the Euclidian distance list)
	Parameters: NeuralNet object, winner neuron index, training set row number
	Returns: NeuralNet object with weights from the input layer modified
`public void netValidation(NeuralNet n)`	Adjusts weights of the winner neuron (on the basis of the Euclidian distance list)
	Parameters: NeuralNet object with the neural net trained
	Returns: -
Class implementation with Java: file Kohonen.java	

Self-Organizing Maps

The class diagram changes are shown in the following figure. Attributes and methods already explained in previous chapters and their configuration methods (getters and setters) are not shown.

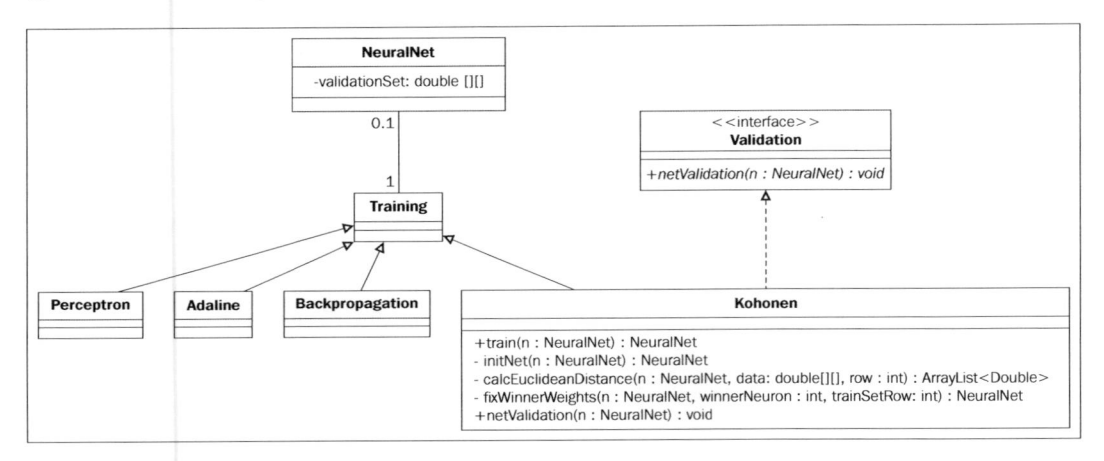

Exploring the Kohonen class

The **Kohonen** class implements a validation interface that provides a validation method to ensure that the correct output neuron was chosen. Let's concentrate on three key methods present in this class: `calcEuclideanDistance`, `fixWinnerWeights`, and `train`.

The Euclidean distance is calculated according to the equation shown in the Section SOM learning algorithm, as can be seen in the following code:

```
    private ArrayList<Double> calcEuclideanDistance(NeuralNet n,
double[][] data, int row) {
      ArrayList<Double> listOfDistances = new ArrayList<Double>();

      int weight_i = 0;
      for(int cluster_i = 0; cluster_i < n.getOutputLayer().
getNumberOfNeuronsInLayer(); cluster_i++) {

        double distance = 0.0;

        for(int input_j = 0; input_j < n.getInputLayer().
getNumberOfNeuronsInLayer(); input_j++) {

          double weight = n.getInputLayer().getListOfNeurons().get(0).
getListOfWeightOut().get(weight_i);
```

```
                    distance = distance + Math.pow(data[row][input_j] - weight,
2.0);
                    weight_i++;

            }

            listOfDistances.add(distance);

            //System.out.println("distance normal "+cluster_i+": 
"+distance);
        }
        return listOfDistances;

    }
```

This method receives as a parameter the dataset for computing the distances of all neurons to a certain row of this dataset. We can see in this method two for loops: The outer loop iterates over all the neurons in the output layer, whereas the inner loop iterates over all the input variables of the corresponding row in the dataset. The distance is finally calculated after the inner loop is executed and is saved in a list of distances that will be returned.

The weight update rule is implemented in the `fixWinnerWeights` method, which already receives as the parameter the winner neuron. The code of this method is listed as follows:

```
    private NeuralNet fixWinnerWeights(NeuralNet n, int winnerNeuron,
int trainSetRow) {
        int start, last;

        start = winnerNeuron * n.getInputLayer().
getNumberOfNeuronsInLayer();

        if(start < 0) {
           start = 0;
        }

        last = start + n.getInputLayer().getNumberOfNeuronsInLayer();

        List<Double> listOfOldWeights = new ArrayList<Double>();
        listOfOldWeights = n.getInputLayer().getListOfNeurons().get( 0 
).getListOfWeightOut().subList(start, last);

        ArrayList<Double> listOfWeights = new ArrayList<Double>();
```

Self-Organizing Maps

```
        listOfWeights = n.getInputLayer().getListOfNeurons().get( 0
).getListOfWeightOut();

    int col_i = 0;
    for (int j = start; j < last; j++) {
      double trainSetValue = n.getTrainSet()[trainSetRow][col_i];
      double newWeight = listOfOldWeights.get(col_i) +
          n.getLearningRate() *
          (trainSetValue - listOfOldWeights.get(col_i));

      //System.out.println("newWeight: " + newWeight);

      listOfWeights.set(j, newWeight);
      col_i++;
    }

    n.getInputLayer().getListOfNeurons().get( 0 ).setListOfWeightOut(
listOfWeights );

    return n;

  }
```

First, the code determines the weights that should be updated, which implies the winner neuron's weights, from start to end. Then, in the inner for loop, the new weight is assigned. Note the subtraction of the input value (trainSetValue) and the old weight.

Finally, let's check how these functions are used together in the Train method. In order to save space, we will focus only on the epoch loop:

```
        for (int epoch = 0; epoch < n.getMaxEpochs(); epoch++) {

      //System.out.println("### EPOCH: "+epoch);

      for (int row_i = 0; row_i < rows; row_i++) {
        listOfDistances = calcEuclideanDistance(n, trainData, row_i);

        int winnerNeuron = listOfDistances.indexOf(Collections.min(listOfDistances));

        n = fixWinnerWeights(n, winnerNeuron, row_i);

      }

    }
```

For every row in the training set, the distances are calculated using the Euclidean distance and right after that, the winner neuron is determined. Then, the weights are updated, and the learning process moves to the next iteration.

Kohonen implementation (clustering animals)

In this section, we will explain the Kohonen algorithm in practice. Imagine that we have some animals and three of their characteristics are: has pelage (Yes/No), is terrestrial (Yes/No), and has mammary glands (Yes/No). Our goal is to cluster the animals in two different groups that we do not know yet. The following table summarizes this data:

#	Animal	Has pelage (Y = 1 / No = -1)	Is terrestrial (Y = 1 / No = -1)	Has mammary glands (Y = 1 / No = -1)
1	Bat	1	-1	1
2	Shark	-1	-1	-1
3	Sea-cow	-1	-1	1
4	Spider	1	1	-1
5	Hippo	-1	1	1
6	Fly	1	-1	-1
7	Viper	-1	1	-1
8	Monkey	1	1	1

The following figure displays the architecture of the Kohonen neural net used for solving this problem:

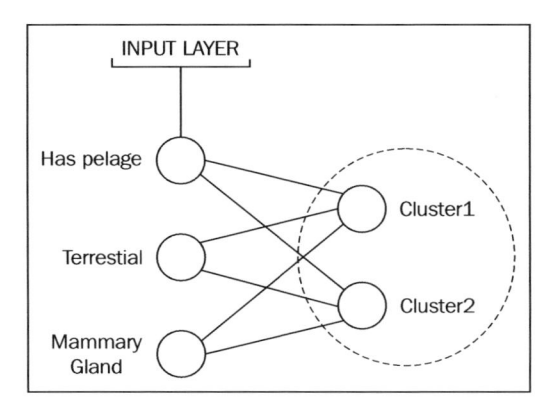

Self-Organizing Maps

Next, let's analyze the test method called `testKohonen()`. It is as follows:

```
private void testKohonen(){
    NeuralNet testNet = new NeuralNet();
    
    //2 inputs because "bias"
    testNet = testNet.initNet(2, 0, 0, 2);
    
    NeuralNet trainedNet = new NeuralNet();
    
    testNet.setTrainSet(new double[][] { { 1.0, -1.0, 1.0 },       {
-1.0, -1.0, -1.0 }, { -1.0, -1.0,  1.0 }, { 1.0, 1.0, -1.0 },      {
-1.0,  1.0,  1.0 }, {  1.0, -1.0, -1.0 } });
    
    //viper and monkey, respectively:
    testNet.setValidationSet(new double[][] { {-1.0, 1.0, -1.0}, {1.0,
1.0, 1.0} } );
    
    testNet.setMaxEpochs(10);
    testNet.setLearningRate(0.1);
    testNet.setTrainType(TrainingTypesENUM.KOHONEN);
    
    trainedNet = testNet.trainNet(testNet);
    
    System.out.println();
    System.out.println("---------KOHONEN VALIDATION NET---------");
    
    testNet.netValidation(trainedNet);
```

The Kohonen test logic follows the same steps as those used in the previous implementations. First, an object of the `NeuralNet` class is created and used for initializing the net with three neurons in the input layer, and two neurons in the output layer that represents the number of clusters to achieve.

After that, samples of rows **1** to **6** from the preceding table are used for the training and those from the last two rows are used for validating the neural net. It is important to ensure that the data used for the validation is not the same as that used for training the neural net. To conclude, a method to train the neural net is called.

When this case of test reaches the end, it generates the validation results shown next.

```java
public class NeuralNetTest {

    public static void main(String[] args) {
        NeuralNetTest test = new NeuralNetTest();

        test.testKohonen();
    }

    private void testKohonen(){
        NeuralNet testNet = new NeuralNet();

        //2 inputs because "bias"
        testNet = testNet.initNet(2, 0, 0, 2);
```

```
run:

---------KOHONEN VALIDATION NET---------
### VALIDATION RESULT ###
CLUSTER 2
### VALIDATION RESULT ###
CLUSTER 1
BUILD SUCCESSFUL (total time: 1 second)
```

By analyzing the validation results, we find that the neural net is able to cluster two different kinds of animals:

- **Cluster 1**: Mammal (monkey)
- **Cluster 2**: Not mammal (viper)

Summary

In this chapter, we've seen how to apply unsupervised learning algorithms to neural networks. We've been presented a new and suitable architecture to that end, the SOMs of Kohonen. Further, unsupervised learning has been proven to be as powerful as the supervised learning methods because it concentrates only on the input data, without the necessity of input–output mappings. We've seen two new training algorithms: competitive learning and its extension for a Kohonen network. The SOMs also play a role in clustering and dimensionality reduction, besides providing a graphical representation of large datasets. With the content learned so far, we can move to the next chapter , which discusses an interesting practical application of weather forecasting.

5
Forecasting Weather

This chapter presents an application of neural networks to the prediction of future weather data. We are going to walk through the entire process of designing a neural network to be applied to this problem, how to choose the neural architecture, the number of neurons, as well as selecting and preprocessing data. Then, the reader will be presented with a dataset on which our neural network is going to make predictions of weather variables using the Java programming language. The topics covered in this chapter are as follows:

- Neural networks for prediction problems
- Selecting data
    - Input/Output variables
    - Filtering
- Preprocessing
    - Normalization
- Java implementation
    - Adaptations
- Empirical design of neural networks

Neural networks for prediction problems

So far, the reader has been presented with a number of neural network implementations and architectures, so now; it is time to get into more complex cases. The power of neural networks in predictions is really astonishing, since they can perform "learning" from historical data in a fashion in which the neural connections are adapted to produce the same results according to some input data. For example, for a given situation (cause), there is a consequence (result) and this is coded as data; the neural network can be used to learn the nonlinear function that maps the situation to the consequence (or the cause to the result).

Prediction problems are an interesting category to apply neural networks to. Let's take a look at a sample table containing weather data:

Date	Avg. temperature	Pressure	Humidity	Precipitation	Wind speed
July 31	23° C	880 mbar	66%	16 mm	5 m/s
August 1	22° C	881 mbar	78%	3 mm	3 m/s
August 2	25° C	884 mbar	65%	0 mm	4 m/s
August 3	27° C	882 mbar	53%	0 mm	3 m/s
...					
December 11	32° C	890 mbar	64%	0 mm	2 m/s

The preceding table depicts five variables containing hypothetical values of weather data collected from a hypothetical city, only for the purpose of this example. Now, let's suppose that each of the variables contains a list of values sequentially taken over time. We can think of each list as a time series. On a time-series chart, one can see how they evolve along with time:

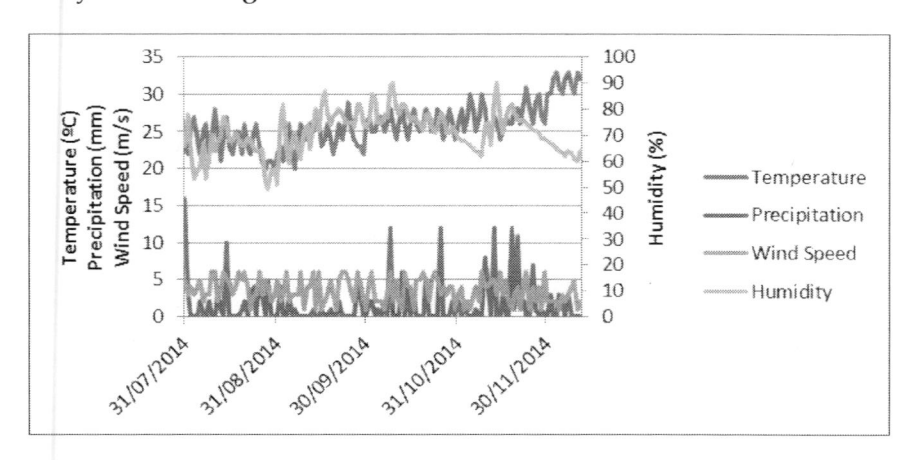

The relationship between these time series denotes a dynamic representation of weather in a certain city, as depicted in the preceding chart. We indeed want the neural network to learn these dynamics; however, it is necessary to understand a little bit more about the phenomena, because we need to structure this data in a way that neural networks can process it.

Only after structuring the data can we structure the neural network, that is, the number of inputs, outputs, and hidden nodes. However, there are many other architectures that may be suitable for prediction problems, such as radial basis functions and feedback networks. In this chapter, we will deal with the feedforward multi layer perceptron with backpropagation learning algorithm, to demonstrate how this architecture can be simply exploited to predict weather variables. Also, this architecture presents very good generalized results with good selected data and there is little complexity involved in the design process.

The overall process for designing neural networks for prediction processes is depicted in the following figure:

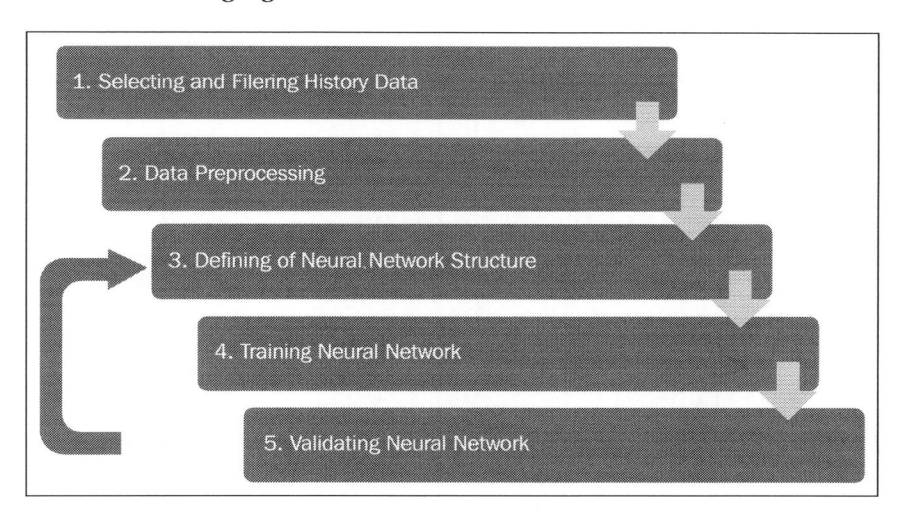

1. Selecting and Filering History Data
2. Data Preprocessing
3. Defining of Neural Network Structure
4. Training Neural Network
5. Validating Neural Network

If the neural network fails to be validated (step 5), then usually, a new structure (step 3) is defined, although sometimes, steps 1 and 2 may be repeated. Each of the steps in the figure will be addressed in the following sections of this chapter.

No data, no neural net – selecting data

The first thing to do is to select appropriate relevant data that carries most of the system's dynamics that we want the neural network to reproduce. In our case, we need to select data that is relevant for weather forecasting.

> While selecting data, getting an expert opinion about the process and its variables can be really helpful. The expert does help a lot in understanding the relationship between the variables, thus selecting them in an appropriate fashion.

In this chapter, we are going to use the data from the Brazilian Institute of Meteorology (INMET - http://www.inmet.gov.br/ in Portuguese), which is freely available on the Internet and we have the rights to apply it in this book. However, the reader may use any free weather database from the Internet while developing applications. Some examples from the English language sources are listed as follows:

- Wunderground (http://wunderground.com/)
- Open weather map (http://openweathermap.org/api)
- Yahoo weather API (https://developer.yahoo.com/weather/)
- U.S. National Climatic Data Center (http://www.ncdc.noaa.gov/)

Knowing the problem – weather variables

Any weather database has almost the same variables:

- Temperature (°C)
- Humidity (%)
- Pressure (mbar)
- Wind speed (m/s)
- Wind direction (°)
- Precipitation (mm)
- Sunny hours (h)
- Sun energy (W/m^2)

This data is usually collected from meteorological stations, satellites, or radars, on an hourly or daily basis.

> Depending on the collection frequency, some variables may be summarized with average, minimum, or maximum values.
>
> The data units may also vary from source to source; that's why the units should always be observed.

Choosing input and output variables

Neural networks work as a nonlinear block that may have a predefined number of inputs and outputs, so we have to select the role that each weather variable will play in this application. In other words, we have to choose which variable(s) the neural network is going to predict and by using which input variables.

> Regarding time series variables, one can derive new variables by applying historical data. This means that given a certain date, one may consider this date's values and the data collected (and/or summarized) from past dates, therefore extending the number of variables.

While defining a problem to use neural networks on, we need to consider one or more predefined target variables: predict temperature, forecast precipitation, measure insolation, and so on. However, in some cases, one may want to model all the variables and to find the causal relationships between them. To identify a causal relationship, there are a number of tools that can be applied:

- Cross-correlation
- Pearson's coefficient
- Statistical analysis
- Bayesian networks

For the sake of simplicity, we are not going to explore these tools in this chapter; however, the reader is recommended to go to the references [*Dowdy & Wearden*, 1983; *Pearl*, 2000; *Fortuna et al.*, 2007] for obtaining more details about these tools. Instead, since we want to demonstrate the power of neural networks in predicting weather, we will choose the average temperature of a given day, based on the other four variables, on the basis of the current technical literature, which is cited in the preceding reference.

Removing insignificant behaviors – Data filtering

Sometimes, some issues are faced while getting data from some source. The common problems are as follows:

- Absence of data in a certain record and variable
- Error in measurement (for example, when a value is badly labeled)
- Outliers (for example, when the value is very far from the usual range)

To handle each of these issues, one needs to perform filtering on the selected data. The neural network will reproduce exactly the same dynamics as those of the data that it will be trained with, so we have to be careful in feeding it with bad data. Usually, records containing bad data are removed from the dataset, ensuring that only "good" data are fed to the network.

To better understand filtering, let's consider the dataset as a big matrix containing n measurements and m variables.

$$A = \begin{bmatrix} a_1(1) & \cdots & a_m(1) \\ a_1(2) & \cdots & a_m(2) \\ \vdots & \ddots & \vdots \\ a_1(n) & \cdots & a_m(n) \end{bmatrix}$$

Where $a_j(i)$ denotes the measurement of variable j at moment i.

So, our task is to find the bad records and delete them. Mathematically, there are a number of ways of identifying a bad record. For error measurement and outlier detection, the following three-sigma rule is very good:

$$|d_i| = \left| \frac{x_i - E[X]}{\sigma_X} \right| = \begin{cases} > 3 \; bad \; record, remove \\ \leq 3 \; good \; record, keep \; it \end{cases}$$

Where x_i denotes the value of the ith measurement, $E[X]$ represents the average value, σX indicates the standard deviation, and d_i refers to the weighted distance from the average. If the absolute distance of the ith measurement fails to fit in less than three records, the ith measurement will be labeled as a bad measurement, and although the other variables from the same instance (row of the matrix) are good, one should discard the entire row of the dataset.

Adjusting values – data preprocessing

Raw data collected from a data source usually presents different particularities, such as data range, sampling, and category. Some variables result from measurements, while the others are a summary or even calculated. Preprocessing means to adapt these variables' values to form neural networks that can handle them properly.

Regarding weather variables, let's take a look at their range, sampling, and type, shown in the following table:

Variable	Unit	Range	Sampling	Type
Mean temperature	°C	23.86–29.25	Hourly	Average of hourly measurements
Precipitation	Mm	0–161.20	Daily	Accumulation of daily rain
Insolation	h	0–10.40	Daily	Count of hours receiving sun radiation
Mean humidity	%	65.50–96.00	Hourly	Average of hourly measurements
Mean wind speed	km/h	0.00–3.27	Hourly	Average of hourly measurements

Except for insolation and precipitation, the variables are all measured and share the same sampling, but if we wanted, for example, to use an hourly dataset, we would have to preprocess all the variables to use the same sample rate. Three of the variables are summarized using daily average values, but if we wanted to, we could use hourly data measurements. However, the range would surely be larger.

Equalizing data – normalization

Normalization is the process to get all the variables into the same data range, usually with smaller values, between **0** and **1** or **-1** and **1**. This helps the neural network to present values within the variable zone in activation functions such as sigmoid or hyperbolic tangent:

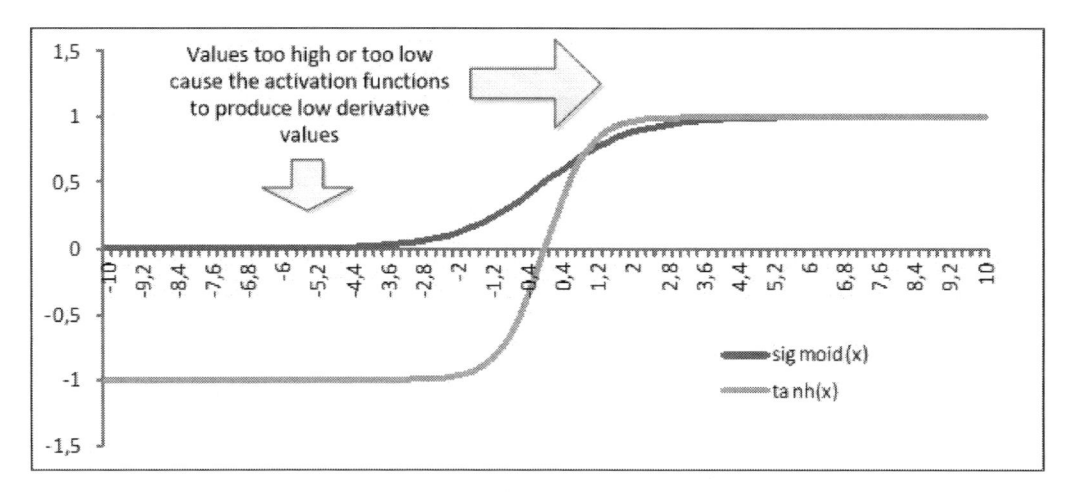

Values too high or too low may drive neurons to produce values that are too high or too low as well for the activation functions, therefore leading the derivative for these neurons to be too small, near zero.

The normalization should consider a predefined range of the dataset. It is performed right away:

$$X_{norm} = (N_{max} - N_{min}) \left[\frac{(X - X_{min})}{(X_{max} - X_{min})} \right] + N_{min}$$

Where N_{min} and N_{max} represent the normalized minimum and maximum limits, respectively; X_{min} and X_{max} denote X variable's minimum and maximum limits, respectively; X indicates the original value; and X_{norm} refers to the normalized value. If we want the normalization to be between **0** and **1**, for example, the equation is simplified as follows:

$$X_{norm} = \frac{(X - X_{min})}{(X_{max} - X_{min})}$$

By applying the normalization, a new "normalized" dataset is produced and is fed to the neural network. One should also take into account that a neural network fed with normalized values will be trained to produce normalized values on the output, so the inverse (denormalization) process becomes necessary as well.

$$X = (X_{max} - X_{min}) \left[\frac{(X_{norm} - N_{min})}{(N_{max} - N_{min})} \right] + X_{min}$$

or:

$$X = (X_{max} - X_{min})[X_{norm}] + X_{min}$$

For the normalization between 0 and 1.

Java implementation for weather prediction

In order to implement this case in Java, we had to make some adjustments in the already written code. The `NeuralNet` class is updated with a new method called `getNetOutputValues()`, to give some output values given a training input dataset. This method performs almost the same operation as the forward method in the backpropagation phase, except for the fact that it returns a matrix containing the output dataset.

In addition, we had to add two components to the project (package `edu.packt.neuralnet.util`): data and chart.

Plotting charts

Charts can be drawn in Java by using the freely available package **JFreeChart** (http://www.jfree.org/jfreechart/). This package is attached with this chapter's source code. So, we designed a class called `Chart`. It implements methods basically for plotting data series by making calls to natively implemented methods of the JFreeChart classes. The following table shows a list of methods contained in this class:

Class name: Chart	
Attributes	

`public enum ChartPlotTypeENUM {`
`   FULL_DATA, COMPARISON;`
`}`
	Enum to store chart types may be plotted

Methods	
`public void plotXYData(Object[] vector, String chartTitle, String xAxisLabel, String yAxisLabel)`	Method to plot XY chart based on a data vector
	Parameters: Vector with data to plot, chart title, x-axis label, and y-axis label
	Returns: -
`public void plotXYData(double[][] matrix, String chartTitle, String xAxisLabel, String yAxisLabel, ChartPlotTypeENUM chartPlotType)`	Method to plot XY chart based on a data matrix
	Parameters: Matrix with data to plot, chart title, x-axis label, y-axis label, and plot type
	Returns: -
`private String selectComparisonSeriesName(int index)`	Method to select comparison series name
	Parameters: Index
	Returns: Series name

Forecasting Weather

`private String selectTemperatureSeriesName(int index)`	Method to select temperature series name
	Parameters: Index
	Returns: Series name
Class Implementation with Java: file Chart.java	

Handling data files

To work with data files, we have to implement a class called `Data`. It currently performs reads from the so-called **CSV** format, which is suitable for data import and export. This class also performs preprocessing on the data by means of normalization.

\multicolumn{2}{c}{Class name: Data}	
\multicolumn{2}{c}{Attributes}	
`private String path;`	Variable to store the CSV file folder path
`private String fileName;`	Attribute to store the CSV file name (with extension)
`public enum NormalizationTypesENUM { MAX_MIN, MAX_MIN_EQUALIZED; }`	Enum to store normalization types may be used
\multicolumn{2}{c}{Constructors}	
`public Data(String path, String fileName)`	Constructor to set path and filename attributes
`public Data( )`	Empty constructor to create an empty object
\multicolumn{2}{c}{Methods}	
\multicolumn{2}{l}{**Note**: The getters and setters methods of this attribute were created too.}	
`public double[][] rawData2Matrix(Data r) throws IOException`	Method to read raw data (CSV file) and convert to a double Java matrix
	Parameters: Data object
	Returns: Double matrix with raw data
`private String defineAbsoluteFilePath(Data r) throws IOException`	Method to define the absolute CSV file path
	Parameters: Data object
	Returns: String with the absolute CSV file path

`public double[][] normalize(double[][] rawMatrix, NormalizationTypesENUM normType)`	Method to normalize a raw data matrix
	Parameters: Double raw data matrix, normalization type
	Returns: Double matrix normalized
`public double[][] denormalize(double[][] rawMatrix, double[][] matrixNorm, NormalizationTypesENUM normType)`	Method to denormalize a raw data matrix
	Parameters: Double raw data matrix, double normalized matrix, normalization type
	Returns: Double matrix denormalized
`public double[][] joinArrays(ArrayList<double[][]> listOfArraysToJoin)`	Method to join arrays (vectors) into a matrix
	Parameters: List of arrays
	Returns: Double matrix
Class implementation with Java: file `Data.java`	

Building a neural network for weather prediction

To forecast weather, we collected daily data from the Brazilian Institute of Meteorology (INMET). The data was measured from a Brazilian city located in the Amazon region.

From the eight variables available at the INMET website, five were selected for use in this project, where the average of the maximum and the minimum temperature became the mean temperature variable. The neural network was trained to forecast the average temperature. So, the structure of the neural network is as shown in the following figure:

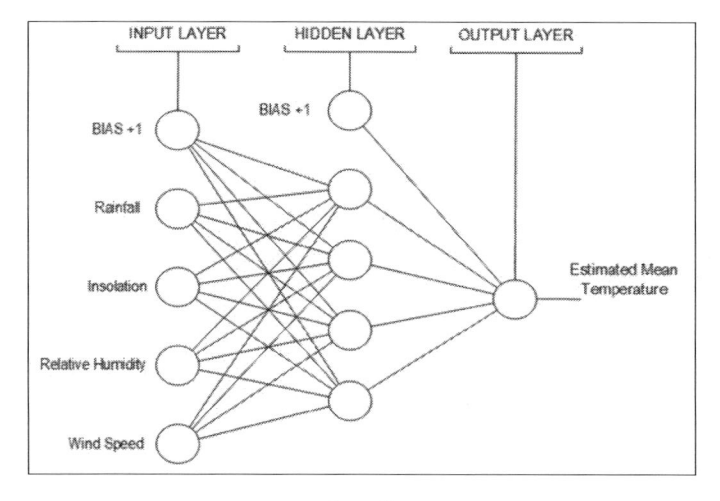

Forecasting Weather

We designed a class called `Weather` exclusively for the weather case. It only has a static main method and is solely aimed at reading the weather data files, creating and training a neural network with this data, and plotting the error for validation. Let's take a glance at how the data files are read inside this class:

```
   Data weatherDataInput  = new Data( "data", "inmet_13_14_input.csv"
);
   Data weatherDataOutput = new Data( "data", "inmet_13_14_output.csv"
);

   //sets the normalisation type
   NormalizationTypesENUM NORMALIZATION_TYPE = Data.
NormalizationTypesENUM.MAX_MIN_EQUALIZED;

   try {
      double[][] matrixInput = weatherDataInput.rawData2Matrix(
weatherDataInput );
      double[][] matrixOutput = weatherDataOutput.rawData2Matrix(
weatherDataOutput );

   //normalise the data
      double[][] matrixInputNorm  = weatherDataInput.normalize(
matrixInput, NORMALIZATION_TYPE );
      double[][] matrixOutputNorm = weatherDataOutput.normalize(
matrixOutput, NORMALIZATION_TYPE );
```

Then, the main method builds a neural network with four hidden neurons and sets the training dataset, as shown in the following code:

```
      NeuralNet n1 = new NeuralNet();
      n1 = n1.initNet(4, 1, 4, 1);

      n1.setTrainSet( matrixInputNorm );
      n1.setRealMatrixOutputSet( matrixOutputNorm );

      n1.setMaxEpochs( 1000 );
      n1.setTargetError( 0.00001 );
      n1.setLearningRate( 0.5 );
      n1.setTrainType( TrainingTypesENUM.BACKPROPAGATION );
      n1.setActivationFnc( ActivationFncENUM.SIGLOG );
         n1.setActivationFncOutputLayer(ActivationFncENUM.LINEAR);

      NeuralNet n1Trained = new NeuralNet();

      n1Trained = n1.trainNet( n1 );

      System.out.println();
```

Here, the network is trained, and then, the charts of the error are plotted. The following lines show how the chart class is used:

```
Chart c1 = new Chart();
c1.plotXYData( n1.getListOfMSE().toArray(), "MSE Error", "Epochs",
"MSE Value" );

//TRAINING:
double[][] matrixOutputRNA = n1Trained.getNetOutputValues( n1Trained
);
double[][] matrixOutputRNADenorm   = new Data().denormalize(
matrixOutput, matrixOutputRNA, NORMALIZATION_TYPE);

ArrayList<double[][]> listOfArraysToJoin = new ArrayList<double[]
[]>();
listOfArraysToJoin.add( matrixOutput );
listOfArraysToJoin.add( matrixOutputRNADenorm );

double[][] matrixOutputsJoined = new Data().joinArrays(
listOfArraysToJoin );

Chart c2 = new Chart();
c2.plotXYData( matrixOutputsJoined, "Real x Estimated -
Training Data", "Weather Data", "Temperature (Celsius)", Chart.
ChartPlotTypeENUM.COMPARISON );
```

In the following graph, it is possible to see the MSE training error plotted. The *x*-axis represents 1000 points (epochs of training), and the *y*-axis shows the variation of the MSE values. It is noticed that before the 100th epoch, the MSE value establishes.

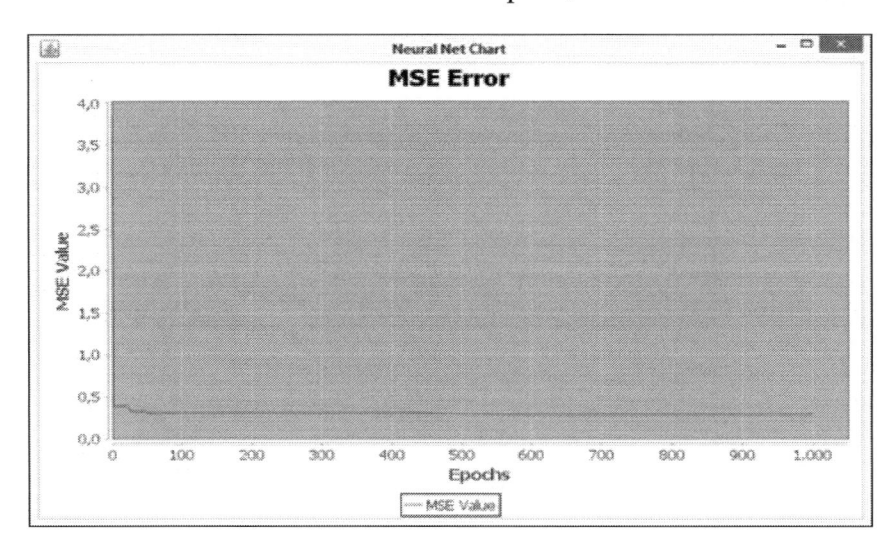

Forecasting Weather

Another graph is displayed next. It shows a comparison between the real (red line) and the estimated (blue line) average temperature. Dotted black lines symbolize the margins of error (-1.0 °C and +1.0 °C).

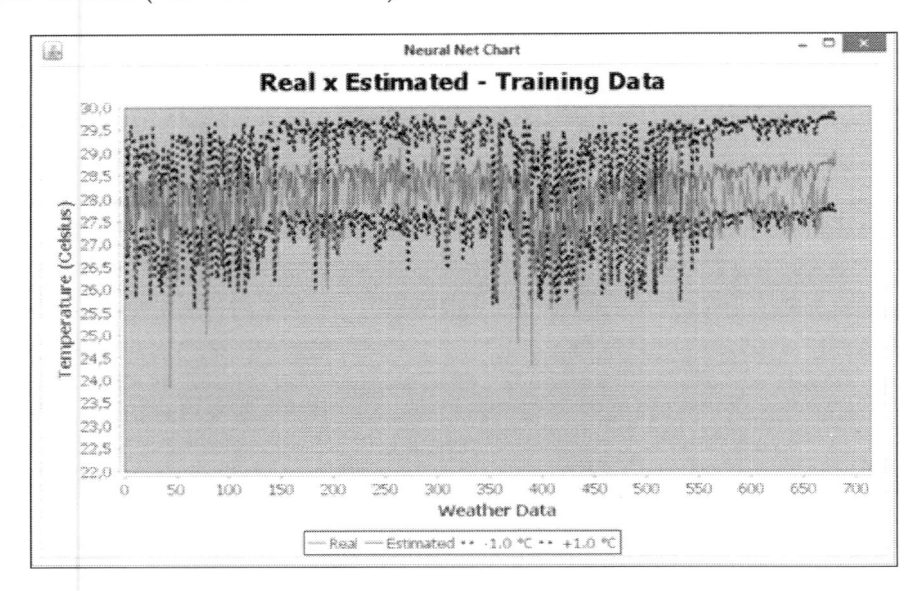

Empirical design of neural networks

While using neural networks in regression problems (that include prediction), there is no fixed number of hidden neurons, so usually, the solver chooses an arbitrary number of neurons and then varies it according to the results produced by the networks created. This procedure may be repeated a number of times until a network with a satisfying criterion is found.

Choosing training and test datasets

In order to attest the neural network's capability to properly respond to new data, it is useful to have two separate datasets, called training and test datasets. In this application, we worked with two distinct periods, one for each dataset.

Period	Begin	End	Type	Number of records	%
1	01/01/2013	31/12/2014	Training	730	93.8
2	30/04/2015	16/06/2015	Test	48	6.2
Total				778	100

The recommendation is for the training set to have at least 75% of the overall dataset.

Designing experiments

Experiments can be performed on the same training and test datasets, but by varying the other network parameters, such as the learning rate, normalization, and the number of hidden units. In this case, we performed 12 experiments, whose parameters were chosen as shown in the following table:

Experiment	Number of neurons in hidden layer	Learning rate	Data normalization type
1	2	0.1	MAX_MIN
2	2	0.1	MAX_MIN_EQUALIZED
3	2	0.5	MAX_MIN
4	2	0.5	MAX_MIN_EQUALIZED
5	2	0.9	MAX_MIN
6	2	0.9	MAX_MIN_EQUALIZED
7	4	0.1	MAX_MIN
8	4	0.1	MAX_MIN_EQUALIZED
9	4	0.5	MAX_MIN
10	4	0.5	MAX_MIN_EQUALIZED
11	4	0.9	MAX_MIN
12	4	0.9	MAX_MIN_EQUALIZED

The objective is to choose a neural network that presents the best performance from the experiments. The best performance is assigned to the network that presents the lowest MSE error, but an analysis of generalization with the test data is also useful.

> While designing experiments, consider starting always from a relatively low number of hidden neurons, since it is desirable to have low computational cost.

Results and simulations

After running the 12 experiments, we found the following MSE errors:

Experiment	MSE training error
1	3.6551720491360E-4
2	0.3034120360203837
3	3.8543681112765E-4
4	0.3467096464653794

Forecasting Weather

Experiment	MSE training error
5	4.6319274448088E-4
6	0.4610935945738937
7	2.6604395044000E-4
8	0.2074979827120087
9	2.7763926432754E-4
10	0.2877786584371894
11	3.4582006086257E-4
12	0.4610935945709355

The following graph exhibits neural net 5th experiment's comparison between real and estimated values, and the respective margins of error:

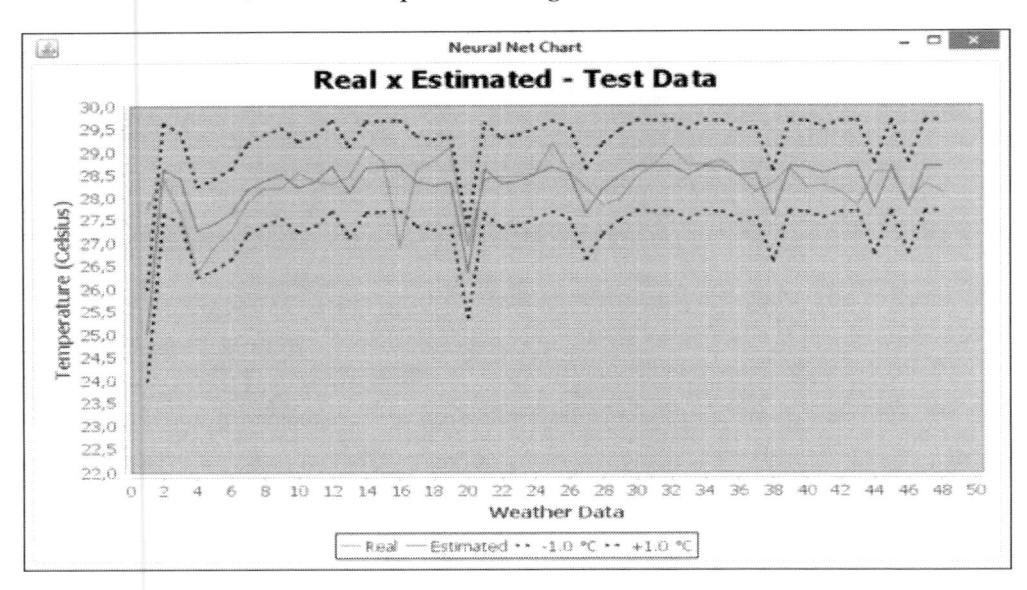

The following graph shows that the same results as those discussed in the previous paragraph, but for neural network 10th experiment:

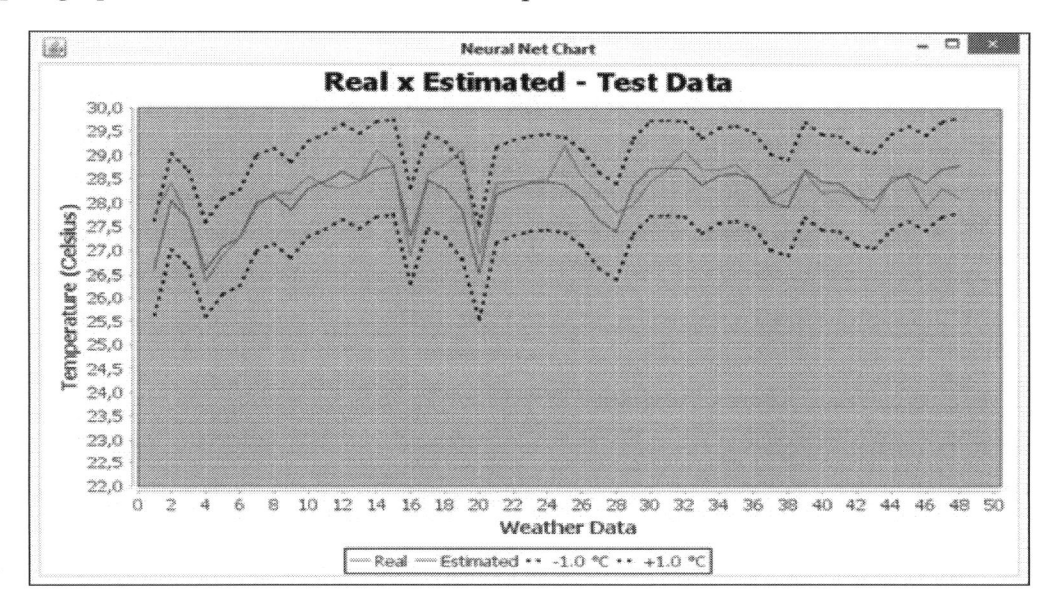

Real x Estimated - Test Data

Although experiment 10 has a larger MSE than experiment 5 and 10's chart presents a better generalization behavior. Therefore, we can conclude the following:

- Considering only the final MSE value to decide about the neural net quality is not recommended.
- Estimated value from experiment 10 follows the real value closer than that from experiment 5.
- Neural net obtained in experiment 10 preserves the trending by ascent and descent better than that obtained in 5, as may be viewed between weather data 1 and 17.

Therefore, by viewing the corresponding charts, we chose network 10 to be the most suitable for weather prediction.

Summary

In this chapter, we've seen an interesting practical application of neural networks. Weather forecasting has always been a rich research field, and indeed, neural networks are widely used for these tasks. In this chapter, the reader also learned how to prepare similar experiments for prediction problems. The correct application of techniques for data selection and preprocessing can save a considerable amount of time while designing a neural network for the prediction. This chapter also serves as a foundation for the following chapters, since all of them will focus on practical cases, so the concepts learned here will be explored widely in the rest of the book.

In the next chapter we will cover classification tasks, which is another common research field where neural networks can be used. Two case studies will be presented, covering the whole process on how neural networks are built for disease diagnosis.

6
Classifying Disease Diagnosis

In this chapter, the reader will be presented with a very didactic but interesting application that neural networks are suitable for: disease diagnosis. We've discovered so far that neural networks can be very well applied to classification problems, where one wants to automatically assign some record to a certain category. This chapter digs deeper into this by presenting the basics on how to design a classification algorithm using neural networks. The topics covered in this chapter are as follows:

- Foundations of classification problems
- Logistic regression
    - Multiple classes vs. binary classes
    - Confusion matrix
    - Sensibility and specificity
- Neural networks for classification
    - Adaptations in Java code
- Disease diagnosis using neural networks
    - Diagnosis for cancer
    - Diagnosis for diabetes

What are classification problems, and how can neural networks be applied to them?

One thing that neural networks are really good at is classifying records. A very simple perceptron network draws a decision boundary defining whether a data point belongs to a particular region or to another region, where a region denotes a class. Let's take a look at an **x–y** scatter chart:

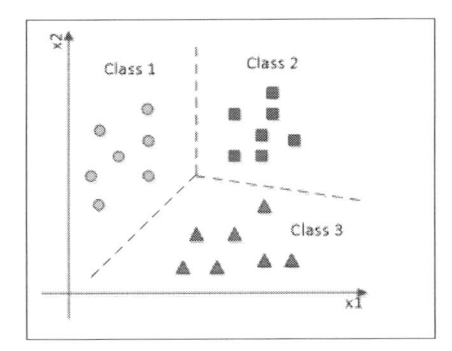

The dashed lines explicitly separate the points into classes. These points represent data records that originally had the corresponding class labels. This implies that their classes were already known; therefore, this classification tasks falls into the supervised learning category.

A classification algorithm seeks to find the boundaries between classes in the data hyperspace. Once the classification boundaries are defined, a new data point, with an unknown class, receives a class label according to the boundaries defined by the classification algorithm. The following figure shows an example of how a new record is classified:

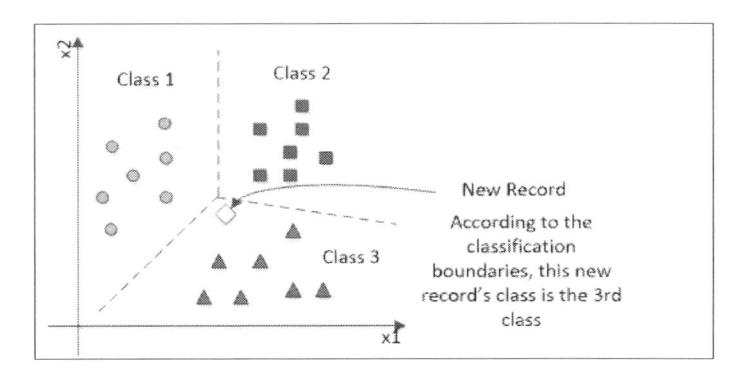

According to the current class configuration, the new record's class is **Class 3**.

A special type of activation function – Logistic regression

We've covered that neural networks can work as data classifiers by establishing decision boundaries onto data in the hyperspace. Such a boundary can be linear in the case of perceptrons or nonlinear in the case of other neural architectures such as MLPs, Kohonen, or Adaline. The linear case is based on linear regression, on which the classification boundary is literally a line, as shown in the preceding figure. If the scatter chart of the data looks like that shown in the following figure, then a nonlinear classification boundary is needed.

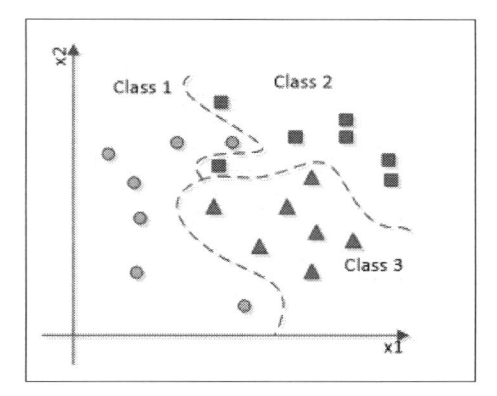

Neural networks are in fact a great nonlinear classifier, and this is achieved by the usage of nonlinear activation functions. One nonlinear function that actually works well for nonlinear classification is the sigmoid function, and the procedure for classification using this function is called logistic regression.

$$f(x) = \frac{1}{1 + e^{-\alpha x}}$$

Classifying Disease Diagnosis

This function returns values bounded between **0** and **1**. In this function, the *a* parameter denotes how hard the transition from **0** to **1** occurs. The following chart shows the difference:

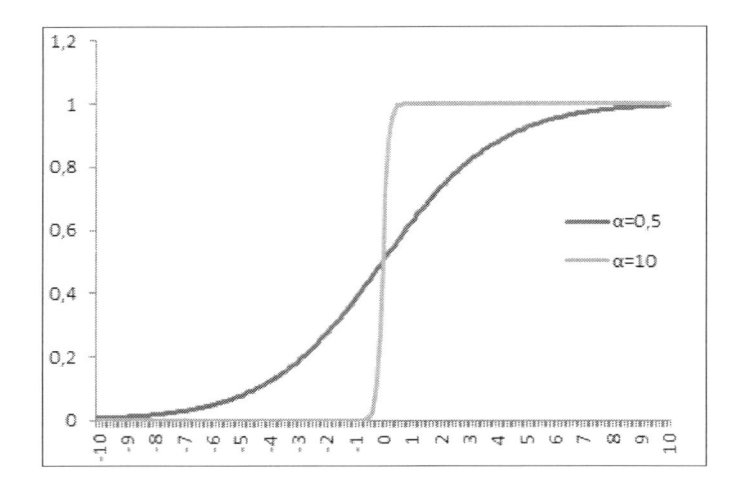

Note that the larger the value of the *a* parameter is, the more the logistic function takes a shape of a hard-limiting threshold function, also known as a step function.

Multiple classes versus binary classes

Classification problems usually deal with a case of multiple classes, where each class is assigned a label. However, a binary classification schema is applied in neural networks. This is because a neural network with a logistic function at the output layer can produce only values between **0** and **1**, meaning that it assigns **(1)** or not **(0)** to some classes.

Nevertheless, there is one approach for multiple classes using binary functions. Consider that every class is represented by an output neuron, and whenever this output neuron fires, the neuron's corresponding class is applied on the input data record. So, let's suppose a network to classify diseases; each neuron output represents a disease to be applied to some symptom:

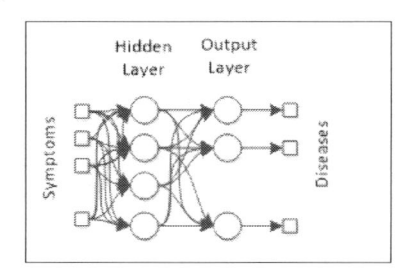

> Note that in this configuration, it is possible to have multiple diseases with the same symptoms. However, if it is desirable to choose only one class, then a schema as a competitive learning algorithm is more suitable.

Comparing the expected versus produced results – the confusion matrix

There is no perfect classifier algorithm; all of them are subjected to errors and biases. However, it is expected that a classification algorithm can correctly classify 70% to 90% of the records.

> Very high correct classification rates are not always desirable because of the possible biases presented in the input data that might affect the classification task, and there is a risk of overtraining, when only the training data are correctly classified.

A confusion matrix shows how many of a given class's records were correctly classified and therefore how many were wrongly classified. The following table depicts what a confusion matrix may look like:

Actual class	Inferred class							Total
	A	B	C	D	E	F	G	
A	92%	1%	0%	4%	0%	1%	2%	100%
B	0%	83%	5%	6%	2%	3%	1%	100%
C	1%	3%	85%	0%	2%	5%	4%	100%
D	0%	3%	0%	92%	2%	1%	1%	100%
E	0%	10%	2%	1%	78%	1%	8%	100%
F	22%	2%	2%	3%	3%	65%	3%	100%
G	9%	6%	0%	16%	0%	3%	66%	100%

Note that the main diagonal is expected to have higher values, as the classification algorithm will always try to extract meaningful information from the input dataset. The sum of all rows must be equal to 100% because all elements of a given class are to be classified in one of the available classes. However, note that some classes may receive more classifications than expected.

The more a confusion matrix looks like an identity matrix, the better the classification algorithm will be.

Classification measures – sensitivity and specificity

When the classification is binary, the confusion matrix is found to be a simple 2 x 2 matrix, and therefore, its positions are specially named:

Actual Class	Inferred Class	
	Positive (1)	Negative (0)
Positive (1)	True Positive	False Negative
Negative (0)	False Positive	True Negative

In disease diagnosis, which is the subject of this chapter, the concept of a binary confusion matrix is applied in the sense that a false diagnosis may be either a false positive or a false negative. The rate of false results can be measured by using sensitivity and specificity indexes.

Sensitivity denotes the true positive rate; it measures how many of the records are correctly classified positively.

$$Sensitivity = \frac{Number\ of\ True\ Positives}{Total\ of\ Actual\ Positive\ Records}$$

Specificity in turn represents the true negative rate; it indicates the proportion of negative record identification.

$$Specificity = \frac{Number\ of\ True\ Negatives}{Total\ of\ Actual\ Negative\ Records}$$

High values of both sensitivity and specificity are desired; however, depending on the application field, sensitivity may carry more meaning.

Applying neural networks for classification

Classification tasks can be performed by using any of the supervised neural networks that this book has covered so far. However, it is recommended to use more complex architectures, such as MLPs. In this chapter, we are going to use the `NeuralNet` class to build an MLP with one hidden layer and the sigmoid function at the output. Every output neuron denotes a class.

We've added to framework a special class called `Classification` in order to handle concepts such as confusion matrix, sensitivity, and specificity. The following table shows a list of the methods and parameters contained in this class:

Class name: Classification	
Methods	
`public double[][] calculateConfusionMatrix( double marginError, double[][] matrix )`	Method to calculate confusion matrix
	Parameters: Margin error and matrix with real output and estimated output
	Returns: Confusion matrix
`public void printConfusionMatrix( double[][] matrix )`	Method to print confusion matrix
	Parameters: Confusion matrix
	Returns: -
`public double calculateSensitivity( double[][] matrix )`	Method to calculate sensitivity of classification
	Parameters: Matrix with real output and estimated output
	Returns: Sensitivity value
`public double calculateSpecificity( double[][] matrix )`	Method to calculate specificity of classification
	Parameters: Matrix with real output and estimated output
	Returns: Specificity value
`public double calculateAccuracy( double[][] matrix )`	Method to calculate accuracy of classification
	Parameters: matrix with real output and estimated output
	Returns: specificity value

Classifying Disease Diagnosis

Class name: Classification	
Methods	
`public double[][] convertToOneColumn( double[][] matrix )`	Method to convert a matrix with more than one column to one column. It has been used when neural net has more than one neuron in output layer
	Parameters: Matrix with more than one column
	Returns: Matrix with one column
Class implementation with Java: file Classification.java	

The implementation of a neural network for classification would follow the following steps:

1. Data loading (training and test data)
2. Data normalization
3. Creating neural network
4. Training neural network
5. Analyze and take conclusions from the classifier via a classification object

First, let's load the data and normalize it:

```
    //Training data
Data dataInput    = new Data("data", "inputs_training.csv");
    Data dataOutput = new Data("data", "output_training.csv");
    // test data
    Data dataInputTestRNA  = new Data("data", "inputs_test.csv");
    Data dataOutputTestRNA = new Data("data", "output_test.csv");

    // normalization
    NormalizationTypesENUM NORMALIZATION_TYPE = Data.
NormalizationTypesENUM.MAX_MIN_EQUALIZED;
```

It is important to convert the data to the matrix format so that it can be fed into the neural network:

```
        //convert the raw data to matrix
        double[][] matrixInput  = dataInput.rawData2Matrix( 
diseaseDataInput );
        double[][] matrixOutput = dataOutput.rawData2Matrix( 
diseaseDataOutput );
```

```
        //Normalize the data. Normalization code for test data is
suppressed.
        double[][] matrixInputNorm = dataInput.normalize(matrixInput,
NORMALIZATION_TYPE);
```

Now, let's create the neural network here with 8 inputs, 3 hidden neurons, and 2 outputs:

```
        NeuralNet n1 = new NeuralNet();
        n1 = n1.initNet(8, 1, 3, 2);
```

Next, we perform the training. Since we've already seen how this can be set up in *Chapter 3, Handling Perceptrons*, we're leaving this out here to save space. Then, we create a new network to receive the trained network:

```
        //Create a new network to receive the trained network
        NeuralNet n1Trained = new NeuralNet();
        n1Trained = n1.trainNet(n1);

        //Plot the error:
        Chart c1 = new Chart();
        c1.plotXYData(n1.getListOfMSE().toArray(), "MSE Error",
"Epochs", "MSE Value");
```

After the training has been finished, we instantiate a classification object to carry out some analyses on the results:

```
        Classification classif = new Classification();

        //Load the test data:
        n1Trained.setTrainSet( matrixInputTestRNANorm );
        n1Trained.setRealMatrixOutputSet( matrixOutputTestRNA );

        double[][] matrixOutputRNATest = n1Trained.
getNetOutputValues(n1Trained);

        //Check the number of outputs to adapt the test data to the
neural multiple outputs
        if(n1Trained.getOutputLayer().getNumberOfNeuronsInLayer() > 1) {

            matrixOutputTestRNA = classif.convertToOneColumn(matrixOutput
TestRNA);
            matrixOutputRNATest = classif.convertToOneColumn(matrixOutput
RNATest);


        }
```

Finally, we apply some processing for exhibiting the charts and the confusion matrix:

```
        ArrayList<double[][]> listOfArraysToJoinTest = new 
ArrayList<double[][]>();
        listOfArraysToJoinTest.add( matrixOutputTestRNA );
        listOfArraysToJoinTest.add( matrixOutputRNATest );
        double[][] matrixOutputsJoinedTest = new Data().joinArrays(listO
fArraysToJoinTest);
        
        //Plot a bar chart
        Chart c3 = new Chart();
        c3.plotBarChart(matrixOutputsJoinedTest, "Real x Estimated - 
Test Data", " Data", "Result (0: NO / 1: YES)");
        
        
        //plots the confusion matrix and the sensitivity and specificity 
indexes
        double[][] confusionMatrix = classif.
calculateConfusionMatrix(0.6, matrixOutputsJoinedTest);
        classif.printConfusionMatrix(confusionMatrix);
        System.out.println("SENSITIVITY = " + classif.calculateSensitivi
ty(confusionMatrix));
        System.out.println("SPECIFICITY = " + classif.calculateSpecifici
ty(confusionMatrix));
        
        //Finally the final accuracy of classification
        System.out.println("ACCURACY    = " + classif.calculateAccuracy(
confusionMatrix));
```

Disease diagnosis with neural networks

For disease diagnosis, we are going to use the free dataset proben1, which is available on the web (http://www.filewatcher.com/m/proben1.tar.gz.1782734-0.html). Proben1 is a benchmark set of several datasets from different domains. We are going to use the cancer and the diabetes dataset. We added two new classes to run the experiments of each case: `CancerDisease` and `DiabetesDisease`.

Using ANN to diagnose breast cancer

Ten variables compose the breast cancer dataset, where nine are inputs and one is a binary output. The dataset has 699 records, but we excluded 16 from them, which were found to be incomplete; thus, we used 683 records to train and test a neural network.

> In real practical problems, it is common to have missing or invalid data. Ideally, the classification algorithm must handle these records, but sometimes, it is recommended to exclude them since there would not be information to produce an accurate result.

The following table shows the configuration of this dataset:

Variable name	Type	Maximum value and minimum value
Diagnosis result	OUTPUT	[0; 1]
Clump thickness	INPUT #1	[1; 10]
Uniformity of cell size	INPUT #2	[1; 10]
Uniformity of cell shape	INPUT #3	[1; 10]
Marginal adhesion	INPUT #4	[1; 10]
Single epithelial cell size	INPUT #5	[1; 10]
Bare nuclei	INPUT #6	[1; 10]
Bland chromatin	INPUT #7	[1; 10]
Normal nucleoli	INPUT #8	[1; 10]
Mitoses	INPUT #9	[1; 10]

Therefore, the proposed neural topology will be that of the following figure:

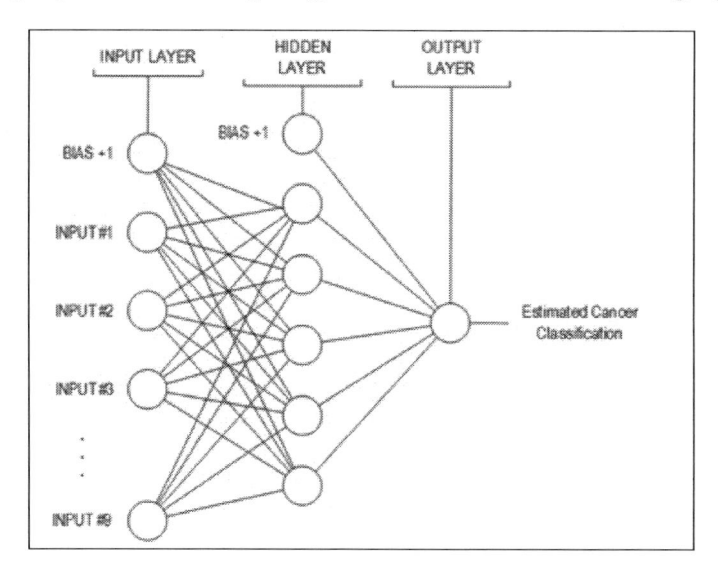

The dataset division was performed as follows:

- **Training**: 600 records
- **Test**: 83 records

As in the previous cases, we performed many experiments to try to find the best neural net to classify whether the cancer is benign or malignant. So, we conducted 12 different experiments to analyze the MSE and accuracy values. After that, the confusion matrix, sensitivity, and specificity were generated with the test dataset and analyzed. At last, an analysis of generalization was conducted. The neural networks involved in the experiments are shown in the table:

Experiment	Number of neurons in hidden layer	Learning rate	Activation function
1	3	0.1	**Hidden layer**: HYPERTAN **Output layer**: SIGLOG
2	3	0.1	**Hidden layer**: SIGLOG **Output layer**: SIGLOG
3	3	0.5	**Hidden layer**: HYPERTAN **Output layer**: SIGLOG
4	3	0.5	**Hidden layer**: SIGLOG **Output layer**: SIGLOG
5	3	0.9	**Hidden layer**: HYPERTAN **Output layer**: SIGLOG
6	3	0.9	**Hidden layer**: SIGLOG **Output layer**: SIGLOG
7	5	0.1	**Hidden layer**: HYPERTAN **Output layer**: SIGLOG
8	5	0.1	**Hidden layer**: SIGLOG **Output layer**: SIGLOG
9	5	0.5	**Hidden layer**: HYPERTAN **Output layer**: SIGLOG
10	5	0.5	**Hidden layer**: SIGLOG **Output layer**: SIGLOG
11	5	0.9	**Hidden layer**: HYPERTAN **Output layer**: SIGLOG
12	5	0.9	**Hidden layer**: SIGLOG **Output layer**: SIGLOG

After each experiment, we collected the MSE values (shown in the following table); **experiment 7** and **experiment 12** resulted in the highest accuracy values. Both MSE training rates are acceptable.

Experiment	MSE training rate	Accuracy
1	0.03972135063712551	0.975903614457831
2	0.03995188471687546	0.975903614457831
3	0.03933513091403112	0.975903614457831
4	0.03930199248652969	0.975903614457831
5	0.04320989863852442	0.963855421686747
6	0.03906524721664331	0.975903614457831
7	0.02833532990528998	0.987951807228915
8	0.02996896005224385	0.975903614457831
9	0.02516212161358099	0.975903614457831
10	0.02510190111178650	0.975903614457831
11	0.02062000996870342	0.963855421686747
12	0.02466074197562852	0.987951807228915

Graphically, the MSE evolution over time is very fast, as can be seen in the following chart of the **experiment 7**:

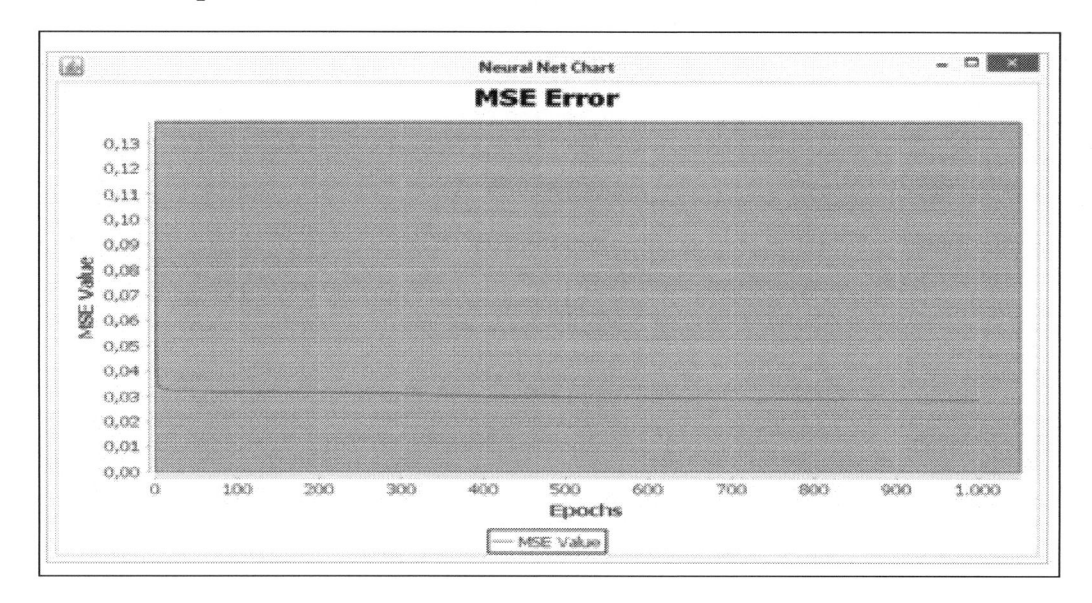

Classifying Disease Diagnosis

The confusion matrix is shown in the table with the sensitivity and specificity for both experiments:

Experiment	Confusion matrix	Sensitivity	Specificity
7	14.0 | 1.0 0.0 | 68.0	1.0	0.9855072463768
11	13.0 | 0.0 1.0 | 69.0	0.9285714285714	1.0

Now, let's analyze generalization. This feature is better observed with bar charts showing for each case the expected class along with the classification estimated by the neural network. Red bars denote the actual positive diagnosis, while blue bars represent the neural output values. It is worth to note that when the output is zero, the patient is diagnosed with benignant cancer and when the output is one, the patient is diagnosed with malignant cancer. This feature is better observed with bar charts as shown in the following figure:

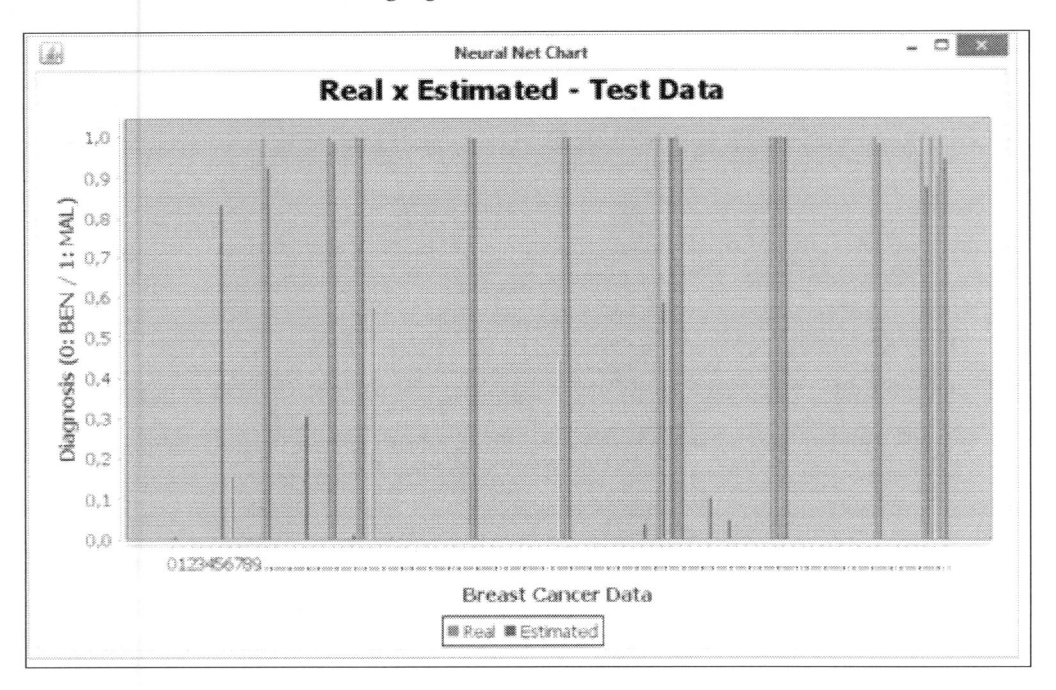

Applying NN for an early diagnosis of diabetes

An additional example to be explored is the diagnosis of diabetes. This dataset has eight inputs and one output, as shown in the following table. There are 768 records, all complete. However, Proben1 states that there are several senseless zero values, probably indicating missing data. We're handling this data as if it were real, thereby introducing some errors (or noise) into the dataset.

Variable name	Type	Maximum value and minimum value
Diagnosis result	OUTPUT	[0; 1]
Number of times pregnant	INPUT #1	[0.0; 17]
Plasma glucose concentration every 2 hours in an oral glucose tolerance test	INPUT #2	[0.0; 199]
Diastolic blood pressure (mm Hg)	INPUT #3	[0.0; 122]
Triceps skin fold thickness (mm)	INPUT #4	[0.0; 99]
Two-hour serum insulin (μU/ml)	INPUT #5	[0.0; 744]
Body mass index (weight in kg/(height in m)^2)	INPUT #6	[0.0; 67.1]
Diabetes pedigree function	INPUT #7	[0.078; 2420]
Age (years)	INPUT #8	[21; 81]

The dataset division was as follows:

- **Training**: 690 records
- **Test**: 78 records

To discover the best neural net topology to classify diabetes, we used the same schema of neural networks with the same analysis as that described in the last section. However, we use a multiple class classification in the output layer: two neurons in this layer will be used, one for the presence of diabetes and the other for the absence.

So, the proposed neural architecture looks like that shown in the following figure:

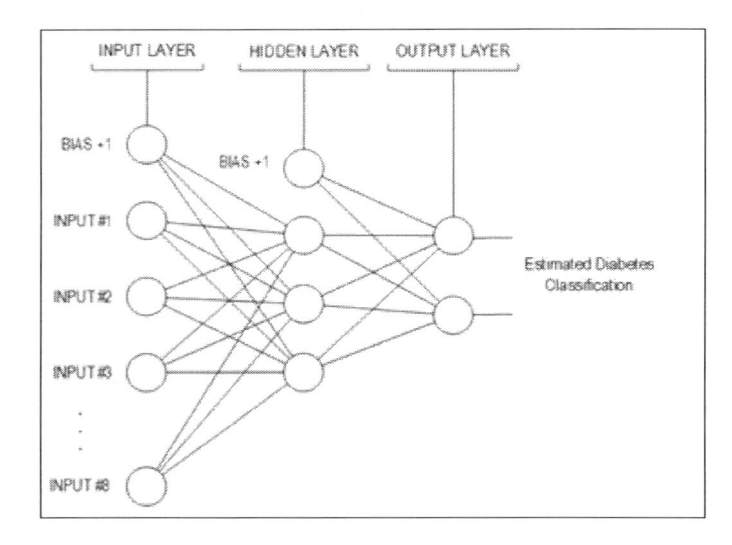

The following table shows the MSE training value and the accuracy of the first six experiments and of the last six experiments:

Experiment	MSE training rate	Accuracy
1	0.1613790087603789	0.692307692307692
2	0.1621959590254118	0.692307692307692
3	0.1643117235316208	0.653846153846153
4	0.1617892991111149	0.692307692307692
5	0.1726829994853517	0.641025641025641
6	0.1617000829026907	0.692307692307692
7	0.1568402004414977	0.666666666666666
#8	0.1577266938606883	0.692307692307692
9	0.1643499270371965	0.666666666666666
10	0.1538651388477906	0.666666666666666
11	0.1747411925925356	0.692307692307692
12	0.1532305775075525	0.679487179487179

[132]

The fall of the MSE is fast as in the first case; nevertheless, the eight experiments showed a slight delay in the decrease in the first epoch.

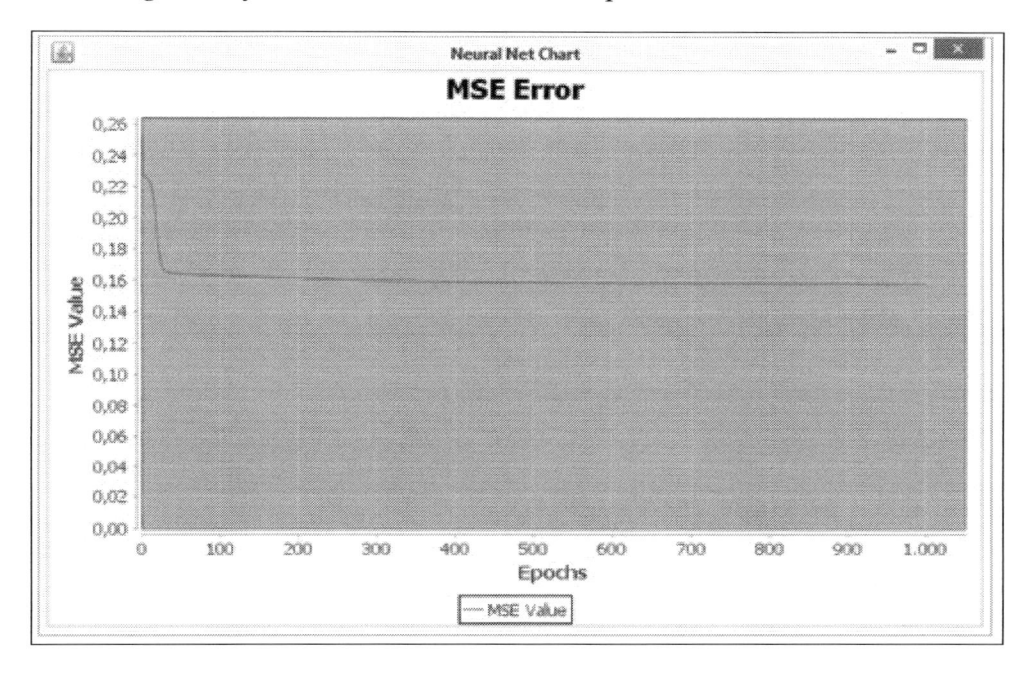

By analyzing the confusion matrix, it can be seen that sensitivity and specificity are not as high as in the first case, and the confusion matrix shows a more homogeneous distribution.

Experiment	Confusion matrix	Sensitivity	Specificity
1	19.0 | 11.0 13.0 | 35.0	0.59375	0.7608695652173914
8	21.0 | 13.0 11.0 | 33.0	0.65625	0.717391304347826

Although this may suggest that the classifier is bad because of the number of false positives or negatives, we should take into account that the original dataset contained bad records, which could not be timely filtered. This explains the false negatives appearing in the generalization bar chart.

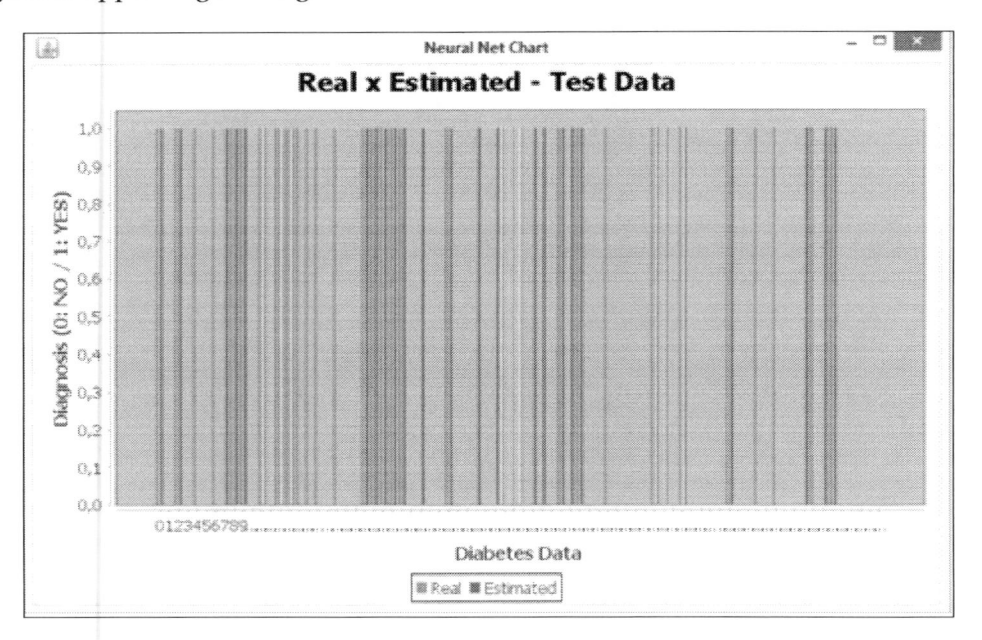

Summary

In this chapter, we've seen two examples of the application of neural networks to disease diagnosis. The fundamentals of the classification problems are briefly reviewed in order to level the knowledge explored in this chapter. Classification tasks belong to one of the most frequently used types of supervised tasks in the fields of machine learning/data mining, and neural networks proved to be very appropriate for application to such problems. The reader was also presented with the concepts used for evaluating the classification tasks, such as sensitivity, specificity, and the confusion matrix. These notations are very useful for all classification tasks, including those that are handled with other algorithms besides neural networks. The next chapter will explore a similar kind of tasks but by using unsupervised learning, which means without expected output data, but the fundamentals presented in this chapter will be somewhat helpful.

Clustering Customer Profiles

One of the amazing capabilities of neural networks applying unsupervised learning is their ability to find hidden patterns that even experts may not have any clue about. In this chapter, we're going to explore this fascinating feature through a practical application to find customer clusters by using a transactions database. We'll go through a review on unsupervised learning and the clustering task. To demonstrate this application, the reader will be provided with a practical example on customer profiling and their respective implementations in Java. In this chapter, we will cover the following topics:

- Clustering Task
    - Cluster Analysis
    - Cluster Evaluation

- Applied Unsupervised Learning
    - Neural Network of Radial Basis Functions
    - Kohonen Network for Clustering
    - Handling Different Types of Data

- Customer Profiling
    - Preprocessing

- Implementation in Java
    - Credit Analysis and Profiles of Customers

Clustering task

Clustering is a part of a broader set of tasks in data analysis, whose objective is to group elements that look alike, more similar to each other, into clusters or groups. A clustering task is fully based on unsupervised learning since there is no need to include any target output data in order to find clusters; instead, the solution designer may choose a number of clusters that he/she wants to group the records into and check the response of the algorithm to it.

> A clustering task may seem to overlap with a classification task with the crucial difference that in clustering, there is no need to have a predefined set of classes before the clustering algorithm is run.

One may wish to apply clustering when there is little or no information at all about the how the data can be gathered into groups. Provided a dataset, we want our neural network to identify both the groups and their members. While this may seem easy and straightforward to perform visually in a two-dimensional dataset, as shown in the following figure, with a higher number of dimensions, this task becomes not so trivial to perform and needs an algorithmic solution. an example of 2-dimensional clustering is shown as follows:

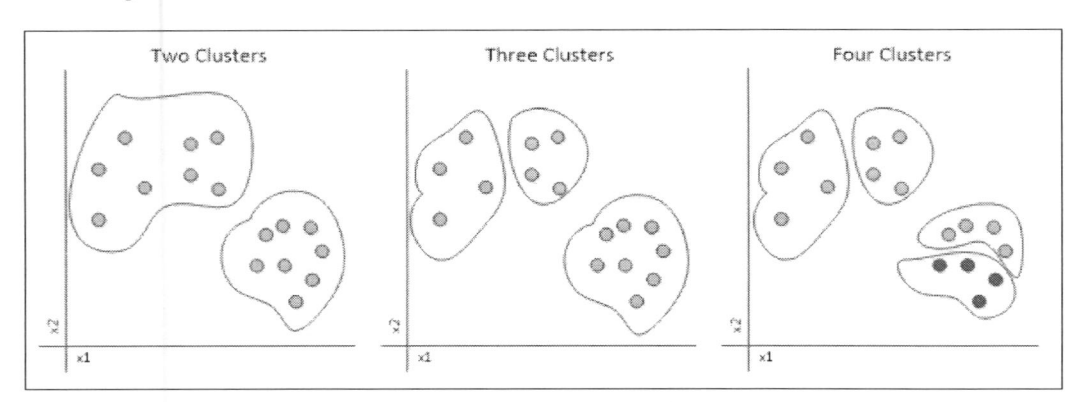

In clustering, the number of clusters is not determined by the data, but by the data analyst who is looking to cluster the data. Here, the boundaries are little bit different than those of classification tasks because they depend primarily on the number of clusters.

Cluster analysis

One difficulty in the clustering tasks, and also in unsupervised learning tasks, is the accurate interpretation of the results. While in supervised learning, there is a defined target from which we can derive an error measure or confusion matrix, in unsupervised learning, the evaluation of quality is totally different and totally dependent on the data itself. The validation criteria involve indexes that assert how well the data is distributed across the clusters as well as external opinions from experts on the data, which is also a measure of quality.

> For example, let's suppose a task of clustering of plants given their characteristics (sizes, leave colors, period of fruiting, and so on). If a neural network mistakenly groups cacti and pine trees in the same cluster, a botanist would certainly not endorse the classification on the basis of his/her specific knowledge in the field and state that this grouping does not make any sense.

Two major issues happen in clustering. One is the fact that one neural network's output is never activated, meaning that one cluster does not have any data point associated with it. The other one is the case of nonlinear or sparse clusters, which could be erroneously grouped into several clusters, while actually, there might be only one, as shown in the following figure:

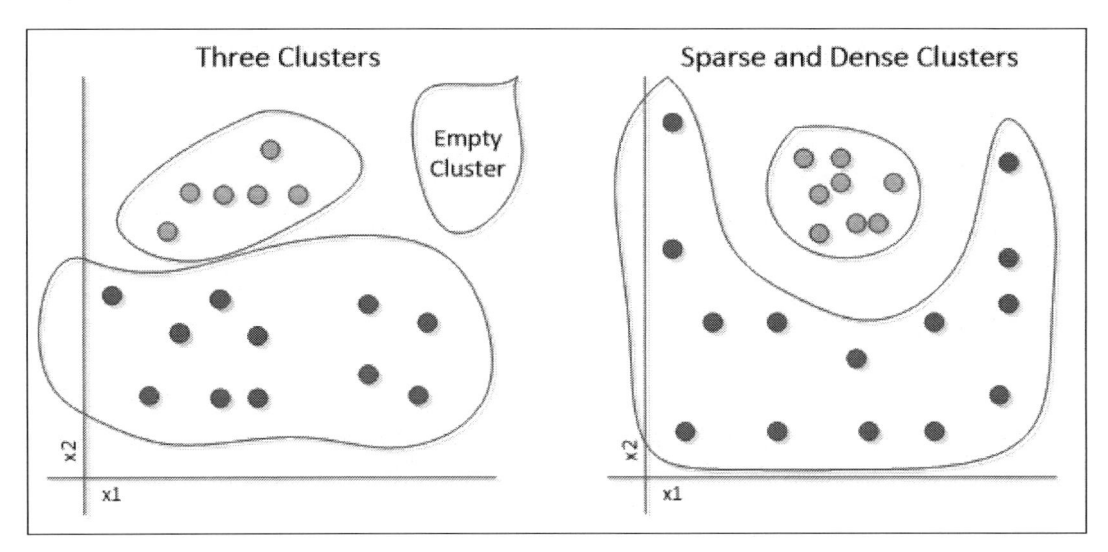

Cluster evaluation and validation

Unfortunately, if the neural network clusters badly, one needs to either redefine the number of clusters or perform additional data preprocessing. To evaluate how good the clustered data is, the **Davies–Bouldin** and **Dunn** index may be applied.

The Davies–Bouldin index takes into account the cluster's centroids in order to find the inter- and intra-distances between clusters and cluster members.

$$DB = \frac{1}{n}\sum_{i=1}^{n}\max_{j \neq i}\left(\frac{\sigma_i + \sigma_j}{d(c_i, c_j)}\right)$$

Where n is the number of clusters, c_i is the centroid of cluster i, σ_i is the average distance of all elements in cluster i, and $d(c_i, c_j)$ is the distance between clusters i and j. The smaller the value of the DB index, the stronger will be the consideration of the neural network as a cluster.

However, for dense and sparse clusters, the DB index will not give much useful information. This limitation can be overcome with the Dunn index:

$$D = \frac{\min_{1 \leq i < j \leq n} d(i, j)}{\max_{1 \leq k \leq n} d'(k)}$$

where $d(i, j)$ is the inter-cluster distance between i and j, and $d'(k)$ is the intra-cluster distance of cluster k. Here, the higher the Dunn index is, the better will be the clustering because although the clusters may be sparse, they still need to be grouped together, and high intra-cluster distances will denote a bad grouping of data.

External validation

In some cases there is already an expected result for clustering, as in the example of plant clustering. This is called external validation. One may apply a neural network with unsupervised learning to cluster data that is already assigned a value. The major difference against the classification lies in the fact that the target outputs are not considered, so the algorithm itself is expected to draw a borderline based only on the data.

Applied unsupervised learning

In neural networks, there are a number of architectures implementing unsupervised learning; however, the scope of this book will cover only two: a neural network of radial basis functions and a Kohonen neural network.

Neural network of radial basis functions

This neural network architecture has three layers and combines two types of learning, as shown in the following figure:

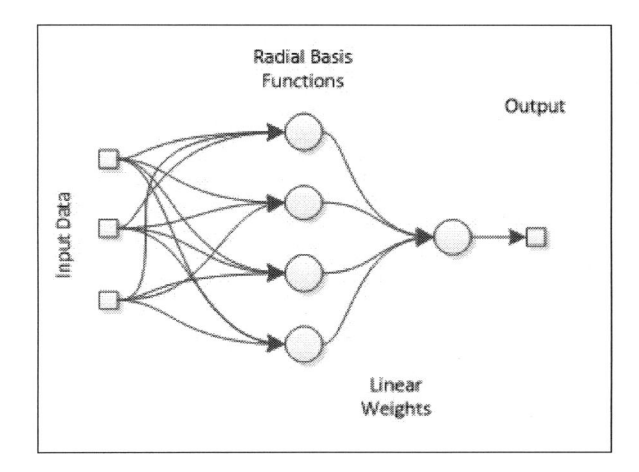

For the hidden layer, competitive learning is applied in order to activate one of the radial basis functions in the hidden neurons. The radial basis function takes the form of Gaussian functions:

$$f_i(d_i) = e^{-\alpha d_i^2}$$

where d is the distance vector between the input x and the weights w of the neuron i:

$$d_i = \|x - w_i\|$$

The output of the neural network will be the linear sum of all the values produced by the neurons of the hidden layer:

$$y(x) = \sum_{i=1}^{N} a_i f_i(\|x - c_i\|)$$

Radial basis functions (RBFs) perform clustering only in the first hidden layer, whereas in the output layer, supervised learning is applied to find the output weights. Because the clusters defined in the RBF network are internal, we are not going to use this network now in this chapter; however, it will be detailed in *Chapter 9*, *Neural Networks Optimization and Adaptation*.

Kohonen neural network

Kohonen networks, which have been covered in *Chapter 4*, *Self-Organizing Maps*, are now used in a modified fashion. Kohonen can produce a shape in one or two dimensions at the output, but here, we are interested in clustering, which can be reduced to only one dimension. In addition, clusters may be related or not to each other, so the vicinity of neurons can be ignored for now in this chapter; this means that only one neuron will be activated and its neighbors will remain unchanged. Therefore, the neural network will adjust its weights to match the data to an array of clusters. The following figure shows a clustering layer in a Kohonen Neural Network:

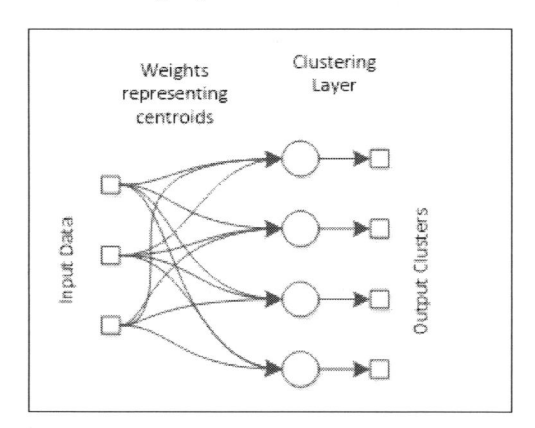

The training algorithm will be competitive learning, wherein the neuron with the greatest output has its weights adjusted. By the end of training, all the clusters of a neural network are expected to be defined. Note that there are no links between output neurons, meaning that only one input is active at the output.

Types of data

In practical applications, data can be classified in the following ways:

- Numerical
    - Continuous or real
    - Discrete
- Categorical
    - Ordinal
    - Unscaled

> So far, we have been working mostly with numerical data, which is in principle easier to handle with neural networks. However, in more complex applications, one needs to handle non-numerical data, which involves translating the data into a "numeric universe," where the neural networks can be applied over it.

Examples of numerical data are values of temperature (continuous) and the number of days (discrete). The non-numerical data (categorical) can be ordinal, where there is a scale between the categories, or be unscaled, when all categories are in the same level, or no scale can be applied to it. Examples of ordinal categorical data are satisfaction degrees (dissatisfied, poorly satisfied, and well satisfied), whereas unscaled categorical data may be city names.

Numerical data can be easily inserted into neural networks, where one may need to only apply some normalization or preprocessing. However, categorical data needs some attention. If the data can be scaled (ordinal), it can be "discretized." Taking the example of satisfaction degree, we may create the following corresponding table:

Satisfaction Degree	Scaled Value
Dissatisfied	0
Poorly Satisfied	1
Very Satisfied	2

However, for unscaled categorical data, it is not recommended to apply numbers that might induce scaling on the considered variable. So, it is better to treat each categorical value as one binary variable, meaning **1** in the presence of the considered value or **0** in the absence of this value:

City Names	Neural Input				
	London	Tokyo	New York	Cape Town	Sydney
London	1	0	0	0	0
Tokyo	0	1	0	0	0
New York	0	0	1	0	0
Cape Town	0	0	0	1	0
Sydney	0	0	0	0	1

This mechanism of binary variables may eventually result in sparse data matrices containing a lot of zeros. However, there are techniques such as **single value decomposition** (**SVD**) that address this problem. The reader will learn more about this in the references.

Customer profiling

One of the interesting tasks in unsupervised learning is the profiling of customers or clustering of customers. Given one dataset of customer information, one wants to find groups of customers that either share similar characteristics or buy the same products. This task results in a number of benefits for business owners because they are provided the information regarding the groups of customers that they have, whereby therefore enabling a more strategic customer relationship.

Preprocessing data

Customer information can contain both numerical and categorical data. Whenever we face a categorical unscaled variable, we need to split it into the number of values that the variable may take. For example, let's suppose that we have the following transaction list of customer purchases:

Transaction ID	Customer ID	Products	Discount	Total
1399	56	Milk, Bread, Butter	0.00	4.30
1400	991	Cheese, Milk	2.30	5.60
1401	406	Bread, Sausage	0.00	8.80
1402	239	Chipotle Sauce, Spice	0.00	6.70

Transaction ID	Customer ID	Products	Discount	Total
1403	33	Turkey	0.00	4.50
1404	406	Turkey, Butter, Spice	1.00	9.00

It can be easily seen that the products is unscaled categorical data, and for each transaction, there is an undefined number of products purchased, that is, the customer may purchase only one or several units of these products. In order to transform this dataset into a numerical dataset, one needs to apply preprocessing. For each product, there will be a variable added to the dataset, resulting in the following:

Cust. ID	Milk	Bread	Butter	Cheese	Sausage	Chipotle Sauce	Spice	Turkey
56	1	1	1	0	0	0	0	0
991	1	0	0	1	0	0	0	0
406	0	1	1	0	1	0	1	1
239	0	0	0	0	0	1	1	0
33	0	0	0	0	0	0	0	1

In order to save space, we ignored the numerical variables and considered the presence of the product purchased by a client as **1** and the absence as **0**. Alternative preprocessing may consider the number of occurrences of a value, therefore no longer remaining binary, but becoming discrete.

Implementation in Java

In this section, we will explore the application of a Kohonen neural network to customer clustering on the basis of the customer information collected from Proben1 (Card dataset).

Card credit analysis for customer profiling

The **Card dataset** is composed of 16 variables in total. Fifteen are inputs, and one is an output variable. For security reasons, all variable names have been changed to meaningless symbols. This dataset brings a good mix of variable types (continuous, categorical with small values, and categorical with larger values). The following table shows a summary of the data:

Clustering Customer Profiles

Variable	Type	Values
V1	OUTPUT	-1; 1
V2	INPUT #1	b, a
V3	INPUT #2	continuous
V4	INPUT #3	continuous
V5	INPUT #4	u, y, l, t.
V6	INPUT #5	g, p, gg
V7	INPUT #6	c, d, cc, i, j, k, m, r, q, w, x, e, aa, ff
V8	INPUT #7	v, h, bb, j, n, z, dd, ff, o
V9	INPUT #8	continuous
V10	INPUT #9	t, f
V11	INPUT #10	t, f
V12	INPUT #11	continuous
V13	INPUT #12	t, f
V14	INPUT #13	g, p, s
V15	INPUT #14	continuous
V16	INPUT #15	continuous

For simplicity, we didn't use the inputs **V5–V8** and **V14** in order to not inflate the number of inputs too much. Further, we applied the following transformation:

Variable	Type	Values	Conversion
V1	OUTPUT	-1; 1	-
V2	INPUT #1	b, a	b = 1, a = 0
V3	INPUT #2	continuous	-
V4	INPUT #3	continuous	-
V9	INPUT #8	continuous	-
V10	INPUT #9	t, f	t = 1, f = 0
V11	INPUT #10	t, f	t = 1, f = 0
V12	INPUT #11	continuous	-
V13	INPUT #12	t, f	t = 1, f = 0
V15	INPUT #14	continuous	-
V16	INPUT #15	continuous	-

The proposed neural net topology is shown in the following figure:

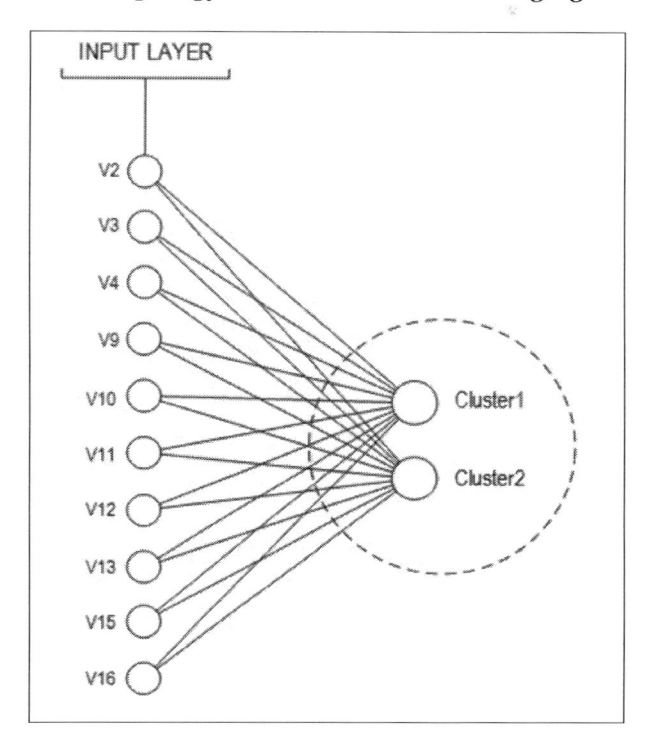

The number of examples stored is **690**, but **37** of them have missing values. These **37** records were discarded. Therefore, **653** examples were used to train and test the neural network. The dataset division was made as follows:

- **Training**: **583** records
- **Test**: **70** records

The Kohonen training algorithm to cluster similar behavior depends on some parameters, such as the following:

- Normalization type
- Learning rate

It is important to note that the Kohonen training algorithm is unsupervised. So, this algorithm is used when the output is not known. In the card example, there are output values in the dataset and they will be used here only to attest clustering.

Clustering Customer Profiles

In this specific case, because the output is known, as classification, the clustering quality may be attested as follows:

- Sensitivity (true positive rate)
- Specificity (true negative rate)
- Accuracy

In a Java project, the calculations of these values are done through the `Classification` class, previously developed in *Chapter 6, Classifying Disease Diagnosis*.

It is a good practice to perform many experiments to try to find the best neural net for clustering customer profiles. Ten different experiments will be conducted, and the quality rates will be analyzed for each, as mentioned earlier. The following table summarizes the strategy that will be followed:

Experiment	Learning Rate	Normalization Type
1	0.1	MIN_MAX
2		MAX_MIN_EQUALIZED
3	0.3	MIN_MAX
4		MAX_MIN_EQUALIZED
5	0.5	MIN_MAX
6		MAX_MIN_EQUALIZED
7	0.7	MIN_MAX
8		MAX_MIN_EQUALIZED
9	0.9	MIN_MAX
10		MAX_MIN_EQUALIZED

The `Card` class was created to run each experiment. Regarding the training, we applied the Euclidian distance, as previously explained in *Chapter 4, Self-Organizing Maps*.

The following piece of code shows a bit of its implementation:

```
Data cardDataInput = new Data("data", "card_inputs_training.csv");

Data cardDataInputTestRNA  = new Data("data", "card_inputs_test.csv");
Data cardDataOutputTestRNA = new Data("data", "card_output_test.csv");

NormalizationTypesENUM NORMALIZATION_TYPE = Data.NormalizationTypesENUM.MAX_MIN;
```

```
try {
    double[][] matrixInput = cardDataInput.rawData2Matrix(
cardDataInput );

    double[][] matrixInputTestRNA = cardDataInput.rawData2Matrix(
cardDataInputTestRNA );

    double[][] matrixOutput = cardDataInput.rawData2Matrix(
cardDataOutputTestRNA );

    double[][] matrixInputNorm = cardDataInput.normalize(matrixInput,
NORMALIZATION_TYPE);

    double[][] matrixInputTestRNANorm = cardDataInput.
normalize(matrixInputTestRNA, NORMALIZATION_TYPE);

    NeuralNet n1 = new NeuralNet();
    n1 = n1.initNet(10, 0, 0, 2);

    n1.setTrainSet( matrixInputNorm );

    n1.setValidationSet( matrixInputTestRNANorm );
    n1.setRealMatrixOutputSet( matrixOutput );

    n1.setMaxEpochs(100);
    n1.setLearningRate(0.1);
    n1.setTrainType(TrainingTypesENUM.KOHONEN);
    n1.setKohonenCaseStudy( KohonenCaseStudyENUM.CARD );

    NeuralNet n1Trained = new NeuralNet();

    n1Trained = n1.trainNet( n1 );

    System.out.println();
    System.out.println("---------KOHONEN TEST---------");

    ArrayList<double[][]> listOfArraysToJoin = new ArrayList<double[]
[]>();

    double[][] matrixReal = n1Trained.getRealMatrixOutputSet();
    double[][] matrixEstimated = n1Trained.netValidation(n1Trained);

    listOfArraysToJoin.add( matrixReal );
    litOfArraysToJoin.add( matrixEstimated );
```

```java
        double[][] matrixOutputsJoined = new Data().
joinArrays(listOfArraysToJoin);

        //CONFUSION MATRIX
        Classification classif = new Classification();

        double[][] confusionMatrix = classif.
calculateConfusionMatrix(-1.0, matrixOutputsJoined);
        classif.printConfusionMatrix(confusionMatrix);

        //SENSITIVITY
        System.out.println("SENSITIVITY = " + classif.calculateSensitivity
(confusionMatrix));

        //SPECIFICITY
        System.out.println("SPECIFICITY = " + classif.calculateSpecificity
(confusionMatrix));

        //ACCURACY
        System.out.println("ACCURACY     = " + classif.calculateAccuracy(co
nfusionMatrix));

    } catch (IOException e) {
      e.printStackTrace();
    }
```

After running each experiment using the Card class and saving the accuracy rates, it is possible to observe that experiments 1 and 6 have the same accuracy. Data from the first experiment was normalized with the MIN_MAX method and data from the second experiment with MAX_MIN_EQUALIZED.

Experiment	Accuracy
1	0.9142857142857143
2	0.6285714285714286
3	0.3714285714285714
4	0.6000000000000000
5	0.5857142857142857
6	0.9142857142857143
7	0.0857142857142857
8	0.3714285714285714
9	0.4142857142857143
10	0.5857142857142857

The following table displays the confusion matrix, sensitivity, and specificity of experiments 1 and 6. Again, please note that it is possible to observe the equivalence between the neural nets in both experiments. Only 6 patterns from 70 (less than 10%) could not be clustered correctly.

Experiment	Confusion Matrix	Sensitivity	Specificity
1	31.0 | 2.0 4.0 | 33.0	0.8857142857142	0.9428571428571
6	31.0 | 2.0 4.0 | 33.0	0.8857142857142	0.9428571428571

Summary

In this chapter, we discussed an application of customer profiling using the Kohonen neural network. Unlike the classification task, the clustering task does not consider any previous knowledge on the desired output; instead, it is desirable that the neural network finds the clusters. However, we've seen that the validation techniques may include external validation, which is a comparison with what could be understood as the "target output." Customer profiling is important because it gives more accurate and clean information about customers to a business owner, without the "human interference" in pointing which customers are in some groups or which ones in others, as in the case of supervised learning. This is the advantage of unsupervised learning, enabling the data to draw results solely by itself.

In the next chapter, we are going to present another interesting application of neural networks: digit recognition in images. It is a way to know in practice how pattern recognition works with a neural net.

8
Pattern Recognition (OCR Case)

We have seen so far that neural networks show an amazing capability in learning through data in both supervised and unsupervised ways. In this chapter, we present an additional case of pattern recognition involving an example of **Optical Character Recognition (OCR)**. Neural networks can be trained to strictly recognize text characters written in an image file. A brief review of classification and clusterization is covered prior to presenting the application itself. In this chapter, we will cover the following topics:

- Pattern Recognition
    - Defined Classes
    - Undefined Classes
- Neural Networks in Pattern Recognition
    - Kohonen and MLP
- The OCR Problem
    - Preprocessing and Class Definitions
- Implementation in Java
    - Digit Recognition

What is pattern recognition all about?

Patterns are a bunch of data and elements that look similar to each other, and can occur systematically and repeat from time to time. Pattern recognition is a task that can be performed mainly by unsupervised learning using clusterization; however, when there is labeled data or defined classes of data, this task can be performed by supervised methods. We as humans perform this task more often than we can imagine. When we see objects and recognize them as belonging to a certain class, we are indeed recognizing a pattern. Also, when we analyze charts, discrete events, and time series, we might find evidence of some sequence of events that repeat systematically under certain conditions. In summary, patterns can be learned by data observations.

Examples of pattern recognition tasks include the following:

- Shape recognition
- Object classification
- Behavior clustering
- Voice recognition
- OCR
- Chemical reaction taxonomy

Definition of classes among tons of data

In a list of classes that has been predefined for a specific domain, each class is considered to be a pattern; therefore, every data record or occurrence is assigned one of these predefined classes.

> Classes can usually be predefined by an expert or on the basis of the previous knowledge of the application domain. Also, it is desirable to apply defined classes when we want the data to be classified strictly into one of the predefined classes.

One illustrated example for pattern recognition using defined classes is animal recognition by images, as shown in the following figure. The pattern recognizer however should be trained to catch all the characteristics that formally define the classes. In the example, eight figures of animals are shown, belonging to two classes: mammals and birds. Since this is a supervised mode of learning, the neural network should be provided with a sufficient number of images that allow it to properly classify new images.

Chapter 8

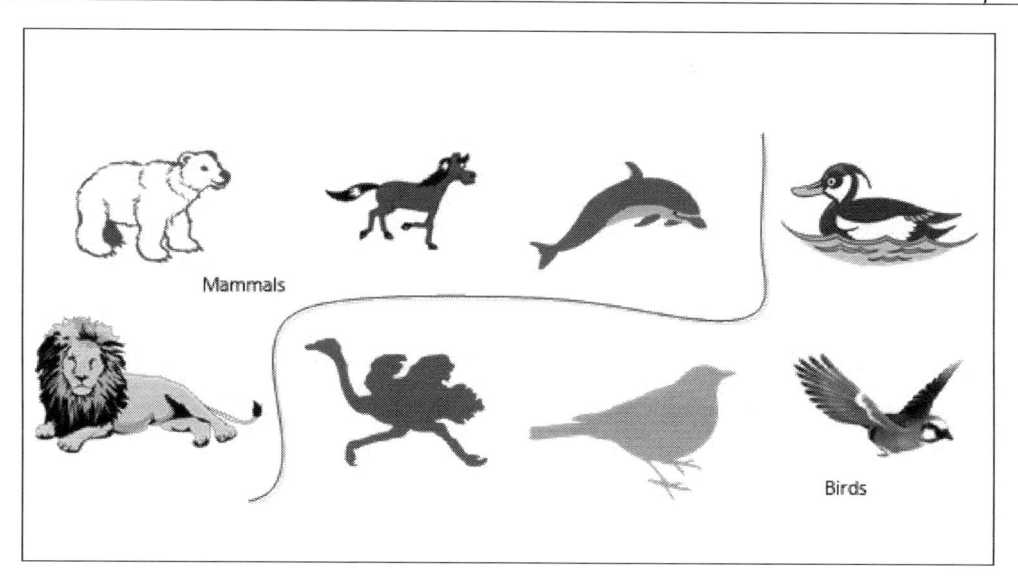

Of course, sometimes, the classification may fail mainly due to similar hidden patterns in the images that neural networks may catch and due to the small nuances present in the shapes. For example, a dolphin has flippers, but it is still a mammal. Sometimes, in order to obtain a better classification, it is necessary to apply preprocessing and ensure that the neural network will receive the appropriate data that would allow for classification.

What if the undefined classes are undefined?

When data are unlabeled and there is no predefined set of classes, it is a scenario for unsupervised learning. Shape recognition is a good example since shapes may be flexible and have an infinite number of edges, vertices, or bindings, as shown in the following figure:

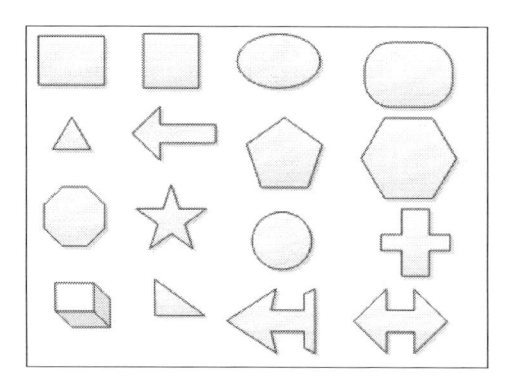

In the preceding image, we can see some types of shapes and we want to arrange them such that the similar ones can be grouped into the same cluster. Based on the shape information that is present in the images, it is likely for the pattern recognizer to classify the rectangle, the square, and the right triangle into the same group. However, if the information were presented to the pattern recognizer, not as an image, but as a graph with edges and vertices coordinates, the classification might have changed a little.

In summary, the pattern recognition task may use both supervised and unsupervised modes of learning, basically depending on the objective of recognition.

External validation

In some cases, there is already an expected result for clustering, as in the example of plant clustering. This is called external validation. One may apply a neural network with unsupervised learning to cluster data that is already assigned a value. The major difference against the classification lies in the fact that the target outputs are not considered, so the algorithm itself is expected to draw a borderline based only on the data.

How to apply neural networks in pattern recognition

For pattern recognition, the neural network architectures that can be applied are the MLPs (supervised) and the Kohonen network (unsupervised). In the first case, the problem should be set up as a classification problem, that is, the data should be transformed into the X-Y dataset, where for every data record in X, there should be a corresponding class in Y. As stated in *Chapter 3, Handling Perceptrons*, and *Chapter 6, Classifying Disease Diagnosis*, the output of the neural network for classification problems should have all of the possible classes, and this may require preprocessing of the output records.

For the other case, the unsupervised learning, there is no need to apply labels on the output; however, the input data should be properly structured as well. To remind the reader, the schemas of both neural networks are shown in the following figure:

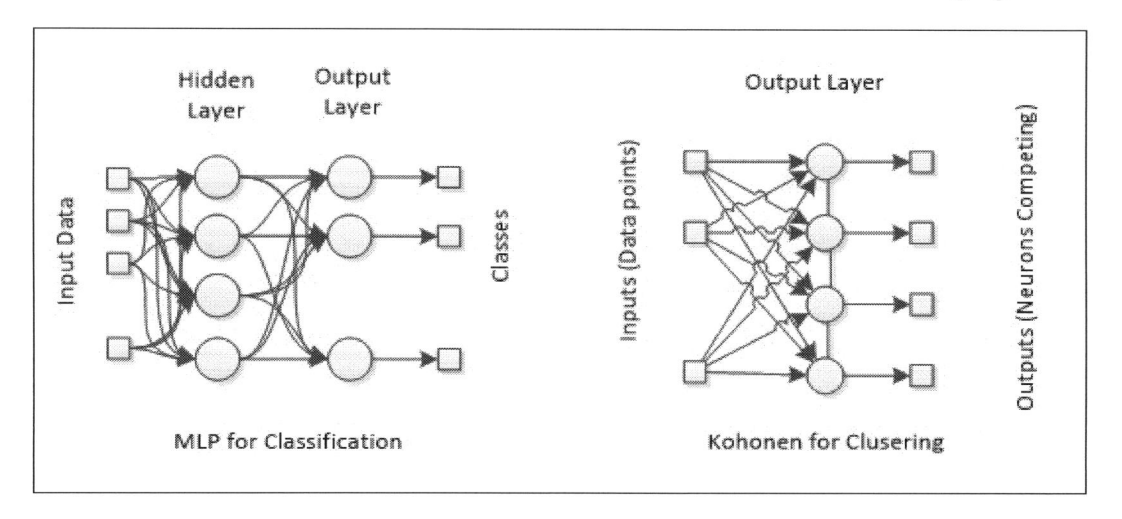

Preprocessing the data

In pattern recognition, we have to deal with all possible types of data, as well as in clustering:

- Numerical
    - Continuous or real
    - Discrete
- Categorical
    - Ordinal
    - Unscaled

However, here, we have the possibility to perform pattern recognition on multimedia content, such as images and videos. So, how should multimedia be handled? The answer to this question lies in the way these contents are stored in files. Images, for example, are written with a representation of small colored points called pixels. Each color can be coded in an RGB notation where the intensity of red, green, and blue defines every color that the human eye is able to see. Therefore, an image of dimensions 100 × 100 would have 10,000 pixels, each one having three values for red, green, and blue, yielding a total of 30,000 points. This is a challenge for image processing in neural networks.

Some methods, which will be reviewed in the next chapter, may reduce this huge number of dimensions. Then, an image can be treated as a big matrix of numerical continuous values.

For simplicity, in this chapter, we discuss only grayscale images with small dimensions.

The OCR problem

Many documents are now being scanned and stored as images, making necessary the task of converting these documents back into text, for a computer to apply editing and text processing. However, this feature involves a number of challenges:

- Variety of text fonts
- Text size
- Image noise
- Manuscripts

In spite of these, humans can easily interpret and read even the text written in a bad-quality image. This can be explained by the fact that humans are already familiar with the text characters and the words in their language. Somehow, the algorithm must become acquainted with these elements (characters, digits, signalization, and so on), in order to successfully recognize text in images.

Simplifying the task – digit recognition

Although there are a variety of tools available in the market for OCR, it is still a big challenge for an algorithm to properly recognize text in images. So, we will be restricting our application to a small domain and deal with relatively simple problems. Therefore, in this chapter, we will implement a neural network to recognize the digits 0 to 9 represented in images. Also, the images will have standardized and small dimensions, for the sake of simplicity.

Approach to digit representation

We applied the standard dimension of 5 × 5 (25 pixels) in grayscale images, resulting in 25 grayscale values for each image, as shown in the following figure:

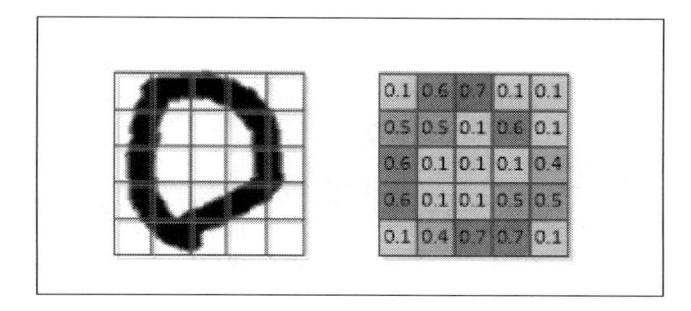

In the preceding image, we have a shape of a circle representing the digit **0** at the left and a corresponding matrix with gray values for the same digit, in grayscale.

We apply this preprocessing in order to represent all the 10 digits in this application.

Let the coding begin!

To recognize optical characters, we produced data to train and to test the neural network. In this example, we considered digits from zero to nine. According to the pixel layout, two versions of each digit data were created, one to train and the other to test. Classification techniques presented in *Chapter 3, Handling Perceptrons*, and *Chapter 6, Classifying Disease Diagnosis* will be used here.

Pattern Recognition (OCR Case)

Generating data

Numbers from zero and nine were represented by matrices in the following figure. Black pixels are typified by the value one and white pixels by the value zero. All pixel values between zero and one are on grayscale. The first dataset is to train the neural network, and the second one is for testing. It's possible to detect some random noise in the test dataset. We performed this procedure deliberately to verify the generalization.

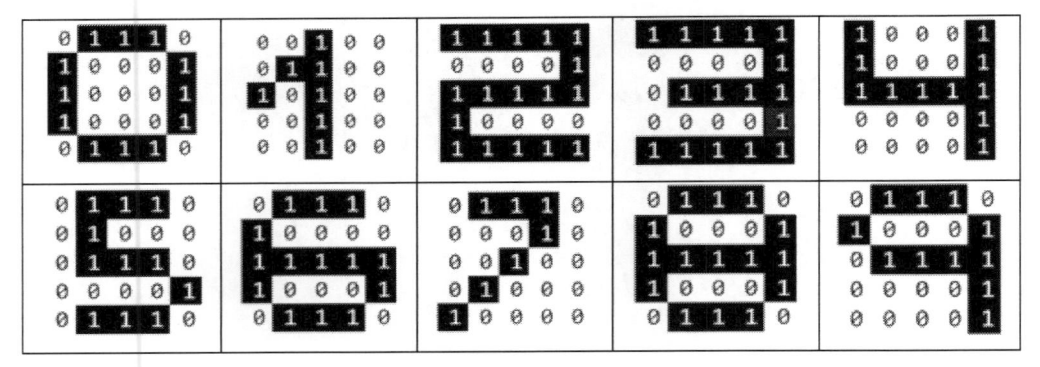

Training dataset

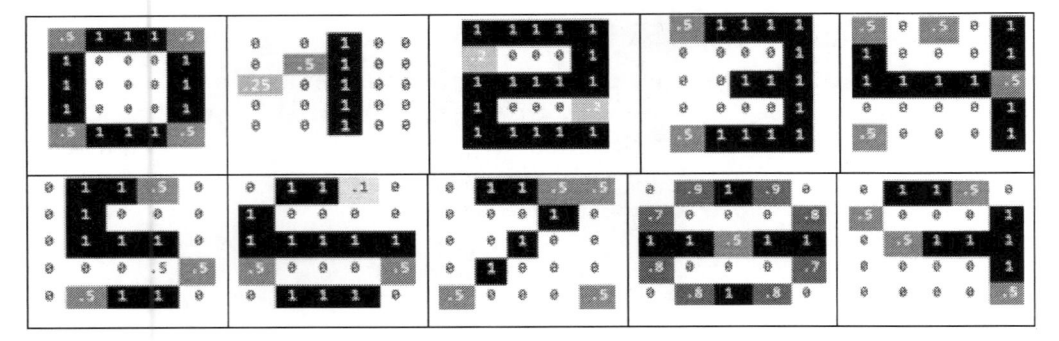

Test dataset

[158]

Each matrix row was merged into vectors (D_{train} / D_{test}) to form a pattern that will be used to train and test the neural network. Therefore, the input layer of the neural network will be composed of 26 neurons. The following tables show this data:

Training Input Dataset
$D_{train}(0) = [1,0,1,1,1,0,1,0,0,0,1,1,0,0,0,1,1,0,0,0,1,0,1,1,1,0]$
$D_{train}(1) = [1,0,0,1,0,0,0,1,1,0,0,1,0,1,0,0,0,0,1,0,0,0,0,1,0,0]$
$D_{train}(2) = [1,1,1,1,1,1,0,0,0,0,1,1,1,1,1,1,1,0,0,0,0,1,1,1,1,1]$
$D_{train}(3) = [1,1,1,1,1,1,0,0,0,0,1,0,1,1,1,1,0,0,0,0,1,1,1,1,1,1]$
$D_{train}(4) = [1,1,0,0,0,1,1,0,0,0,1,1,1,1,1,1,0,0,0,0,1,0,0,0,0,1]$
$D_{train}(5) = [1,0,1,1,1,0,0,1,0,0,0,0,1,1,1,0,0,0,0,0,1,0,0,1,1,1,0]$
$D_{train}(6) = [1,0,1,1,1,0,1,0,0,0,0,1,1,1,1,1,1,0,0,0,1,0,1,1,1,0]$
$D_{train}(7) = [1,0,1,1,1,1,0,0,0,0,1,0,0,0,0,1,0,0,0,0,1,0,0,0,0,1]$
$D_{train}(8) = [1,0,1,1,1,0,1,0,0,0,1,1,1,1,1,1,1,0,0,0,1,0,1,1,1,0]$
$D_{train}(9) = [1,0,1,1,1,0,1,0,0,0,1,0,1,1,1,1,0,0,0,0,1,0,0,0,0,1]$

Test Input Dataset
$D_{test}(0) = [1,0.5,1,1,1,0.5,1,0,0,0,1,1,0,0,0,1,1,0,0,0,1,0.5,1,1,1,0.5]$
$D_{test}(1) = [1,0,0,1,0,0,0,0.5,1,0,0,0.25,0,1,0,0,0,0,1,0,0,0,0,1,0,0]$
$D_{test}(2) = [1,1,1,1,1,1,0.2,0,0,0,1,1,1,1,1,1,1,0,0,0,0,0.2,1,1,1,1,1]$
$D_{test}(3) = [1,0.5,1,1,1,1,0,0,0,0,1,0,0,1,1,1,0,0,0,0,1,0.5,1,1,1,1]$
$D_{test}(4) = [1,0.5,0,0.5,0,1,1,0,0,0,1,1,1,1,1,1,0.5,0,0,0,0,1,0.5,0,0,0,0,1]$
$D_{test}(5) = [1,0,1,1,0.5,0,0,1,0,0,0,0,1,1,1,0,0,0,0,0,0.5,0.5,0,0.5,1,1,0]$
$D_{test}(6) = [1,0,1,1,0.1,0,1,0,0,0,0,1,1,1,1,1,1,0.5,0,0,0,0.5,0,1,1,1,0]$
$D_{test}(7) = [1,0,1,1,0.5,0.5,0,0,0,1,0,0,0,1,0,0,0,1,0,0,0,0.5,0,0,0,0,0.5]$
$D_{test}(8) = [1,0,0.9,1,0.9,0,0.7,0,0,0,0.8,1,1,0.5,1,1,0.8,0,0,0,0,0.7,0,0.8,1,0.8,0]$
$D_{test}(9) = [1,0,1,1,0.5,0,0.5,0,0,0,1,0,0.5,1,1,1,0,0,0,0,1,0,0,0,0,0.5]$

The output dataset was represented by 10 patterns. Each one has a more expressive value (**1**) and the rest are zero. Therefore, the output layer of the neural network will have 10 neurons, as shown in the following table:

Output Dataset
Out(0) = [0,0,0,0,0,0,0,0,0,1]
Out(1) = [1,0,0,0,0,0,0,0,0,0]
Out(2) = [0,1,0,0,0,0,0,0,0,0]
Out(3) = [0,0,1,0,0,0,0,0,0,0]
Out(4) = [0,0,0,1,0,0,0,0,0,0]
Out(5) = [0,0,0,0,1,0,0,0,0,0]
Out(6) = [0,0,0,0,0,1,0,0,0,0]
Out(7) = [0,0,0,0,0,0,1,0,0,0]
Out(8) = [0,0,0,0,0,0,0,1,0,0]
Out(9) = [0,0,0,0,0,0,0,0,1,0]

Building the neural network

So, in this application, our neural network shall have 25 inputs and 10 outputs, so we varied the number of hidden neurons. We created a class called `Digit` in the package `ocr` to handle this application. The neural network architecture was designed with the following parameters and represented by the following figure:

- **Neural network type**: MLP
- **Training algorithm**: Backpropagation
- **Number of hidden layers**: 1
- **Number of neurons in the hidden layer**: 18
- **Number of epochs**: 6000

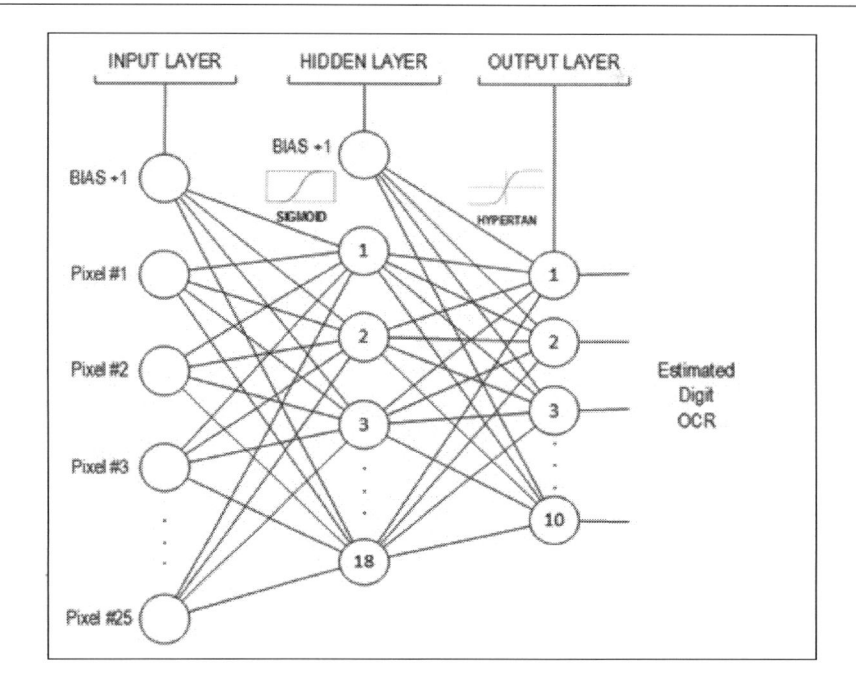

Testing and redesigning – trial and error

Now, as has been done in other case studies presented previously, let's find the best neural network topology training several nets. The strategy to do that is summarized in the following table:

Experiment	Learning Rate	Activation Functions
1	0.5	**Hidden layer**: SIGLOG
		Output layer: SIGLOG
2	0.7	**Hidden layer**: SIGLOG
		Output layer: SIGLOG
3	0.9	**Hidden layer**: SIGLOG
		Output layer: SIGLOG
4	0.5	**Hidden layer**: SIGLOG
		Output layer: HYPERTAN
5	0.7	**Hidden layer**: SIGLOG
		Output layer: HYPERTAN
6	0.9	**Hidden layer**: SIGLOG
		Output layer: HYPERTAN

Pattern Recognition (OCR Case)

Experiment	Learning Rate	Activation Functions
7	0.5	**Hidden layer:** SIGLOG
		Output layer: LINEAR
8	0.7	**Hidden layer:** SIGLOG
		Output layer: LINEAR
9	0.9	**Hidden layer:** SIGLOG
		Output layer: LINEAR

The following piece of code of the `Digit` class defines how to create a neural network to read from digit data:

```
Data ocrDataInput   = new Data("data\\ocr", "ocr_traning_inputs.csv");
Data ocrDataOutput  = new Data("data\\ocr", "ocr_traning_outputs.csv");
//read the data points coded in a csv file
Data ocrDataInputTestRNA  = new Data("data\\ocr", "ocr_test_inputs.csv");
Data ocrDataOutputTestRNA = new Data("data\\ocr", "ocr_test_outputs.csv");

// convert these files into matrices
double[][] matrixInput  = ocrDataInput.rawData2Matrix( ocrDataInput );
double[][] matrixOutput = ocrDataOutput.rawData2Matrix( ocrDataOutput );

//creates a neural network
NeuralNet n1 = new NeuralNet();
//25 inputs, 1 hidden layer, 18 hidden neurons and 10 outputs
    n1 = n1.initNet(25, 1, 18, 10);

    n1.setTrainSet( matrixInput );
    n1.setRealMatrixOutputSet( matrixOutput );

//set the training parameters
    n1.setMaxEpochs(6000);
    n1.setTargetError(0.00001);
    n1.setLearningRate( 0.7 );
    n1.setTrainType(TrainingTypesENUM.BACKPROPAGATION);
    n1.setActivationFnc(ActivationFncENUM.SIGLOG);
    n1.setActivationFncOutputLayer(ActivationFncENUM.SIGLOG);
```

Results

After running each experiment using the `Digit` class and saving the MSE values (according to the following table), we can observe that experiments **2** and **4** have the lowest MSE values. The differences between these two experiments are the learning rate and the activation function used in the output layer.

Experiment	MSE Training Rate
1	0.03007294436333284
2	0.02004457991277001
3	0.03002653392502009
4	0.00119817123282438
5	0.06351562546547934
6	0.23755154264016012
7	0.19155179860965179
8	1.73485602025775039
9	44.1822391373913359

The MSE evolution over the training epochs is plotted in the following figures. It is interesting to note that the curve of experiment **2** stabilizes near the 750th epoch, as shown in the following figure:

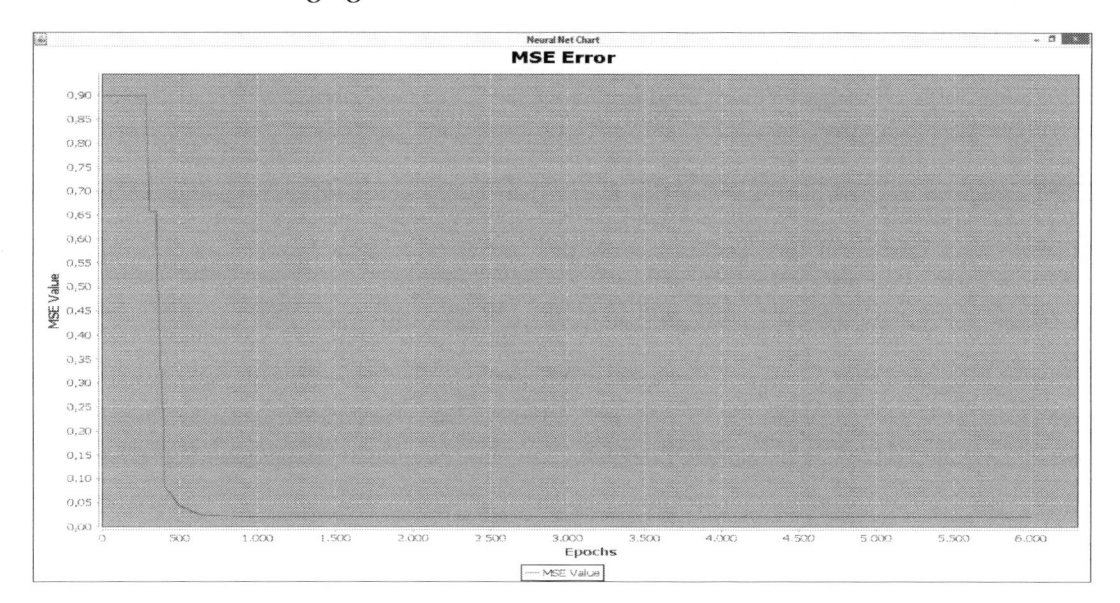

However, the curve of **experiment 4** keeps varying until the 6000th epoch, as shown in the following figure:

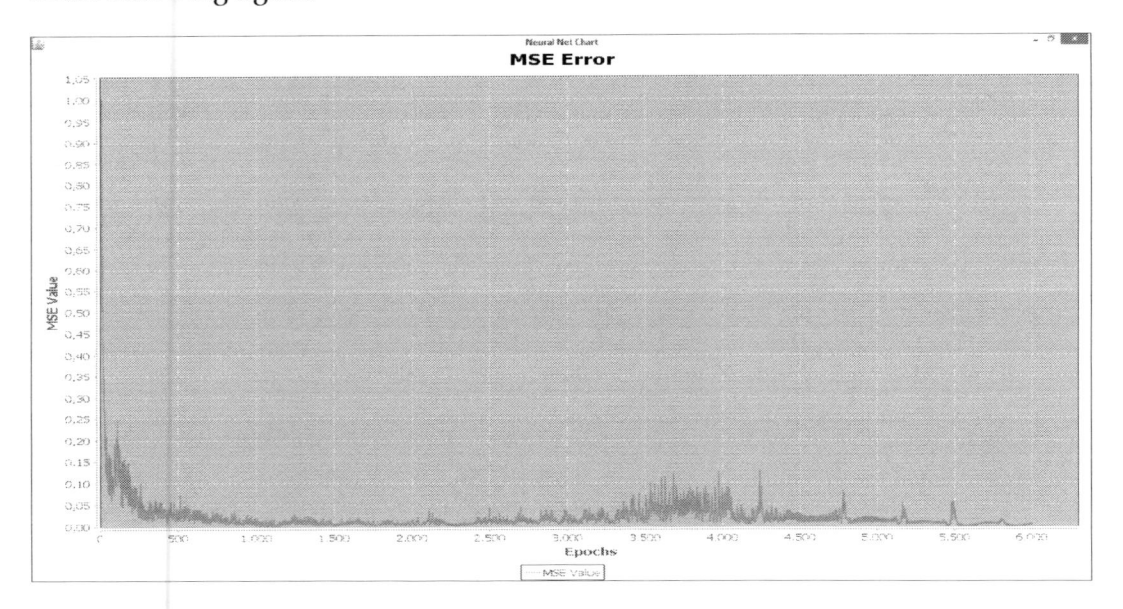

We have already explained that only the MSE value should not be considered to attest to neural net quality. Accordingly, the test dataset was used to verify the neural network generalization capacity. A comparison between the real output with noise and the neural net estimated output of experiments **2** and **4** is depicted in the following table. It is possible to conclude that the neural network weights obtained by experiment **4** are able to better recognize digits from zero to nine even if the images present pixels noisier than those obtained by experiment **2**. While experiment **2** erroneously classified three patterns, experiment **4** classified all patterns correctly.

Output Comparison										
Real Output (Test Dataset)										Digit
0.00	0.00	0.00	0.00	0.00	0.00	0.00	0.00	0.00	**1.00**	0
1.00	0.00	0.00	0.00	0.00	0.00	0.00	0.00	0.00	0.00	1
0.00	**1.00**	0.00	0.00	0.00	0.00	0.00	0.00	0.00	0.00	2
0.00	0.00	**1.00**	0.00	0.00	0.00	0.00	0.00	0.00	0.00	3
0.00	0.00	0.00	**1.00**	0.00	0.00	0.00	0.00	0.00	0.00	4
0.00	0.00	0.00	0.00	**1.00**	0.00	0.00	0.00	0.00	0.00	5
0.00	0.00	0.00	0.00	0.00	**1.00**	0.00	0.00	0.00	0.00	6
0.00	0.00	0.00	0.00	0.00	0.00	**1.00**	0.00	0.00	0.00	7
0.00	0.00	0.00	0.00	0.00	0.00	0.00	**1.00**	0.00	0.00	8
0.00	0.00	0.00	0.00	0.00	0.00	0.00	0.00	**1.00**	0.00	9
Estimated Output (Test Dataset) – Experiment 2										Digit
0.00	0.00	0.00	0.00	0.00	0.01	0.02	0.00	0.00	**0.97**	0 (OK)
0.97	0.00	0.00	0.00	0.03	0.00	0.00	0.00	0.00	0.00	1 (OK)
0.00	0.00	0.00	**0.02**	0.00	0.00	0.00	0.01	0.00	0.00	4 (ERR)
0.00	0.00	0.00	0.02	0.00	0.00	**0.20**	0.00	0.00	0.00	7 (ERR)
0.00	0.00	0.00	**0.96**	0.00	0.00	0.00	0.02	0.00	0.00	4 (OK)
0.01	0.00	0.00	0.00	**0.98**	0.01	0.00	0.00	0.00	0.00	5 (OK)
0.01	0.00	0.00	0.00	0.00	**0.56**	0.00	0.07	0.00	0.00	6 (OK)
0.00	0.00	0.00	0.00	**0.66**	0.00	0.14	0.00	0.00	0.00	5 (ERR)
0.00	0.00	0.00	0.00	0.00	0.03	0.00	**0.93**	0.00	0.01	8 (OK)
0.00	0.00	0.00	0.00	0.01	0.00	0.00	0.01	**0.96**	0.00	9 (OK)
Estimated Output (Test Dataset) – Experiment 4										Digit
0.00	0.16	0.09	0.06	0.06	0.01	0.11	-0.27	-0.09	**0.97**	0 (OK)
1.00	0.00	0.09	0.13	0.21	-0.22	0.42	0.19	0.34	0.14	1 (OK)
0.00	**0.99**	0.04	0.05	0.07	0.10	0.14	0.18	0.22	0.25	2 (OK)
0.01	0.03	**0.81**	0.06	0.09	0.03	0.74	-0.03	-0.03	-0.12	3 (OK)
0.02	-0.11	-0.10	**0.94**	0.08	0.08	0.11	0.85	0.09	0.06	4 (OK)
0.02	-0.01	0.10	0.06	**1.00**	0.11	0.10	0.11	0.10	0.06	5 (OK)
-0.00	-0.07	-0.05	0.22	0.09	**1.00**	0.20	0.11	0.26	0.20	6 (OK)
0.51	-0.05	0.25	0.09	0.96	0.22	**0.99**	0.25	0.34	0.34	7 (OK)
0.00	0.04	0.04	0.04	0.05	0.06	0.05	**0.98**	0.03	0.07	8 (OK)
0.00	0.01	0.05	0.01	0.02	0.00	0.04	0.03	**1.00**	0.02	9 (OK)

Summary

In this chapter, we've seen the power of neural networks with respect to recognizing digits from zero to nine in images. Although the coding of the digits was very small in 5 × 5 images, it was important to see the concept in practice. Neural networks are capable of learning from data, and provided that real-world representations can be transformed into data, it is reasonable to state that character recognition is a very good example of the application of pattern recognition. The application here can be extended to any type of characters, under the condition that the neural network be presented all the predefined characters.

The next chapter will explore all the content seen in this book so far to present the reader with some options for the optimization and improvement of the neural network application, concluding the outline designed for this book.

Neural Network Optimization and Adaptation

In this chapter, the reader will be presented with techniques that help to optimize neural networks, thereby favoring its best performance. Tasks such as input selection, dataset separation and filtering, and choice of the number of hidden neurons are examples of what can be adjusted to improve a neural network's performance. Furthermore, this chapter focuses on methods for adapting neural networks to real-time data. Two implementations of these techniques are presented here. Application problems will be selected for exercises. This chapter deals with the following:

- Input selection
    - Dimensionality reduction
    - Data filtering
- Structure selection
    - Pruning
- Online retraining
    - Stochastic online learning
- Adaptive neural networks
    - Adaptive resonance theory

Common issues in neural network implementations

When developing a neural network application, it is quite common to face problems regarding how accurate the results are. The source of these problems can be various:

- bad input selection
- noisy data
- very big dataset
- unsuitable structure
- inadequate number of hidden neurons
- inadequate learning rate
- insufficient stop condition; and/or
- bad dataset segmentation

The design of a neural network application sometimes requires a lot of patience and trial-and-error methods. There is no methodology stating specifically the number of hidden units and/or which architecture should be used, but there are recommendations on how to properly choose these parameters. Another issue that programmers may face is a long training time, which often causes the neural network to not learn the data. No matter how long the training runs, the neural network won't converge.

> Designing a neural network requires the programmer or designer to test and redesign the neural structure as many times as needed, until an acceptable result is obtained.

On the other hand, one may wish to improve the results. A neural network can learn until the learning algorithm reaches the stop condition, either the number of epochs or the mean squared error. Even so, sometimes, the results are either inaccurate or not generalized. This will require a redesign of the neural structure as well as the dataset.

Input selection

One of the key tasks in designing a neural network application is to select appropriate inputs. For the unsupervised case, one wishes to use only relevant variables on which the neural network will find the patterns. For the supervised case, there is a need to map the outputs to the inputs, so one needs to choose only the input variables that somewhat influence the output.

Data correlation

One strategy that helps in selecting good inputs in the supervised case is the correlation between data series. A correlation between data series is a measure of how one data sequence reacts or influences the other. Suppose that we have one dataset containing a number of data series from which we choose one to be an output. Now, we need to select the inputs from the remaining variables.

We then evaluate the influence of one variable at a time on the output in order to decide whether to include it as an input or not. The **Pearson coefficient** is one of the most used variables:

$$r_{x(k)y(k)} = \frac{S_{x(k)y(k)}}{\sqrt{S_{x(k)x(k)}S_{y(k)y(k)}}}$$

Where $S_{x(k)y(k)}$ denotes the covariance between the x and the y variables:

$$S_{x(k)y(k)} = \sum_{i=\tau}^{n} x(i)y(i) - \frac{\sum_{j=0}^{n} x(j) \sum_{j=0}^{n} y(j)}{n}$$

The correlation takes values from **-1** to **1**, where values close to **+1** indicate a positive correlation, values near **-1** indicate a negative correlation, and values near **0** indicate no correlation at all.

To exemplify, let's see the following three charts of the two variables X and Y:

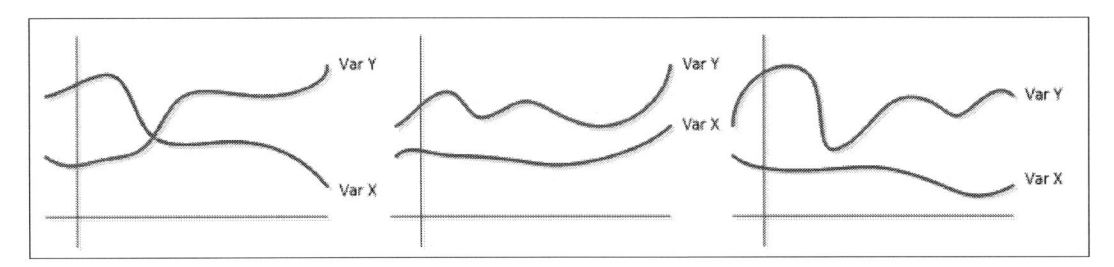

In the first chart, to the left, visually, one can see that as one variable decreases, the other increases its value (corr.: -0.8). The middle chart shows the case when the two variables vary in the same direction, therefore a positive correlation (corr.: +0.7). The third chart, to the right, shows a case where there is no correlation between the variables (corr.: -0.1).

There is no threshold rule as to which correlation should be taken into account as a limit; it depends on the application. While absolute correlation values greater than 0.5 may be suitable for one application, in others, values near 0.2 may add a significant contribution.

Dimensionality reduction

Another interesting point is regarding the removal of redundant data. Sometimes, this is desired when there is a lot of available data in both unsupervised and supervised learning. To exemplify, let's see the following chart of two variables:

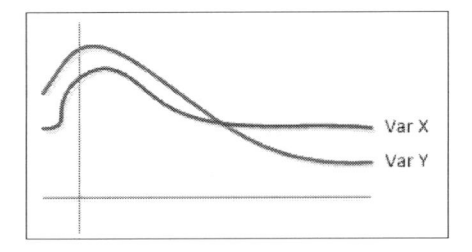

It can be seen that both X and Y variables share the same shape, so this can be interpreted as a redundancy, as both variables are carrying almost the same information because of the high positive correlation. Thus, one can consider a technique called **Principal Component Analysis (PCA)**, which is a good approach for dealing with these cases.

The result of PCA will be a new variable summarizing the previous two (or more) variables. Basically, the original data series are subtracted by the mean and then multiplied by the transposed eigenvectors of the covariance matrix:

$$S = \begin{bmatrix} S_{XX} & S_{XY} \\ S_{YX} & S_{YY} \end{bmatrix}$$

Where SXY denotes the covariance between the variables X and Y.

The derived new data will then be as follows:

$$Z = eig(S)^T [X - E[X] \quad Y - E[Y]]$$

Let's see now how a new variable would look like in a chart, compared to the original variables:

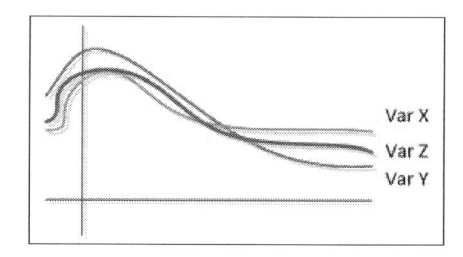

Data filtering

Noisy and bad data are also a source of problems in neural network applications; that's why we need to filter data. One of the common data filtering techniques can be performed by excluding the records that exceed the usual range. For example, temperature values are between -40 and 40, so a value like 50 would be considered an outlier and could be taken out.

The three-sigma rule is a good and effective measure for filtering. It consists of filtering the values that are beyond three times the standard deviation from the mean:

$$d_i = \left|\frac{X_i - E[X]}{std(X)}\right| \leq 3$$

Structure selection

To choose an adequate structure for a neural network is also a very important step. However, this is often done empirically, since there is no rule on how many hidden units a neural network should have. The only measure on how many units are adequate is the neural network performance. One assumes that if the general error is low enough, then the structure is suitable. Nevertheless, they might have a smaller structure that could yield the same result.

In this context, there are basically two methodologies: constructive and pruning. The construction consists of starting with only the input and the output layers, then adding new neurons at a hidden layer, until a good result can be obtained. The destructive approach, also known as pruning, works on a bigger structure on which the neurons having few contributions to the output, are taken out.

The construction approach is depicted in the following figure:

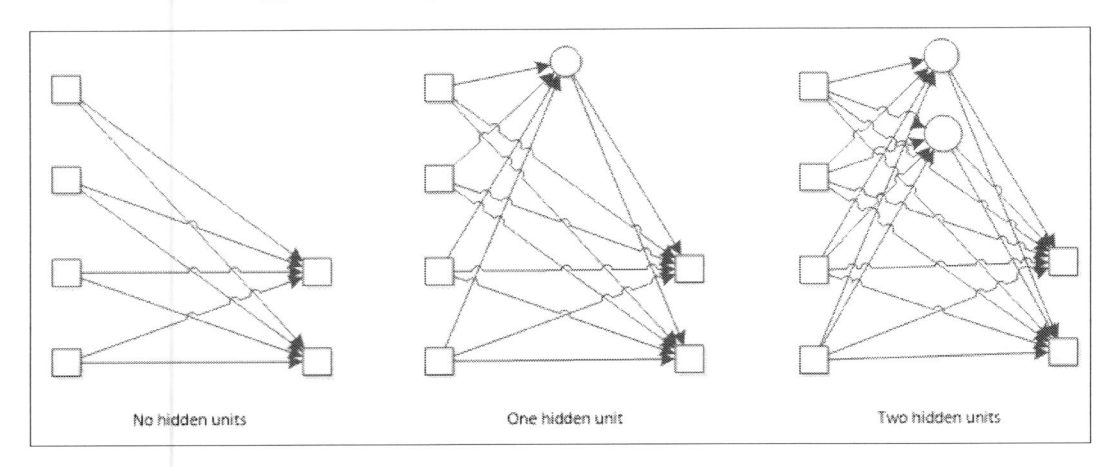

No hidden units   *One hidden unit*   *Two hidden units*

Pruning is the way back; when given a high number of neurons, one wishes to "prune" those whose sensitivity is very low, which means that its contribution to the error is minimal, as shown in the following figure:

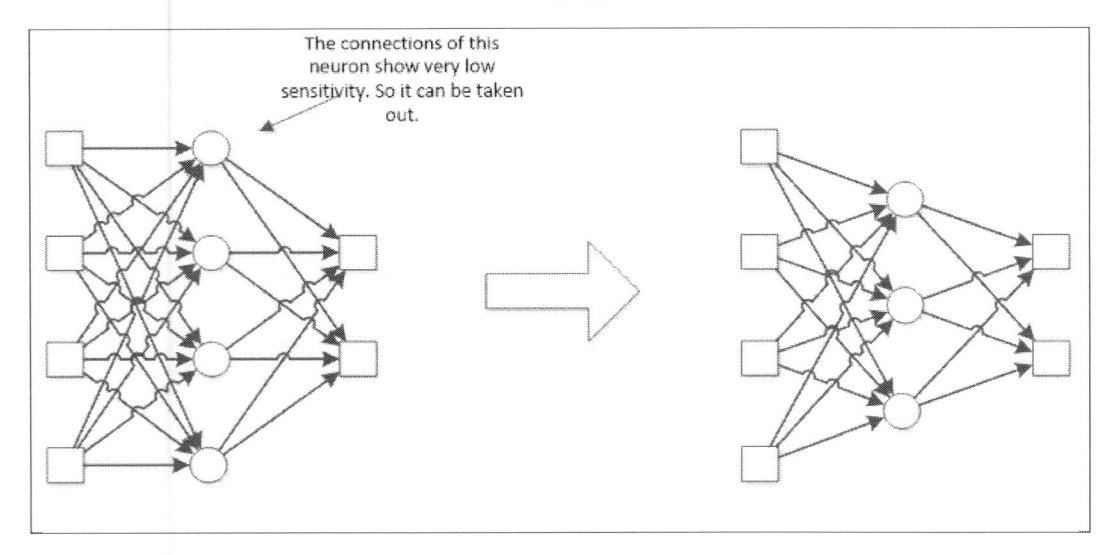

Online retraining

During the learning process, it is important to design how the training should be performed. Two basic approaches are batch and incremental learning.

In batch learning, all the records are fed to the network, so it can evaluate the error and then update the weights.

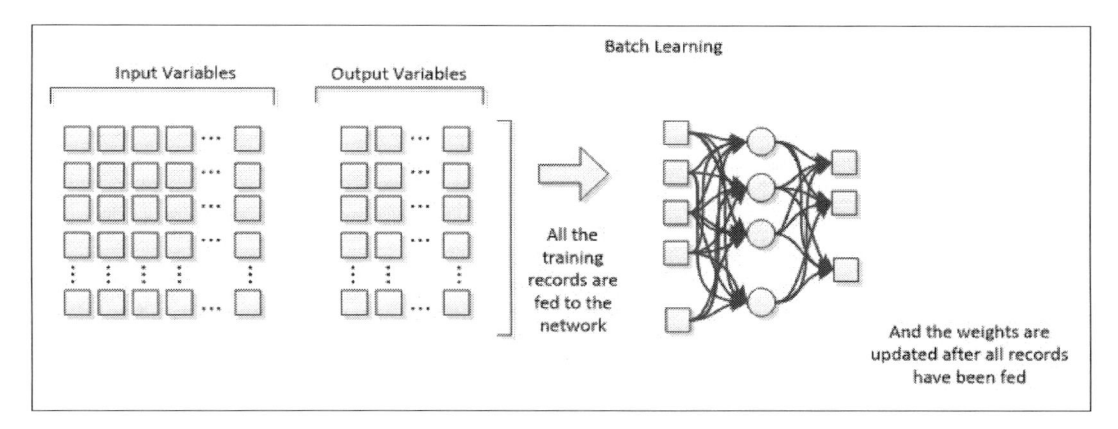

In incremental learning, the update is performed after each record has been sent to the network.

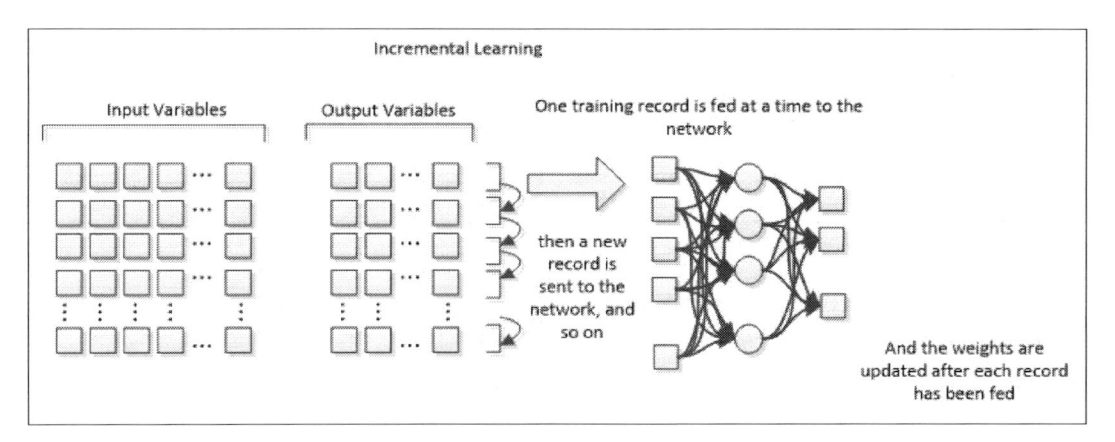

Both approaches work well and have advantages and disadvantages. While batch learning can used for a less often, though more directed weight update, incremental learning provides a way for a finely tuned weight adjustment. In this context, it is possible to design a mode of learning that enables the network to learn continually.

Neural Network Optimization and Adaptation

Stochastic online learning

Offline learning means that the neural network learns while not in "operation." Every neural network application is supposed to work in an environment, and in order to be at production, it should be properly trained. Offline training is suitable to put the network into operation, since its outputs may vary over large ranges of values, which would certainly compromise the system, if it is in operation. However, when it comes to online learning, there are restrictions. While in offline learning, it's possible to use cross-validation and bootstrapping to predict errors, in online learning, this can't be done since there's no "training dataset" anymore. However, one would need online training when some improvement in the neural network's performance is desired.

A stochastic method is used when online learning is performed. This algorithm to improve neural network training is composed of two main features: random choice of samples for training and variation of the learning rate in runtime (online). This training method has been used when noise is found in the objective function. It helps to escape the local minimum (one of the best solutions) and to reach the global minimum (the best solution).

The pseudo algorithm is as follows:

```
Initialize the weights.
    Initialize the learning rate.
    Repeat the following steps:
       Randomly select one (or possibly more) case(s)
          from the population.
       Update the weights by subtracting the gradient
          times the learning rate.
       Reduce the learning rate according to an
          appropriate schedule.
```

> The Source code of the pseudo algorithm can be found at ftp://ftp.sas.com/pub/neural/FAQ2.html#A_styles.

Implementation

In the Java project, it has created the `BackpropagationOnline` class inside the `learn` package. The differences between this algorithm and classic `backpropagation` was programmed by changing the `train()` method and adding two new methods: `generateIndexRandomList()` and `reduceLearningRate()`. The first one generates a random list of indexes to be used in the training step, and the second one executes the learning rate online variation according to the following heuristic:

```
private double reduceLearningRate(NeuralNet n, double percentage) {
```

[174]

```
      double newLearningRate = n.getLearningRate() *
                    ((100.0 - percentage) / 100.0);

      if(newLearningRate < 0.1) {
        newLearningRate = 1.0;
      }

      return newLearningRate;
   }
```

The `train()` method was also modified to comply with the pseudo algorithm presented earlier. The following code is the main part of this method:

```
    ArrayList<Integer> indexRandomList = generateIndexRandomList(rows);

    while(getMse() > n.getTargetError()) {

      if ( epoch >= n.getMaxEpochs() ) break;

      double sumErrors = 0.0;

      for (int rows_i = 0; rows_i < rows; rows_i++) {

        n = forward( n, indexRandomList.get(rows_i) );

        n = backpropagation( n, indexRandomList.get(rows_i) );

        sumErrors = sumErrors + n.getErrorMean();

        n.setLearningRate( reduceLearningRate( n, n.getLearningRatePerce
ntageReduce() ) );

      }

      setMse( sumErrors / rows );

      n.getListOfMSE().add( getMse() );


      epoch++;

    }
```

Application

We have used data from previous chapters to test this new way to train neural nets. This chapter uses the same neural net topology that was defined in *Chapter 5, Forecasting Weather*, and *Chapter 8, Pattern Recognition (OCR Case)*. The first one is the forecast weather problem, and the second one is the OCR. The following table shows the comparison of results.

Values	Forecast weather	OCR
Classic backpropagation learning rate	0.5	0.5
Classic backpropagation MSE value	0.2877786584	0.0011981712
On-line backpropagation learning rate	Found: $\cong\cong$ 0.15	Found: $\cong\cong$ 0.40
On-line backpropagation MSE value	0.4618623052	9.977909980E-6

The following graph shows the MSE evolution found after the new training method. It takes into consideration the forecast weather data. The curve has a saw shape because of the variation of the learning rate. Besides, it's very similar to the curve shown in *Chapter 5, Forecasting Weather*.

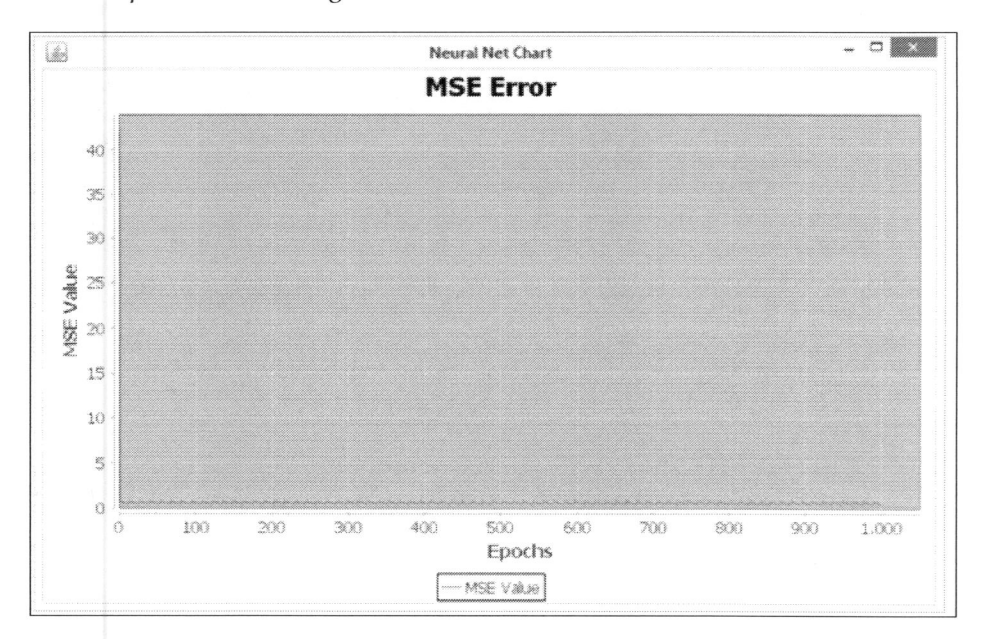

On the other hand, the following graph was produced using the OCR data and shows that the training process was faster and stopped near the 900th epoch because it had a very small MSE error. It's important to remember that in *Chapter 8, Pattern Recognition (OCR Case)*, the training process was slower and continued until the 6000th epoch.

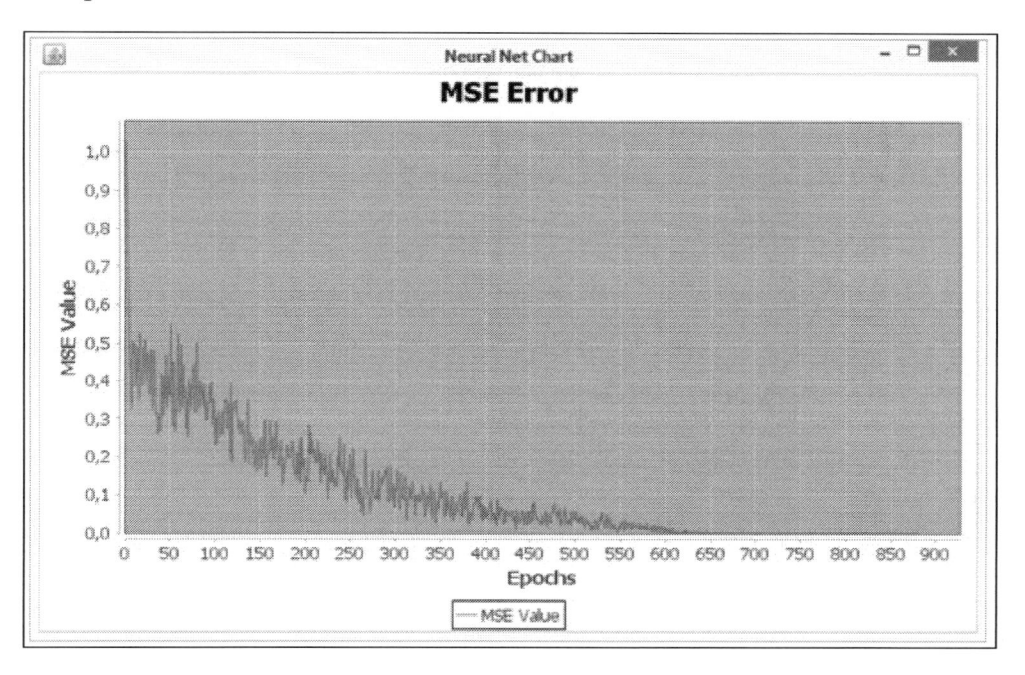

Other experiments were also conducted: train neural nets with the backpropagation algorithm, considering the learning rate found by using an online approach. The MSE values decreased in both problems.

The forecast weather MSE was about 0.206 against 0.287 (found in *Chapter 5, Forecasting Weather*). It's shown in the following figure:

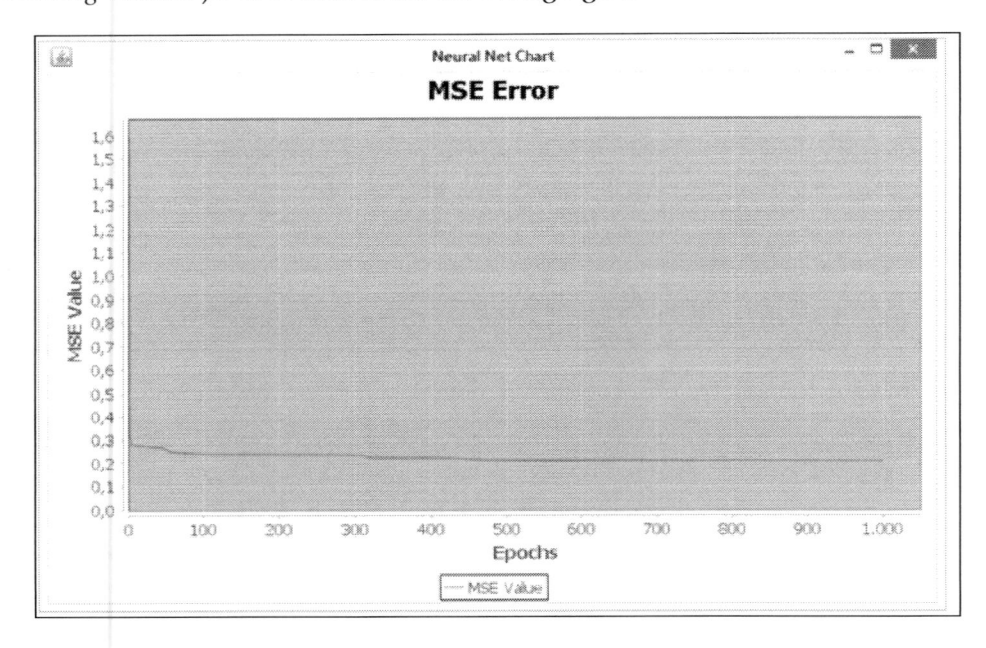

The OCR MSE was about 8.663E-6 against 0.001 (found in *Chapter 8, Pattern Recognition (OCR Case)*). It's possible to see this in the following figure:

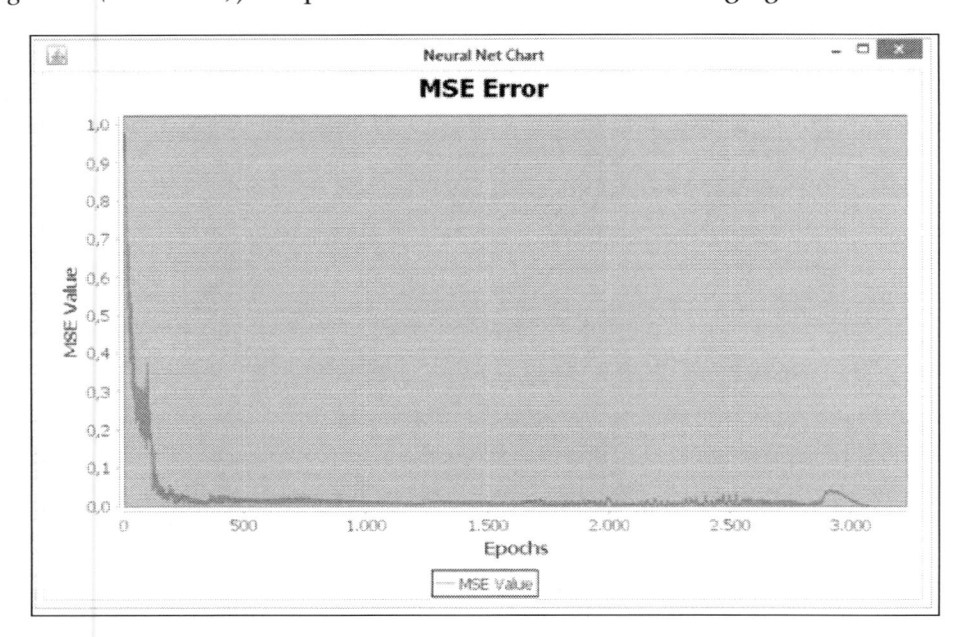

Another important observation is based on the fact that the training process shown in the preceding figure is almost terminated in the 3000th epoch. Therefore, it's faster and better than the training process discussed in *Chapter 8, Pattern Recognition (OCR Case)*, using the same algorithm.

Adaptive neural networks

Analogous to human learning, neural networks may also work in order to not forget the previous knowledge. Using the traditional approaches for neural learning, this is nearly impossible because of the fact that every training involves replacing all the connections already made with the new ones, thereby "forgetting" the previous knowledge, thus arises a need to make the neural networks adapt to new knowledge by incrementing instead of replacing their current knowledge. To address this issue, we are going to explore a method called **adaptive resonance theory (ART)**.

Adaptive resonance theory

The question that drove the development of this theory was the following: "*How can an adaptive system remain plastic to a significant input and yet maintain the stability for irrelevant inputs?*" In other words: "How to retain the previously learned information while learning new information?"

We've seen that the competitive learning in unsupervised learning deals with pattern recognition, wherein similar inputs yield similar outputs or fire the same neurons. In an ART topology, the resonance comes in when the information is being retrieved from the network, by providing the feedback from the competitive layer and the input layer. So, while the network receives the data to learn, there is an oscillation resulting from the feedback between the competitive and the input layers. This oscillation stabilizes when the pattern is fully developed inside the neural network. This resonance then reinforces the stored pattern.

Implementation

A new class called ART has been created in the som package. The following table describes the methods of this class:

Class name: ART	
Attributes	
`private int SIZE_OF_INPUT_LAYER;`	Global variable to store the number of neurons in the input layer
`private int SIZE_OF_OUTPUT_LAYER;`	Global variable to store the number of neurons in the output layer
Methods	
`public NeuralNet train(NeuralNet n)`	Method to train the neural net based on the ART algorithm
	Parameters: Neural net object to train
	Returns: Trained neural net object
`private void initGlobalVars(NeuralNet n)`	Method to initialize global variables
	Parameters: Neural net object
	Returns: -
`private NeuralNet initNet(NeuralNet n)`	Method to initialize neural net weights
	Parameters: Neural net object
	Returns: Neural net object with the initialized weights
`private int calcWinnerNeuron(NeuralNet n, int row_i, double[][] patterns)`	Method to calculate the winner neuron
	Parameters: Neural net object, row of the training set, training set patterns
	Returns: Index of the winner neuron
`private NeuralNet setNetOutput(NeuralNet n, int winnerNeuron)`	Method to attribute the neural net output
	Parameters: Neural net object, index of winner neuron
	Returns: Neural net object with the output attributes
`private boolean vigilanceTest(NeuralNet n, int row_i)`	Method to verify whether the neural net has learned or not
	Parameters: Neural net object, row of the training set
	Returns: True if the neural net learned and false if not

private NeuralNet fixWeights(NeuralNet n, int row_i, int winnerNeuron)	Method to fix the weights of the neural net
	Parameters: Neural net object, row of the training set, index of the winner neuron
	Returns: Neural net object with the weights fixed
Class Implementation with Java: file ART.java	

The training method is shown in the following code. It's possible to notice that first, the global variables and the neural net are initialized. After that, the number of training sets and the training patterns are stored, and then, the training process begins. The first step of this process is to calculate the index of the winner neuron; the second is to make an attribution of the neural net output. The next step involves verifying whether the neural net has learned or not. If it has learned, then the weights are fixed, and if not, another training sample is presented to the net.

```java
public NeuralNet train(NeuralNet n){

    this.initGlobalVars( n );

    n = this.initNet( n );

    int rows = n.getTrainSet().length;

    double[][] trainPatterns = n.getTrainSet();

    for (int epoch = 0; epoch < n.getMaxEpochs(); epoch++) {

      for (int row_i = 0; row_i < rows; row_i++) {

        int winnerNeuron = this.calcWinnerNeuron( n, row_i, trainPatterns );

        n = this.setNetOutput( n, winnerNeuron );

        boolean isMatched = this.vigilanceTest( n, row_i );

        if ( isMatched ) {
          n = this.fixWeights(n, row_i, winnerNeuron);
        }

      }

    }

    return n;

}
```

Summary

In this chapter, we've discussed a few topics that make a neural network work better, either by improving its accuracy or by extending its knowledge. These techniques help a lot in designing solutions with artificial neural networks. The reader is welcome to apply this framework in any desired task that neural networks can be used on, in order to explore the enhanced power that these structures can have. Even simple details such as selecting the input data may influence the entire learning process, as well as the filtering of bad data or the elimination of redundant variables. We demonstrated in two implementations, two strategies that help to improve the performance of a neural network: stochastic online learning and adaptive resonance theory. These methodologies enable the network to extend its knowledge and therefore, adapt to new changing environments.

A
Setting up the NetBeans Environment

This appendix shows a step-by-step procedure of how to set up the development environment for the NetBeans IDE.

Download and install NetBeans

> Before downloading and installing NetBeans, make sure that you have installed the JDK (Java Development Kit), which can be downloaded from https://www.oracle.com/java/index.html.

Setting up the NetBeans Environment

Follow these steps to download and install NetBeans:

1. NetBeans can be freely downloaded at the project's site `https://netbeans.org/downloads/index.html` (shown in the following figure); choose the installer that is to be downloaded according to your operation system, as shown in the drop-down list platform:

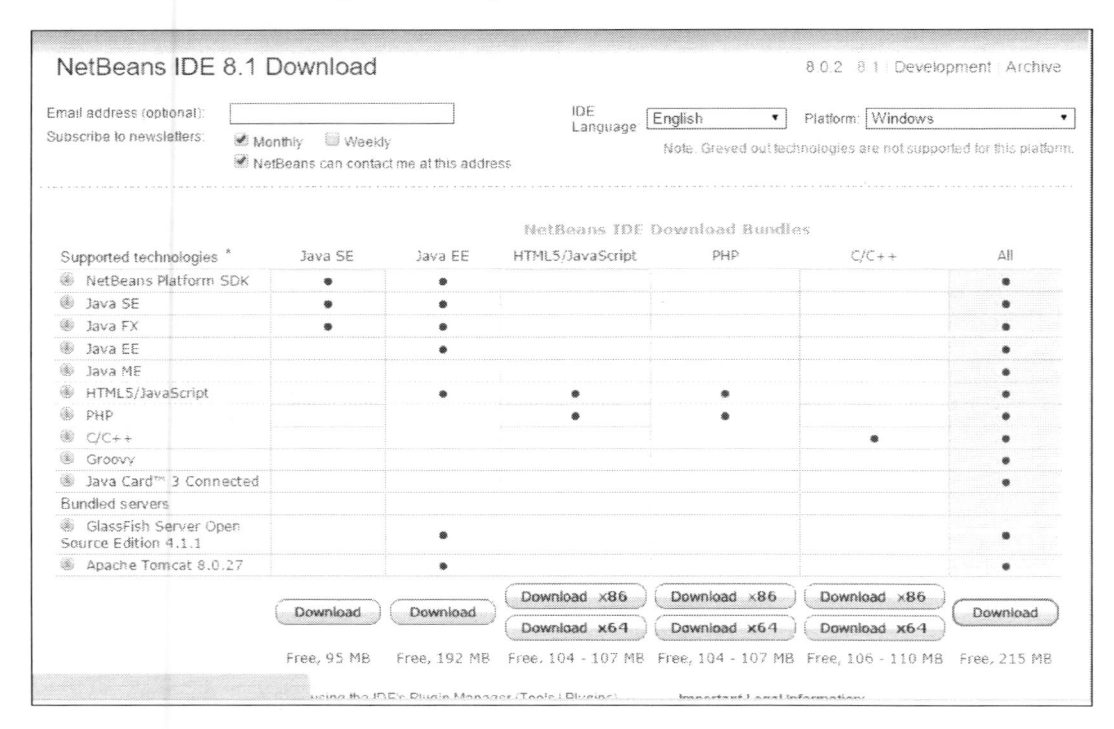

2. You can select from the versions displayed in the web page. For the projects in this book, the Java SE version fits very well; in addition, it is the smallest and lightest version as well. The download should start shortly; in every case, you can click on the **download it here** button, as shown in the following screenshot:

Appendix A

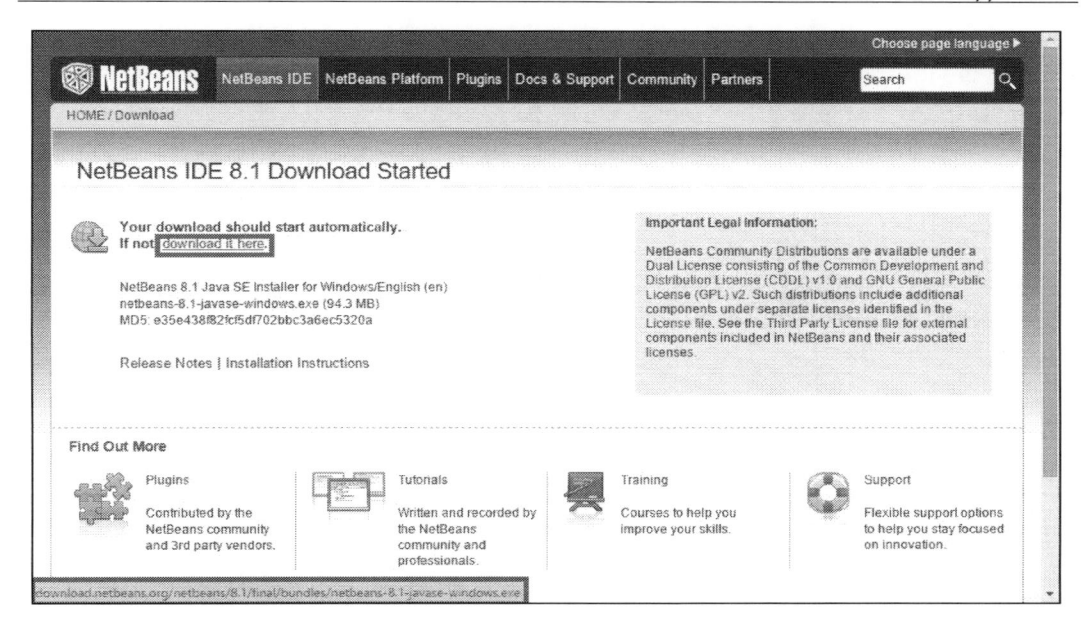

3. After the download, you should run the `netbeans-<version>-javase-<your_os>.exe` executable file. The following screen appears. You can perform the standard installation then. When executing the installer, it tells you about the size of the installation and the version. You can then click on the **Next** button.

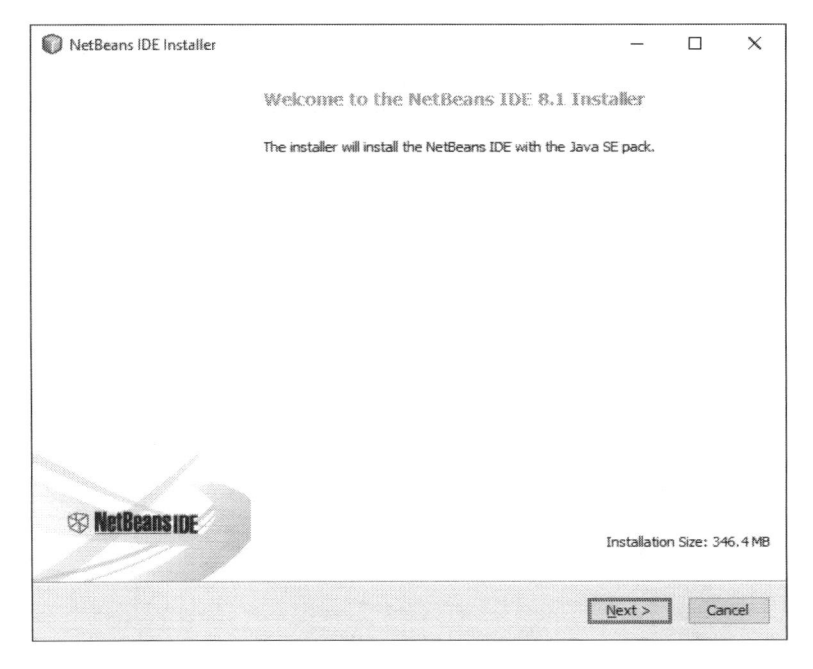

Setting up the NetBeans Environment

4. You must accept the license agreement by marking the checkbox, as shown in the following screenshot, and then click on the **Next** button:

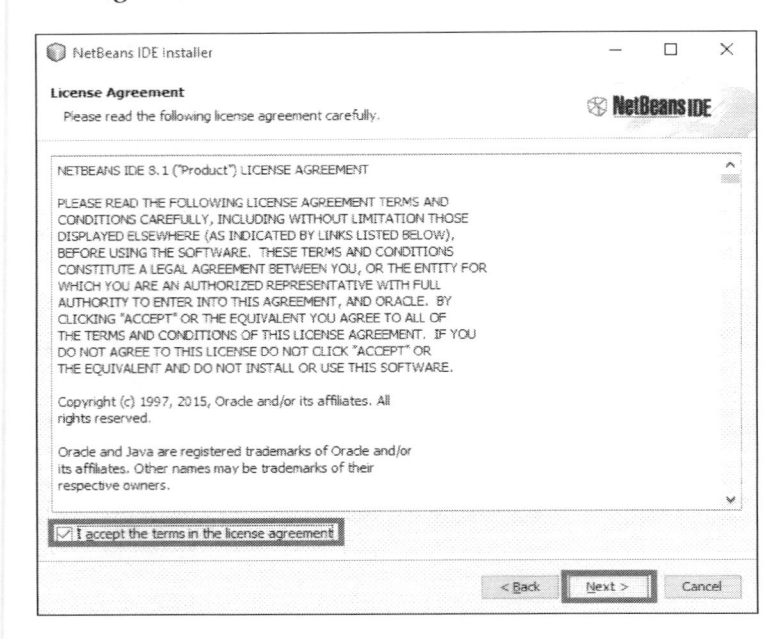

5. Then, you can select the folders where the program will be installed or you can just leave the default folders, as indicated in the following screenshot:

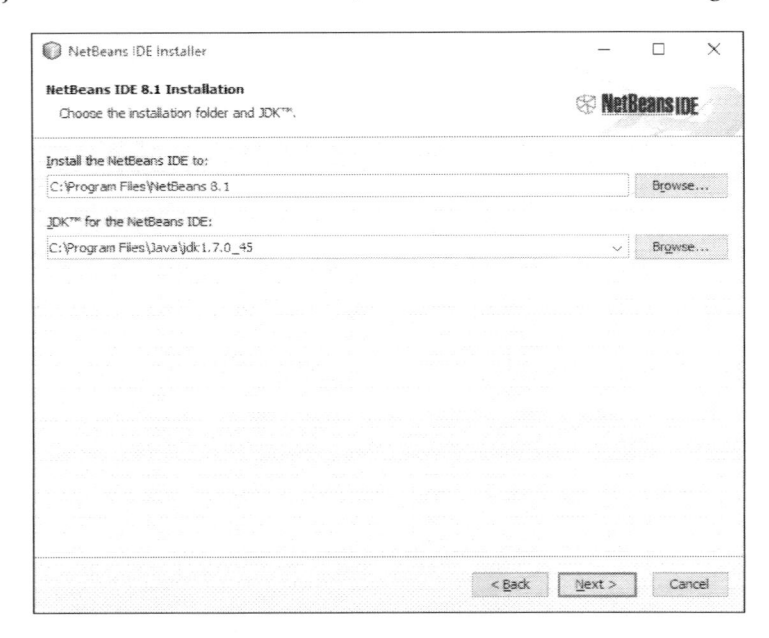

Appendix A

6. Now, we're ready to install. You may the click on the **Check for Updates** checkbox and just click on the **Install** button.

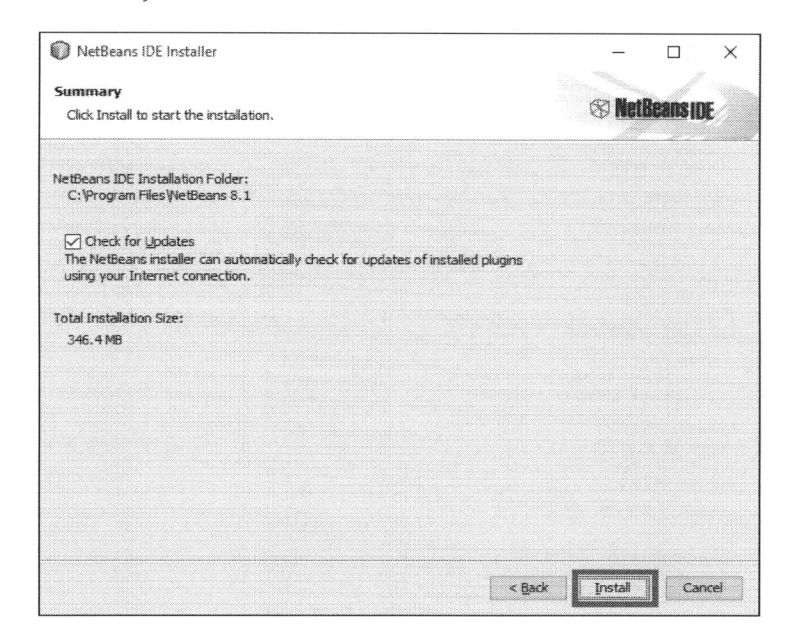

7. After the installation, you may click on the **NetBeans** icon on the desktop to run NetBeans. An initial page will open:

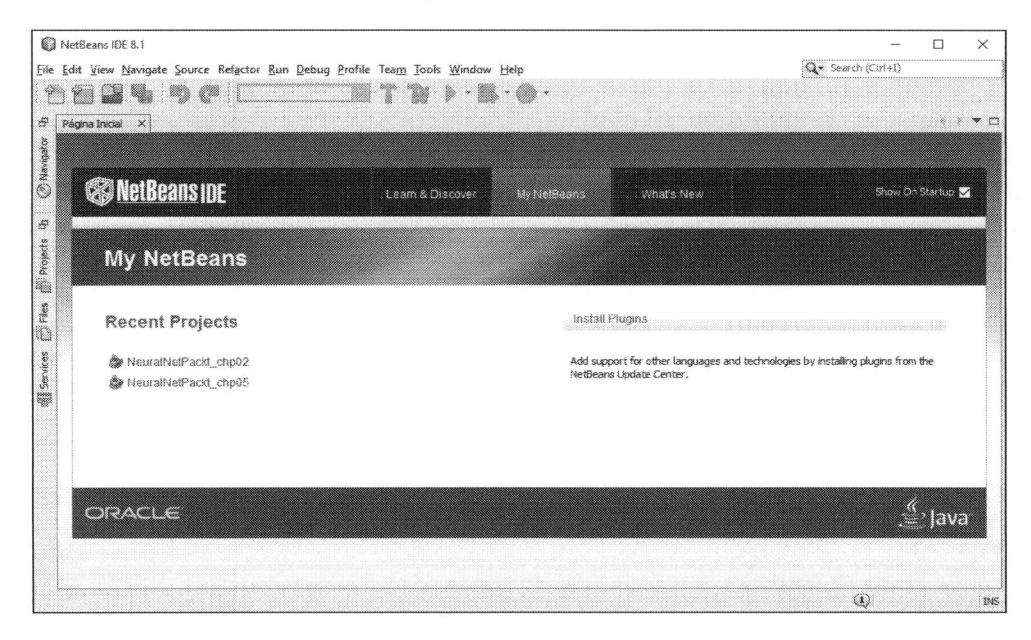

Setting up the NetBeans Environment

Setting up the NetBeans environment

To set up the NetBeans environment, you need to perform the following steps:

1. The NetBeans environment already provides options to create and open new projects. Now, let's create a new project by selecting the menu **File | New Project**. In the dialog window that opens, make sure that you have selected the **Java Project with Existing Sources** project template and then click on **Next**, as shown in the following screenshot:

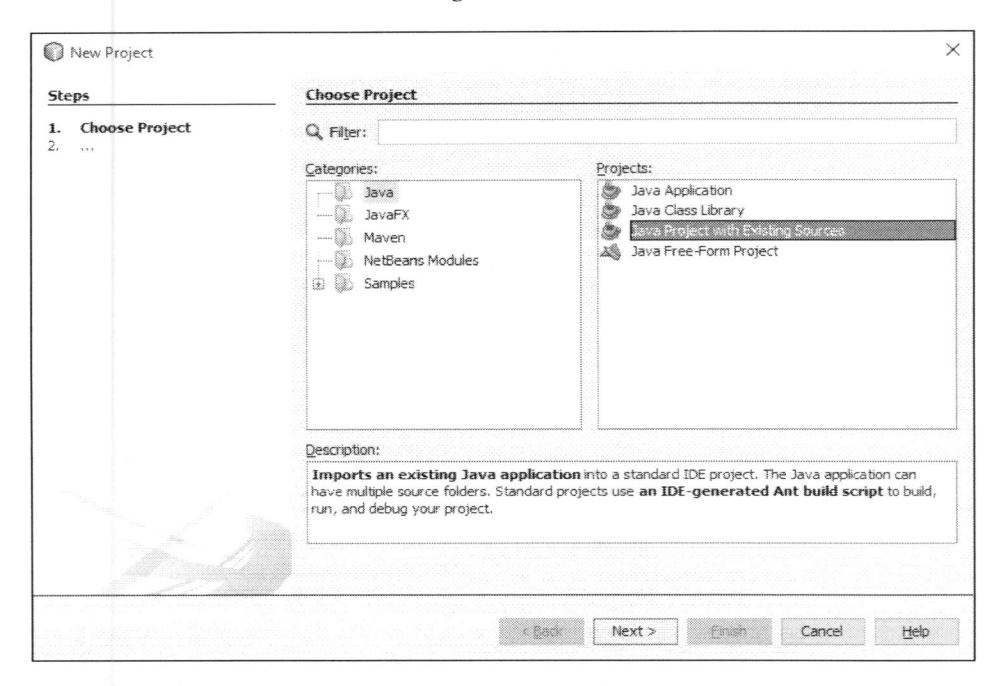

2. Then, you can choose a name for the project, the name **NeuralNetPackt_ch01** is mere a suggestion, and you are free to choose the name you want.

Appendix A

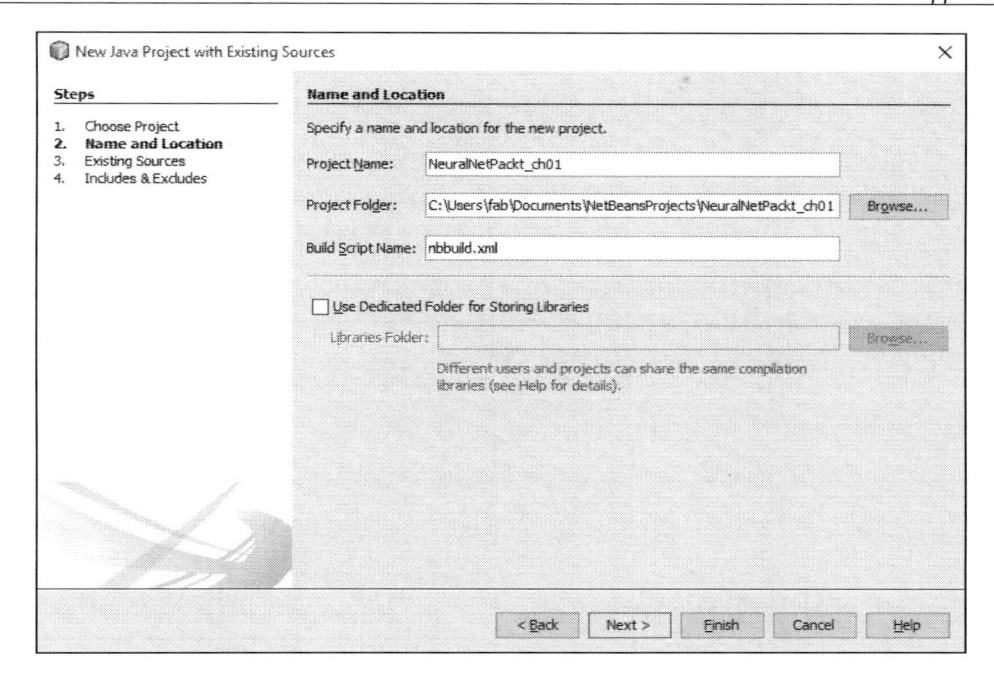

3. In the next screen, you can select the folder where the source codes are stored:

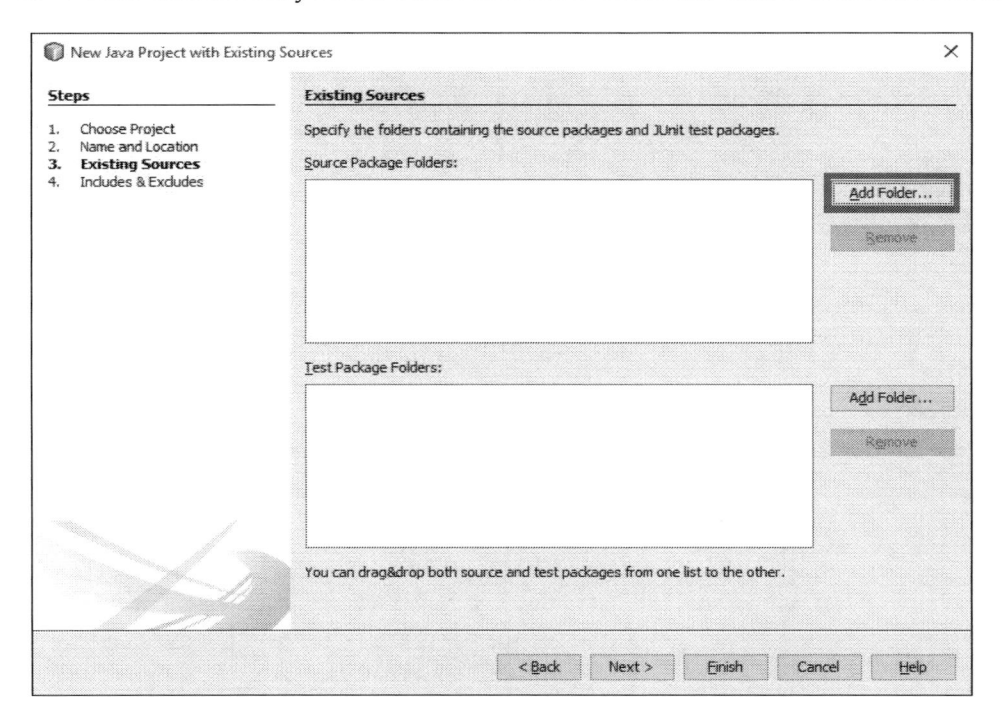

Setting up the NetBeans Environment

4. In the file, open the dialog that opens, browse to the folder where the files are stored, and select it.

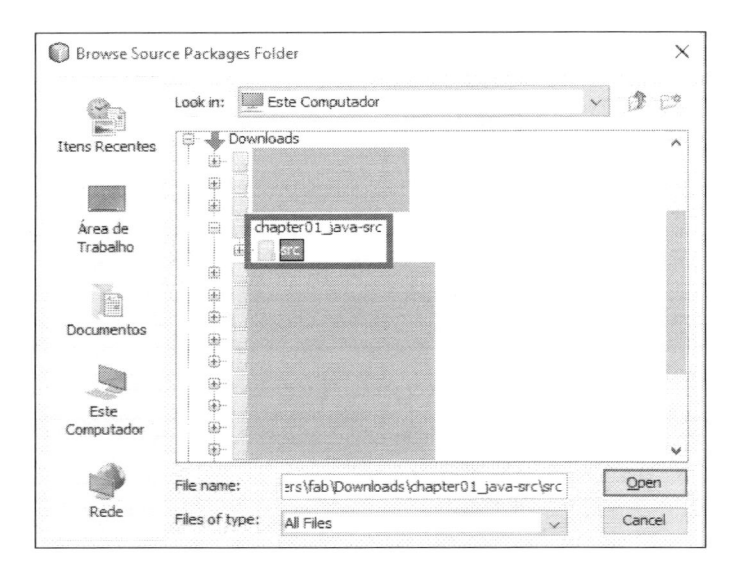

5. Once you've selected the folder, you can click on the **Open** button and then the next button in the parent window. Now, a list of includes and excludes is displayed. You can just leave it as is and click on the **Finish** button.

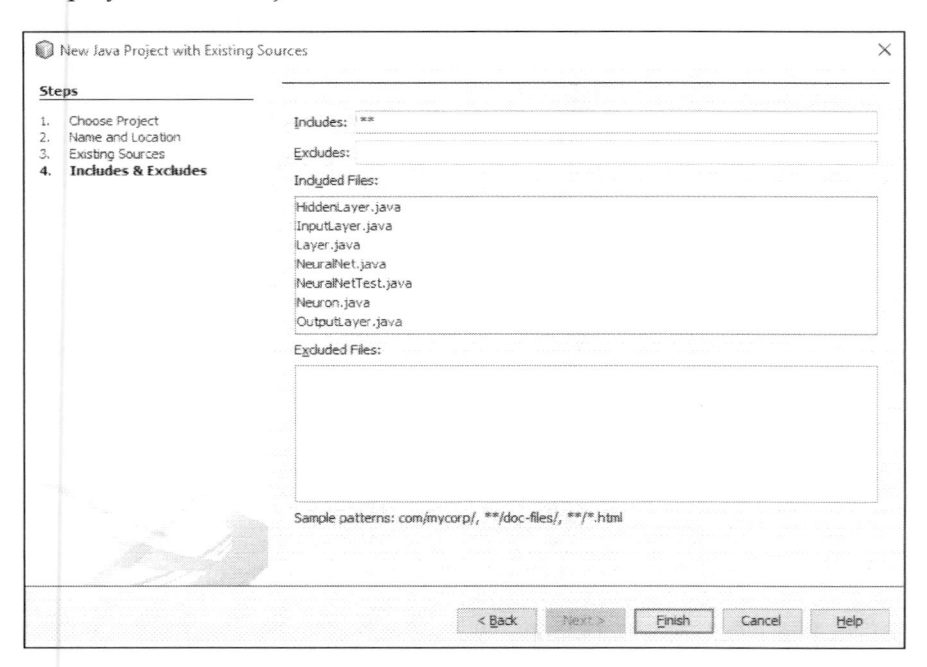

Appendix A

6. And we're done! Now, you are ready to work on the codes of each chapter in your NetBeans installation.

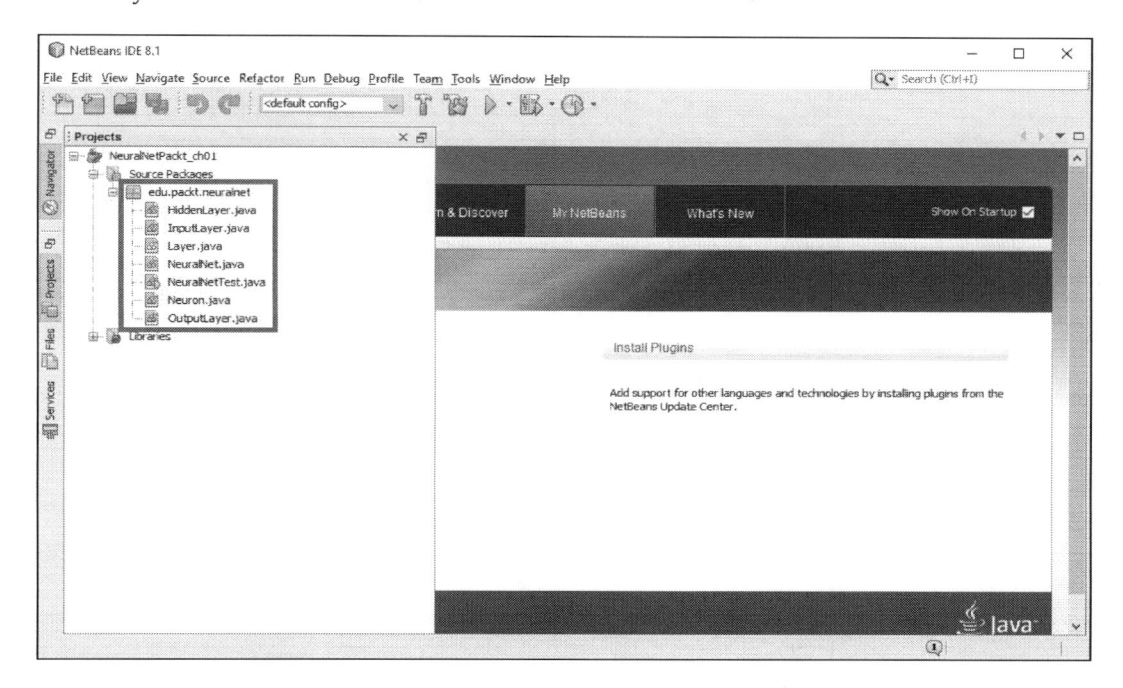

Importing a project

The following are the steps to import a project in NetBeans:

1. NetBeans offers an option to import an existing project, whether created on NetBeans or Eclipse. You can go to the menu **File** | **Import Project** and select the appropriate option.

[191]

Setting up the NetBeans Environment

If you already have Eclipse installed and you want to import it into NetBeans, just select the folder for the workspace location and click on **OK**.

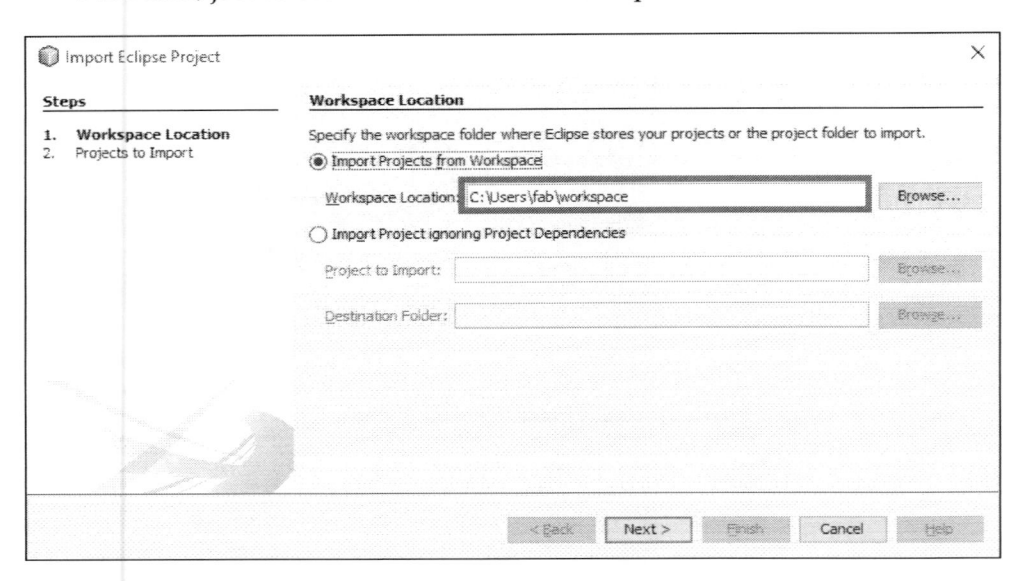

2. Select the project you want to import and click on the **Finish** button.

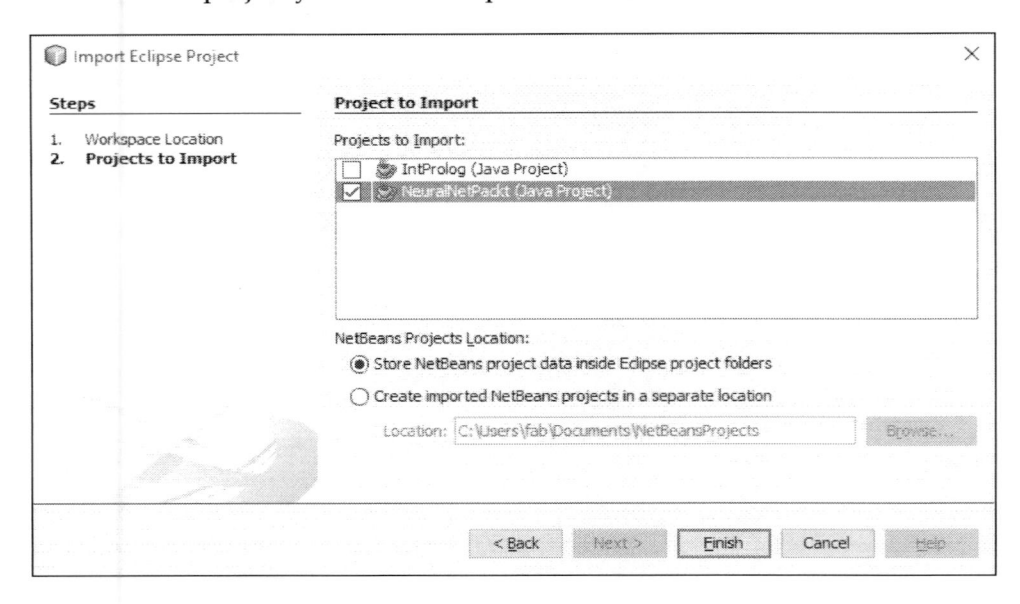

Appendix A

3. And the project is imported successfully.

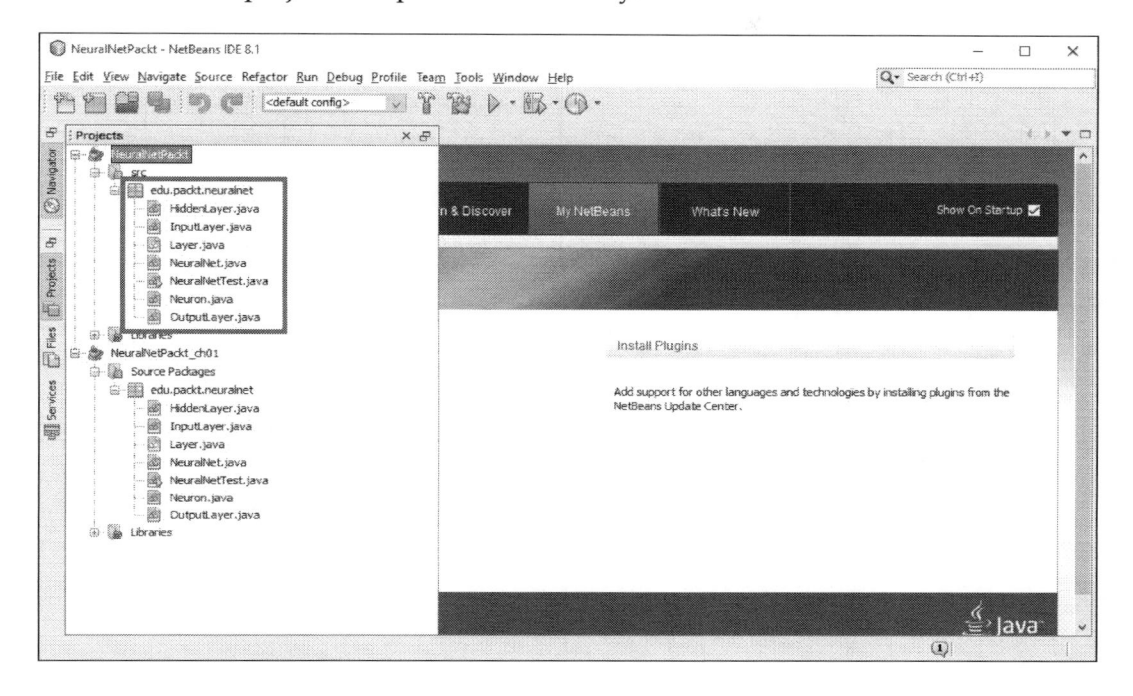

4. If you want to import from a Zip file, you can choose the **From Zip** option by navigating to **File | Import Project**. Just make sure that the Zip file was created from the NetBeans project.

Setting up the NetBeans Environment

Programming and running code with NetBeans

After going through all the previous steps, you are able to start Java programming. The next screenshot shows you the structure of the NetBeans environment:

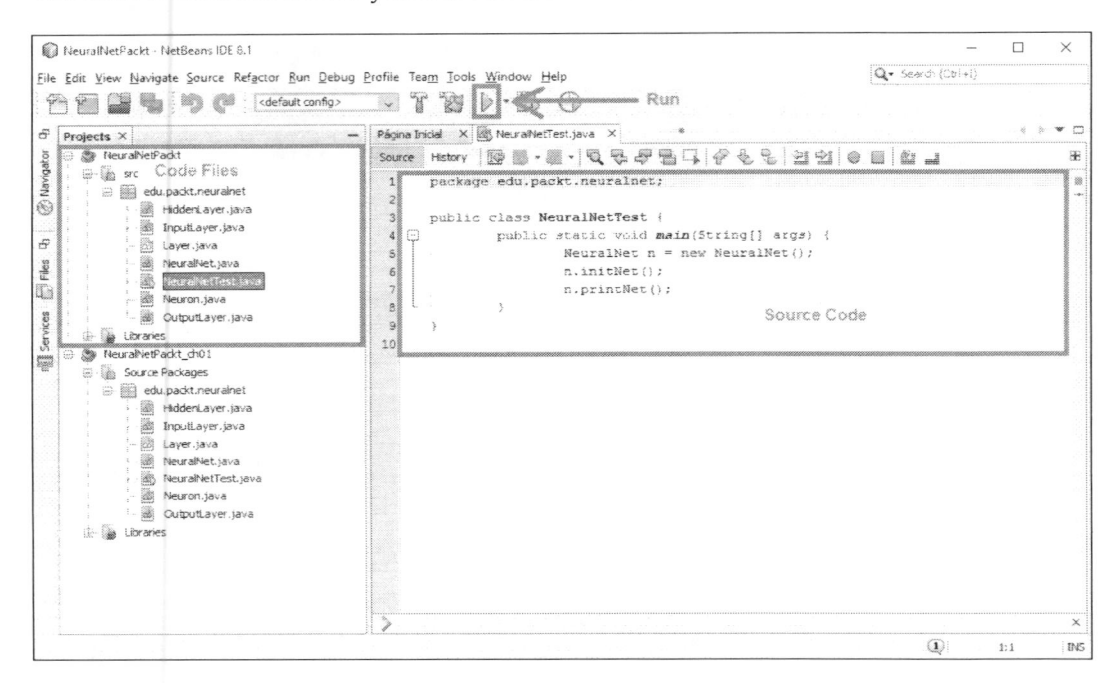

The following are the details of the NetBeans environment's sections:

- **Projects**: This section is displayed on the left-hand side of the packages and classes that compose the Java project
- **Code**: This is shown in the middle of the screen and brings the code you should interact with
- **Run the code**: As displayed in the button indicated on the screen
- **Debug the code**: To debug the code, select the **Debug** menu and then choose a file to debug (or press *Ctrl + Shift + F5*)

> We recommend you to run the IDE as an administrator, but it is not necessary.

Appendix A

Debugging with NetBeans

To debug a Java program in NetBeans, you just select a project to debug or the class file itself, as shown in the following screenshot:

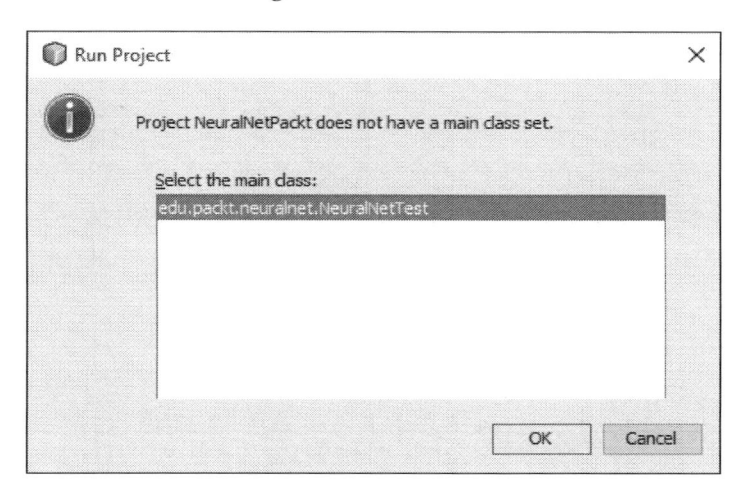

To debug line-by-line, you should add a breakpoint. So, you can place a breakpoint by clicking on the corresponding line number. Let's add a breakpoint in the beginning of the main method.

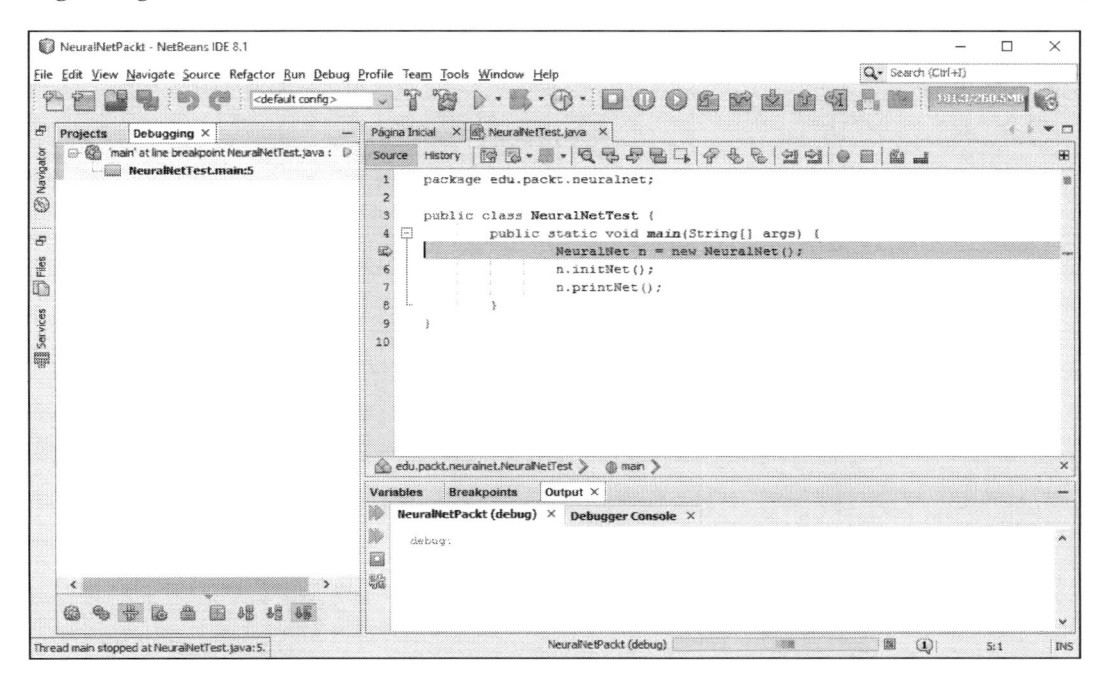

[195]

Setting up the NetBeans Environment

Use the following commands to debug line-by-line on the source code:

- *F5*: This is used to step into the method
- *F6*: This is used to step over the method
- *F7*: This is used to return to the step
- *F8*: This is used to resume debugging
- *Ctrl + F2*: This is used to terminate the debug

To inspect the value of a variable, just right-click on the code screen and select the **New Watch** option (or just press *Ctrl + Shift + F7*). Insert the name of the variable or expression you want to watch and click on **Ok**. You can see at the bottom of the screen a section called variables, where all the user custom expressions and relevant variables are displayed with their current values, as shown in the following screenshot:

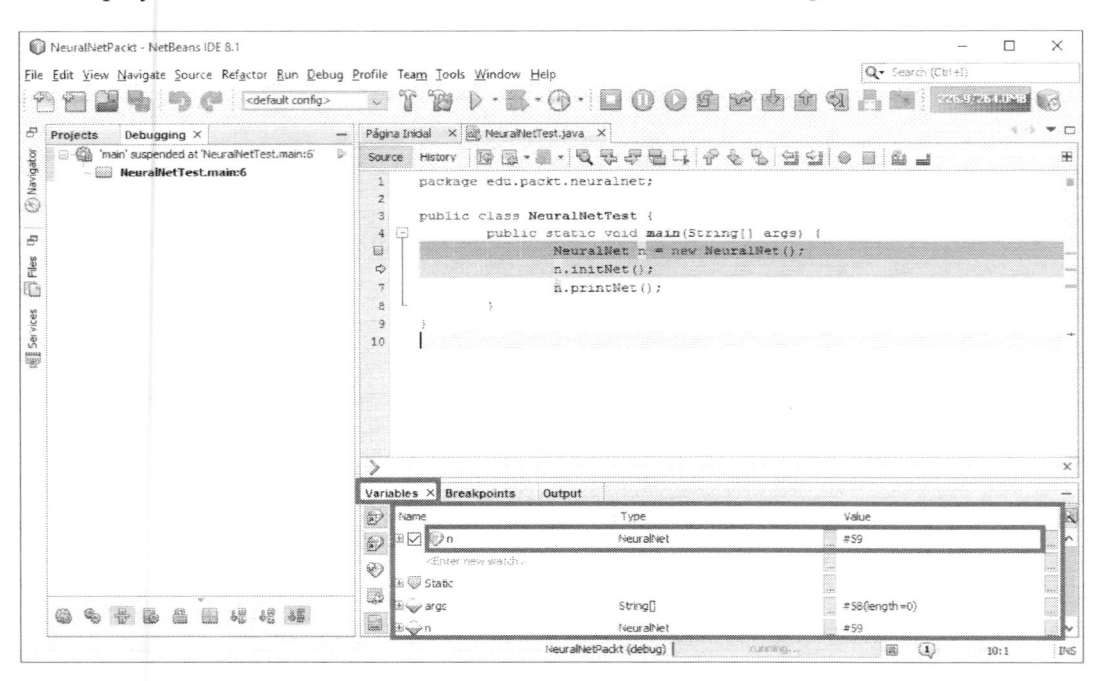

[196]

In the preceding case, n is an object, so you can expand all its attributes by clicking on the + sign on the left-hand side. And there you are; all the attributes are shown as follows:

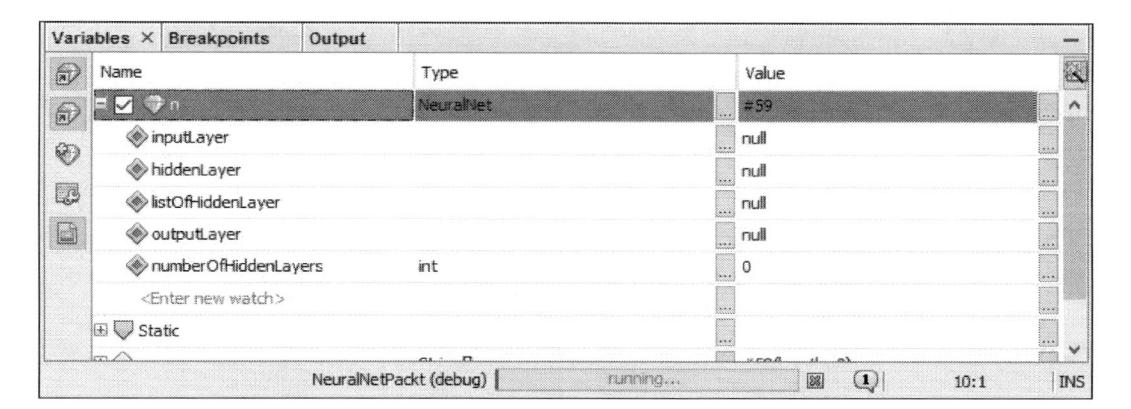

Name	Type	Value
n	NeuralNet	#59
inputLayer		null
hiddenLayer		null
listOfHiddenLayer		null
outputLayer		null
numberOfHiddenLayers	int	0
<Enter new watch>		
Static		

B
Setting Up the Eclipse Environment

This appendix shows you a step-by-step procedure of how to set up your development environment if you want to use the Eclipse IDE.

Download and install Eclipse

> Before downloading and installing Eclipse, ensure that you have installed its JDK (Java Development Kit), accessing https://www.oracle.com/java/index.html.

Setting Up the Eclipse Environment

The following are the steps to install Eclipse:

1. Access `http://www.eclipse.org/downloads` (shown in the following figure); choose **Eclipse Installer** to download the installer according to your operating system. Recently, the Eclipse team made the installation process easier through **Eclipse Installer**.

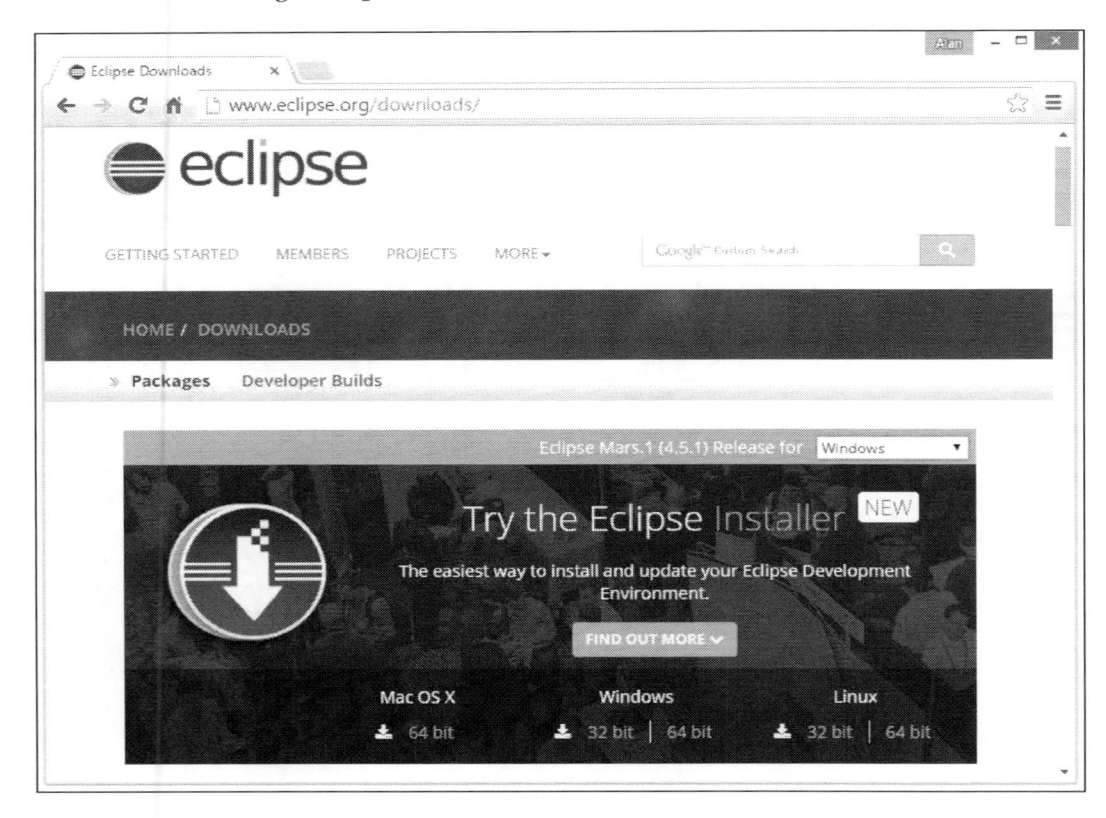

2. The web page represented in the following screenshot appears after this. You should click on the **Download** button. The best mirror to download is selected automatically, but if you want to choose another one, you may do so at the bottom of the page.

[200]

Appendix B

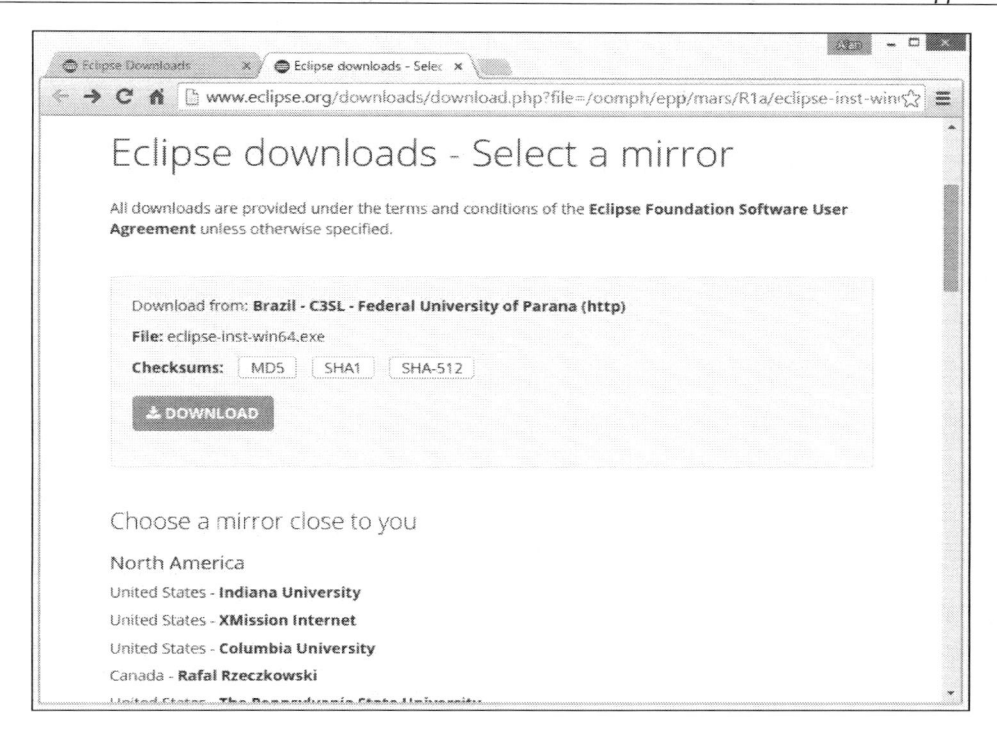

3. After the download, you should run the `eclipse-inst-<your_os>.exe` executable file. The following screen appears after this. As we will not develop web applications, you should click on the first option, that is, **Eclipse IDE for Java Developers**.

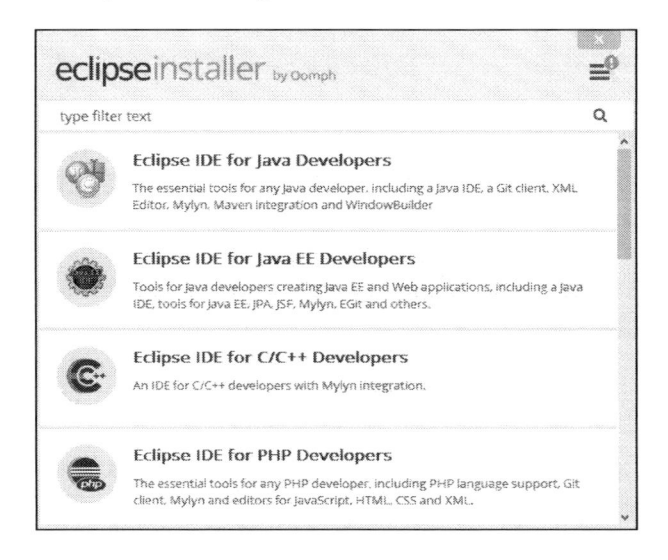

Setting Up the Eclipse Environment

4. Now, you should select the installation folder and decide whether you want to create the start menu entry and desktop shortcut. Then, click on the **INSTALL** button.

5. You must accept the license by clicking on the **Accept Now** button.

6. Finally, the installation process begins.

7. After the installation, you may click on the **LAUNCH** button to run Eclipse.

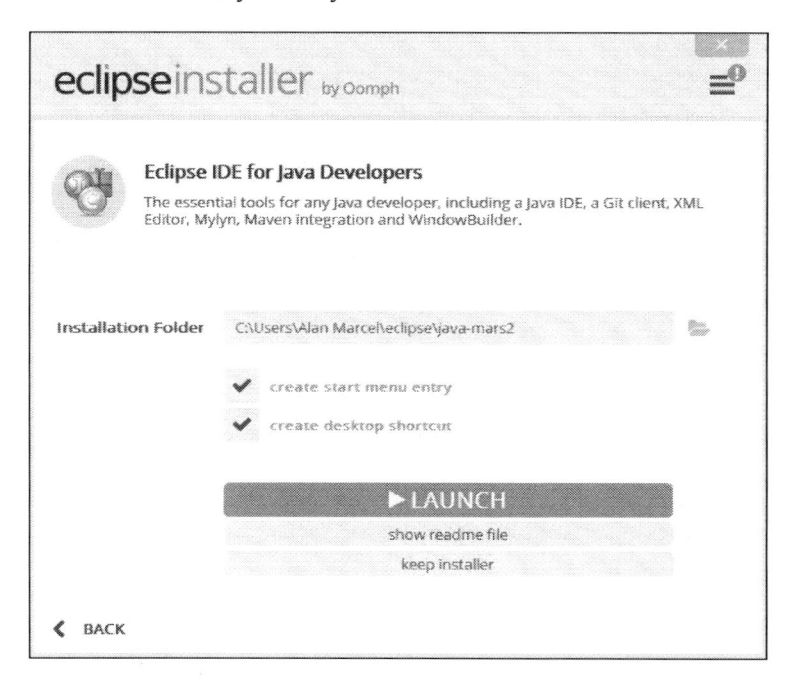

Setting up the Eclipse environment

Follow the next steps to set up the environment:

1. In the next step, we choose the workspace folder where your projects will be placed. If you mark the **Use this as the default and do not ask again** option, then the next time you run Eclipse, it will not be necessary to inform the `workspace` folder again. Now, click on the **OK** button.

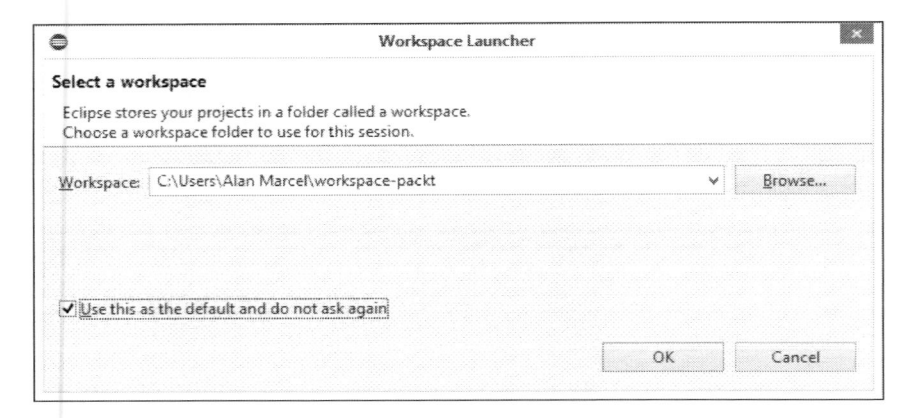

2. The welcome screen is displayed and you are ready to start the Java programming.

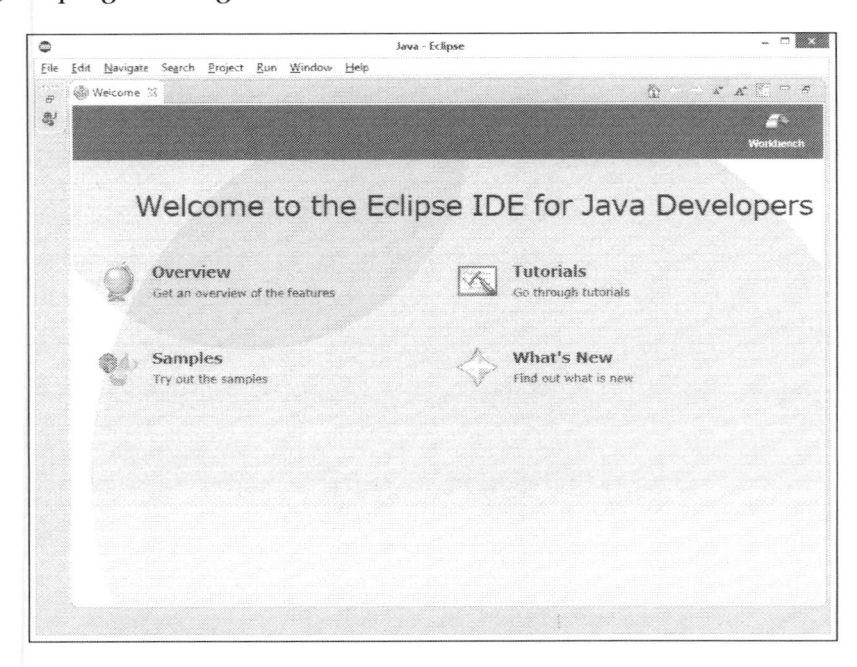

Importing a project

> Before importing the project, make sure that you unzip it in a folder you know.

The following are the steps to import a project in Eclipse:

1. To import a project that is already developed in your Eclipse IDE, navigate to **File** | **Import**.

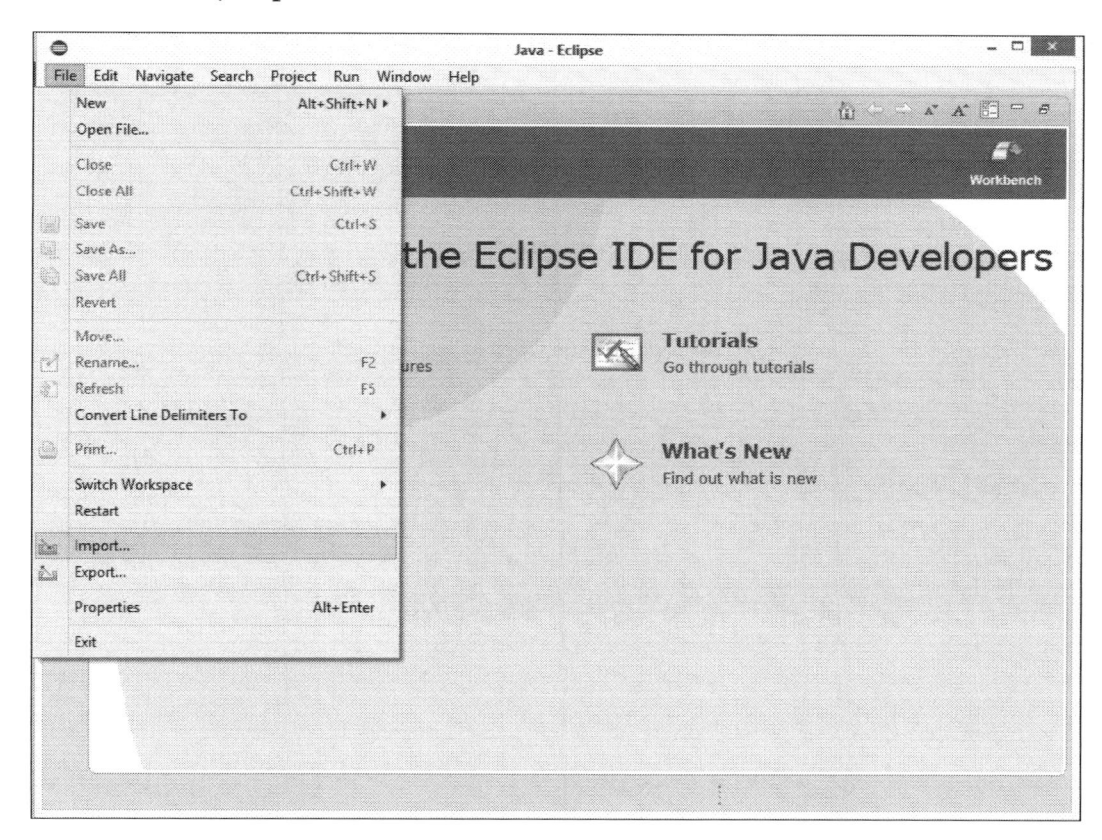

Setting Up the Eclipse Environment

2. After the import prompt is displayed, you should expand the **General** option, choose **Existing Projects into Workspace**, and click on the **Next** button.

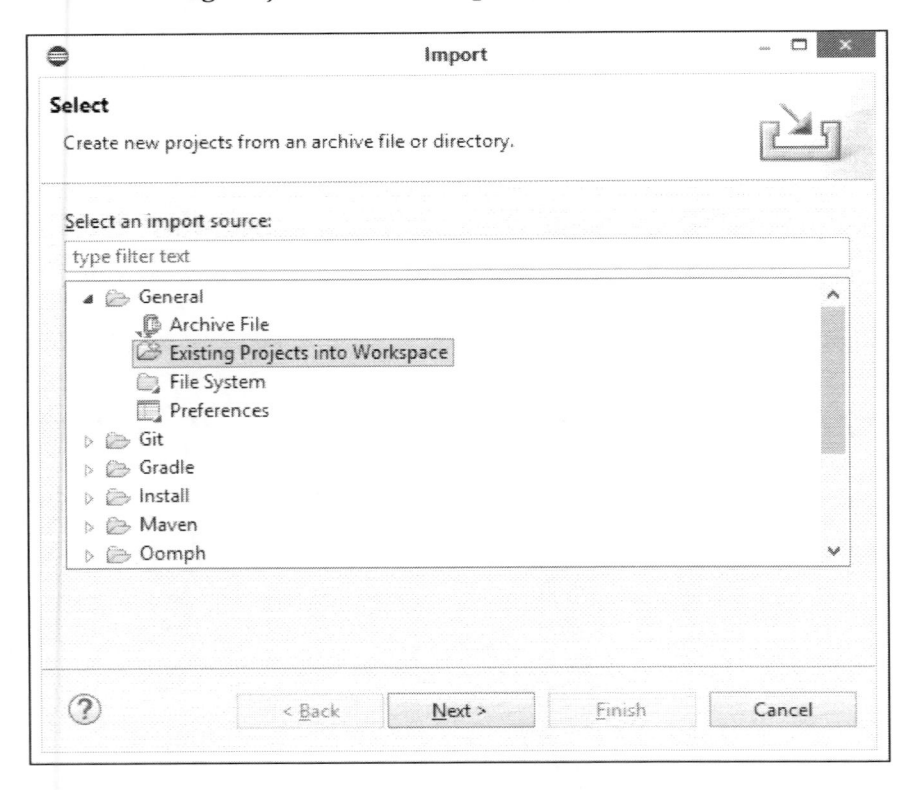

3. Now, click on the **Browse...** button to search for the project unzip folder. After that, do not forget to mark the **Search for nested projects** option and click on the **Finish** button.

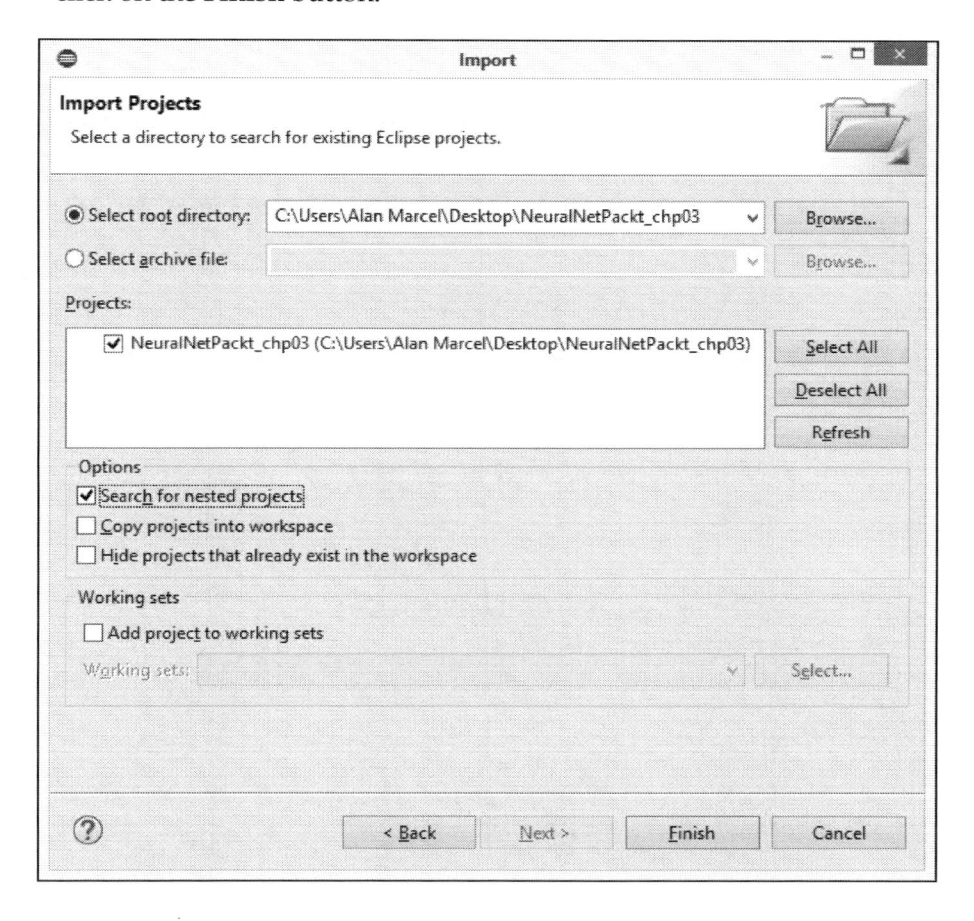

Setting Up the Eclipse Environment

4. In this step, you should close the welcome screen, and you will see in **Package explorer** the project you've imported to Eclipse.

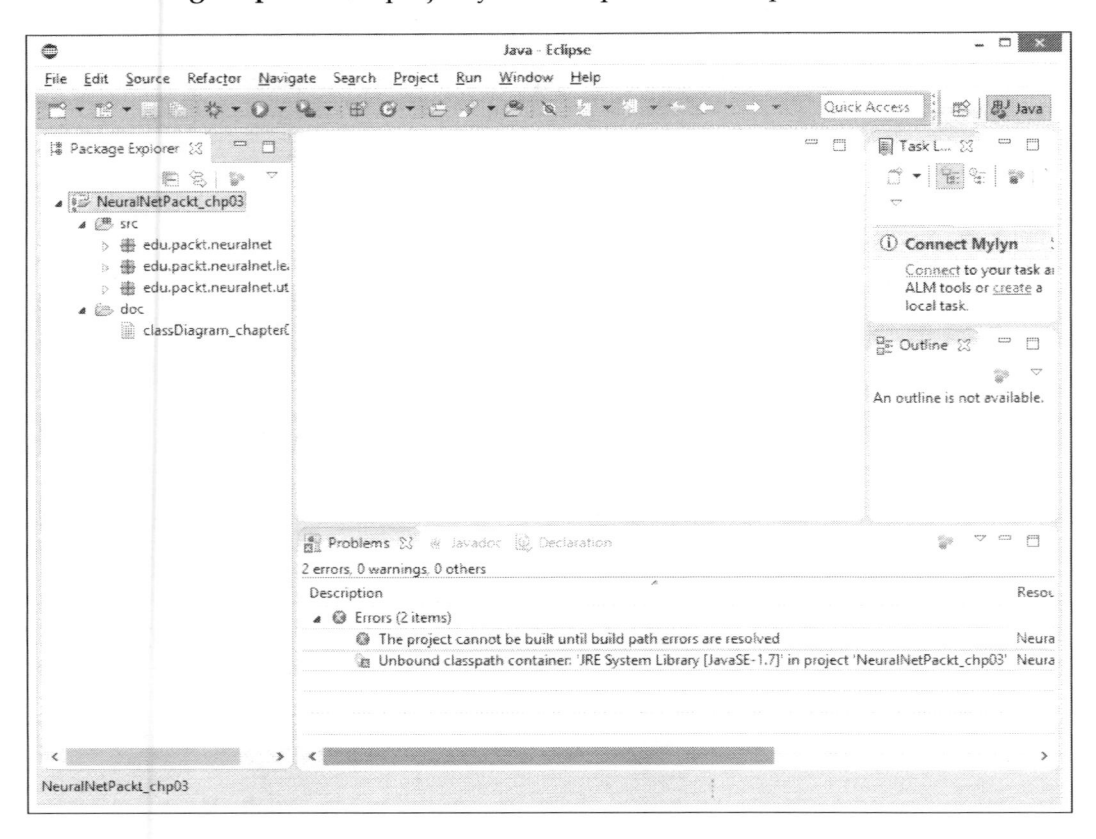

5. If you see a JRE version error, you should open the **Problems** tab. Right-click on **Unbound classpath container...**, and choose **Quick Fix**. The next screen will be exhibited.

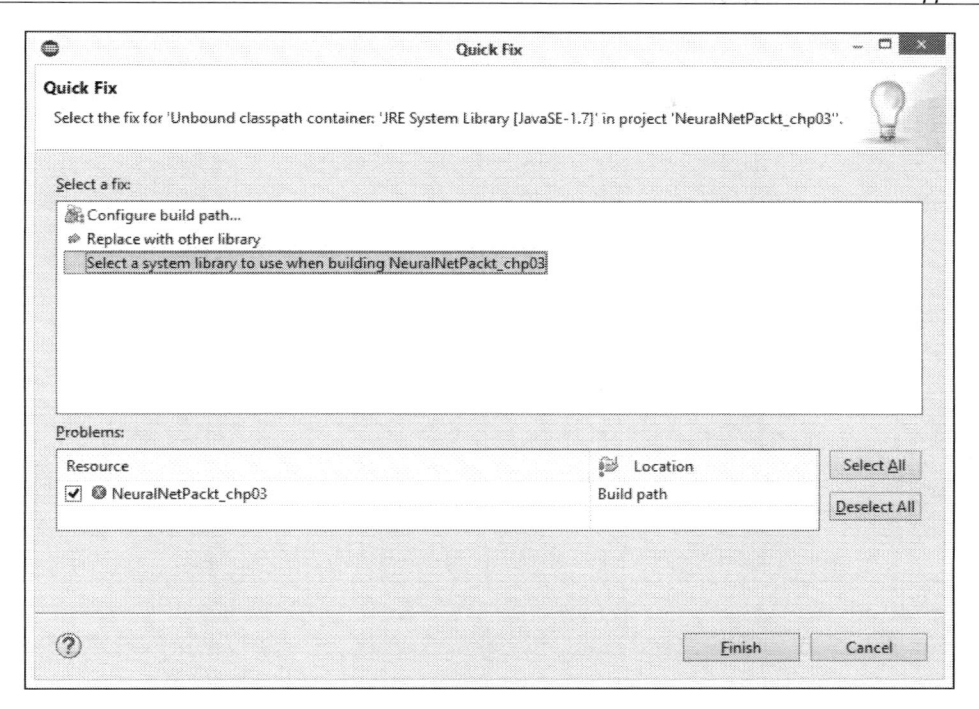

6. Now, click on the **Select a system library to use...** option and the **Finish** button. The **Edit Library** window appears, and you should select the **Workspace default JRE (jre1.8.0_40)** option then and click on the **Finish** button.

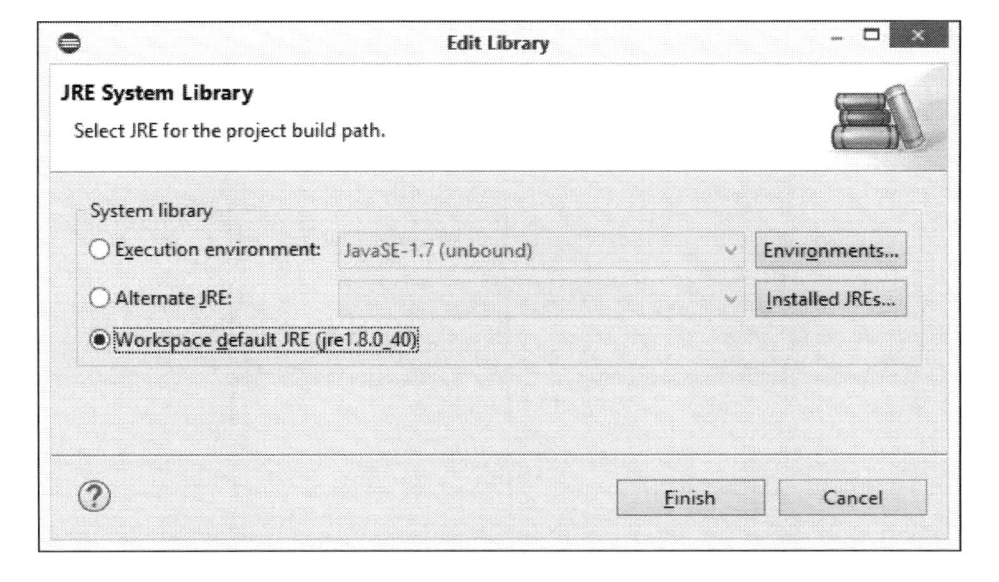

Programming and running code with the Eclipse IDE

[💡 Make sure that you run the Eclipse IDE as an administrator.]

After all the previous steps, you are now able to start Java programming. The next screenshot shows the structure of Eclipse:

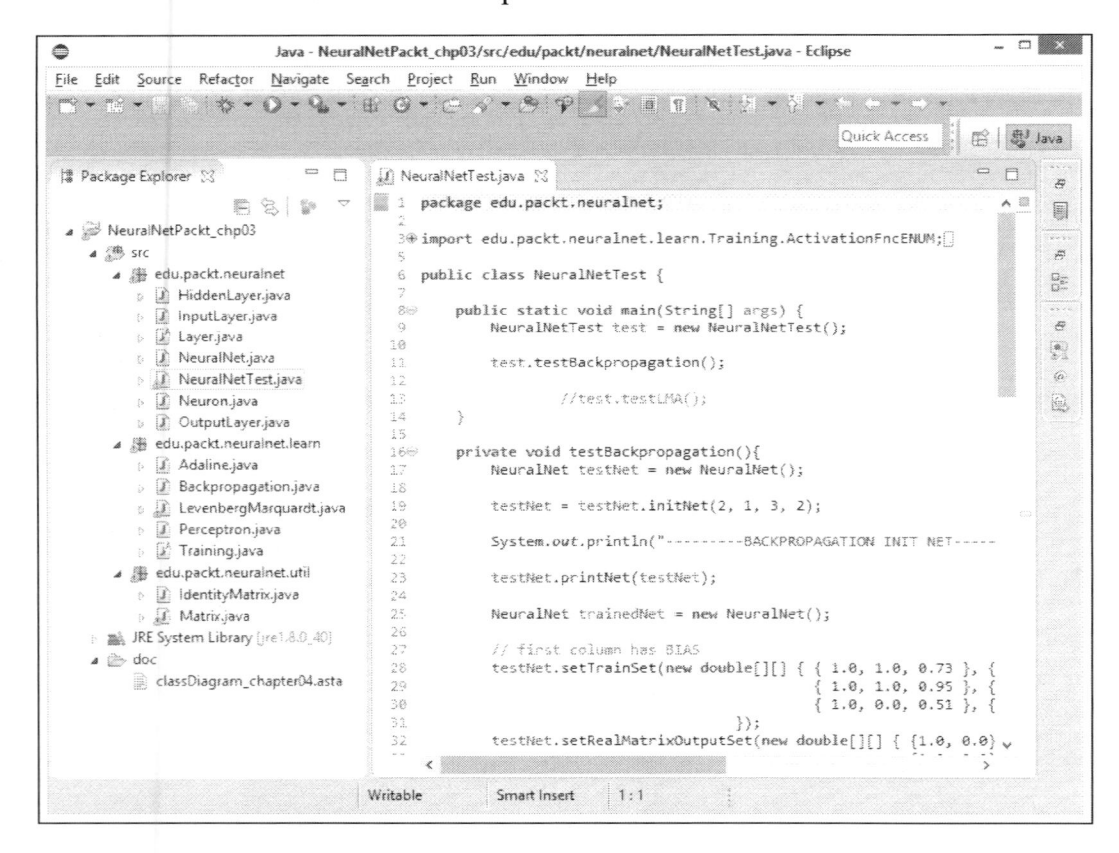

The following are the four sections of Eclipse:

- **Package Explorer**: This section is displayed on the left-hand side of the packages and classes that compose the Java project
- **Code**: This is shown in the middle of the screen and brings the code that you should interact with

- **Run the code**: There are many ways to run code. Perhaps, the easiest one is the play button indicated by arrow **A**
- **Debug the code**: There are also many ways to debug code. The easiest one is the bug button appointed by arrow **B**.

When you click on the button to run the code, it runs in the **Console** tab, as shown in the following screenshot:

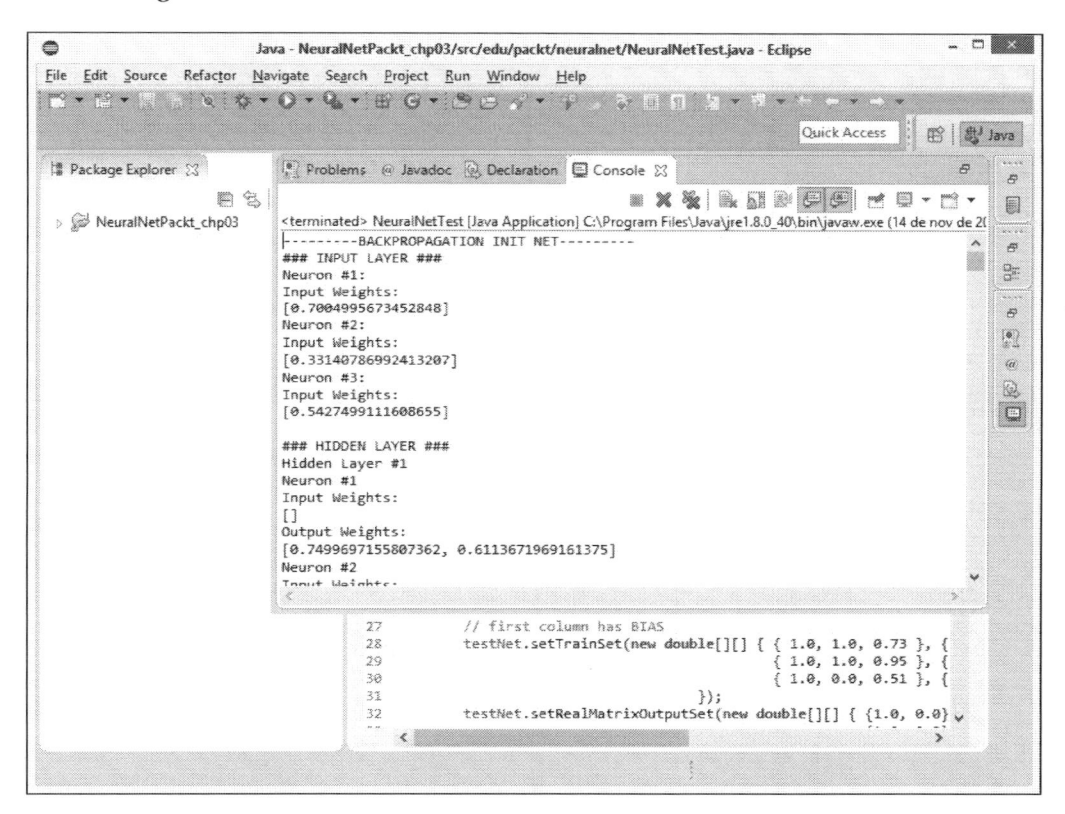

Debugging with the Eclipse IDE

To debug a Java class using the Eclipse IDE, you must create a breakpoint. It can be made by simply double-clicking near the line number (a blue round will be displayed). Then, when you click on the debug button to run the debugging process, the execution of the class will stop right on the line marked with the breakpoint, and you may type the following keys on the keyboard:

- *F5*: This is used to step into a method
- *F6*: This is used to step over a method

Setting Up the Eclipse Environment

- *F7*: This is used to step return
- *F8*: This is used to resume debugging
- *Ctrl + F2*: This is used to terminate the debug

The following screenshot shows the Eclipse debug screen. There is an important section in this screen on the right-top corner named **Variables** that shows the variables and its respective current values.

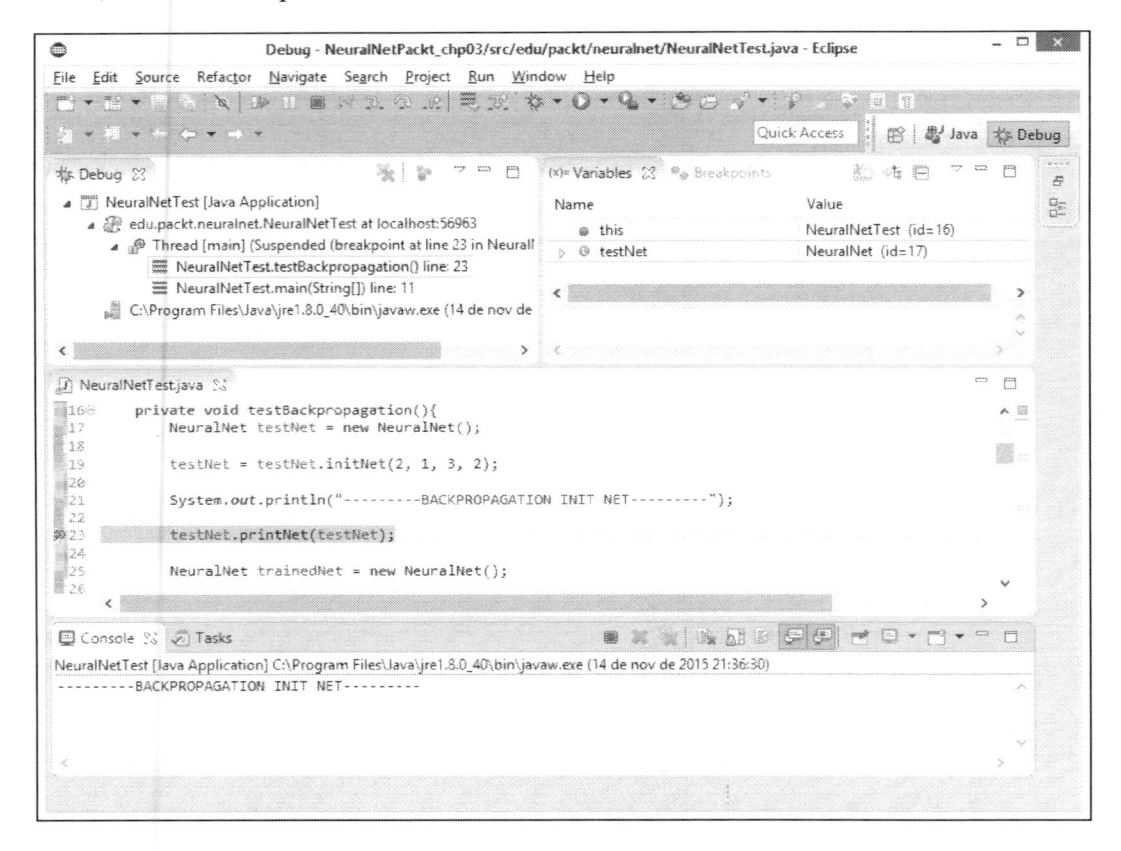

C
References

Here are some references for you if you want to know more about a specific topic covered in this book.

Chapter 1 – Getting Started with Neural Networks

- Kevin L. Priddy, Paul. E.Keller.. *Artificial Neural Networks: An introduction*. SPIE Press. . January 1, 2005.
- James Levenick . *Simply Java: An introduction to Java Programming*. Charles River Media; 1st ed., September 8, 2005.

Chapter 2 – How Neural Networks Learn

- Terrence J. Sejnowski. *Neural Network Learning Algorithms*. Neural Computers Volume 41. Springer Study Edition, pp. 291-300, 1989.
- Derrick H. Hguyen, Bernard Widrow. *Neural Networks for Self-Learning Control Systems*. IEEE Control Systems Magazine, April 1990.

Chapter 3 – Working with Perceptrons

- Simon O. Haykin. *Neural Networks and Leaning Machines*. Prentice Hall, 3rd ed., November 28, 2008.
- David E. Rumelhart, Geoffrey E. Hinton, Ronald J. Williams. *Learning Representations by back-propagating errors*. Nature v. 323 (6088), pp. 533-536, October 8, 1986.

References

- K. Levenberg. *A Method for the Solution of Certain Non-Linear Problems in Least Squares*. Quaterly of Applied Mathematics, vol 2, pp. 164-168, 1944.
- D. Marquardt. *An Algorithm for Least-Squares Estimation of Nonlinear Parameters*. SIAM Journal on Applied Mathematics, vol 11 (2), pp. 431-441, 1963.

Chapter 4 – Self-Organizing Maps

- Richard O Duda, Peter E. Hart, David G. Stork. *Unsupervised Learning and Clustering, Pattern Classification 2nd ed.*. Wiley, 2001.
- Geoffrey Hinton, Terrence, J. Sejnowski. *Unsupervised Learning: Foundations of Neural Computation*. MIT Press, 1999.
- David E. Rummelhart, David Zipser. *Feature discovery by competitive learning*. Cognitive science 9.1, pp. 75-112, 1985.
- Teuvo Kohonen. *Self-Organized Formation of Topologically Correct Feature Maps*. Biological Cybernetics, v. 43 (1), pp. 59-69, 1982.

Chapter 5 – Forecasting the Weather

- S. Dowdy, S. Wearden. *Statistics for Reasearch*. Wiley, pp. 230, 1983.
- Judea Pearl. *Causality: Models, Reasoning, and Inference*. Cambridge University Press, 2000.
- Luigi Fortuna, Salvatore Graziani, Alessandro Rizzo, Maria G. Xibilia. *Soft Sensors for Monitoring and Control of Industrial Processes*. Springer Advances in Industrial Control, 2007.

Chapter 6 – Disease Diagnosis

- Edward I. Altman, Giancarlo Marco, Varetto Franco. *Corporate distress diagnosis: Comparison using linear discriminant analysis and neural networks (the Italian experience)*. Journal of Banking and Finance v. 18, pp. 505-529, 1994.
- C. M. Bishop. *Neural Networks for Pattern Recognition*. Oxford University Press, 1995.
- Qeethara K. Al-Shayea. *Artificial Neural Networks in Medical Diagnosis*. International Journal of Computer Science Issues, Vol. 8, Issue 2, pp. 150-154, March 2011.

- David A. Freedman. *Statistical Models: Theory and Practice*. Cambridge University Press, 2009.
- Tom Fawcett. *An Introduction to ROC Analysis*. Pattern Recognition Letters, vol. 27, is. 8 pp. 861-874, 2006.

Chapter 7 – Clustering Customer Profiles

- Du, K.L. *Clustering: A Neural Network Approach*. Neural Networks, Vol. 23, Is. 1, pp. 89-107, January 2010.
- J. Park, I.W. Sandberg. *Universal Approximation using Radial-Basis-Function Networks*. Neural Computation, vol. 3 is. 2, pp. 246-257, 1991.
- Michael E. Wall, Andreas Rechtsteiner, Luis M. Rocha, *Singular value decomposition and principal component analysis*. A Practical Approach to Microarray Data Analysis, pp. 91-109, 2003.
- Glendon Cross, Wayne Thompson. *Understanding your Customer: Segmentation Techniques for Gaining Customer Insight and Predicting Risk in the Telecom Industry*. SAS Global Forum, 2008.

Chapter 8 – Pattern Recognition (the OCR Case)

- Jayanta K. Basu, Debnath Bhattacharyya, Tai-hoon Kim. *Use of Artificial Neural Network in Pattern Recognition*. International Journal of Software Engineering and Its Applications, Vol. 4, No. 2, April 2010.
- Vivek Shrivastava, Navdeep Sharma. *Artificial Neural Network Based Optical Character Recognition*. Signal and Image Processing: An International Journal (SIPIJ), Vol. 3, No. 5, October 2012.

Chapter 9 – Neural Network Optimization and Adaptation

- Utrans J. Moody, Rehfuss S., Siegelmann H. *Input variable selection for neural networks: application to predicting the U.S. business cycle*. Computational Intelligence for Financial Engineering, Proceedings of the IEEE/IAFE, 1995
- Saxén H., Pettersson, F. *Method for the selection of inputs and structure of feedforwaed neural networks*. Computers and Chemical Enginnering, Vol. 30, Is. 6-7, pp. 1048-1045, May 15, 2006.

References

- Alan M. F. Souza, Carolina M. Affonso, Fábio M. Soares, Roberto C.L. *De Oliveira. Soft Sensor for Fluoridated Alumina Inference in Gas Treatment Centers.* Intelligent Data Engineering and Automated Learning 2012, Lecture Notes in Computer Science v. 7435, pp. 294-302, Spinger Verlab Berlin Heidelberg, 2012.

- Jollife. *I.T. Principal Component Analysis.* 2nd ed. Springer Wiley, 2002.

- Karmin, E.D. *A simple procedure for pruning back-propagation trained neural networks.* IEEE transactions on Neural Networks, pp. 239-242, June 1990.

- P.E. Gill, W. Murray, M.H. Wright. *Practical Optimization.* Academic Press: London, 1981.

- Gail A. Carpenter, Stephen Grossberg. *Adaptive Resonance Theory.* The Handbook of Brain Theory and Neural Networks, 2nd ed., pp. 1-11, 2002.

Index

A

abstraction 11
activation function 5, 6
ADALINE (traffic forecast) 41-45
adaptive neural networks
　about 179
　implementation 180, 181
adaptive resonance theory (ART) 179
AND logic 37
applied unsupervised learning
　about 139
　Kohonen neural network 140
　neural network, of radial basis
　　functions 139, 140
　types of data 141
artificial intelligence 2
artificial neural networks (ANNs)
　about 2
　need for 2
　used, for diagnosing breast cancer 126-130
artificial neuron 5

B

backpropagation algorithm 61, 62, 68
Best Matching Unit (BMU) 88
bias 7
binary classes
　versus multiple classes 120, 121

C

card credit analysis
　for customer profiling 143-149
categorical data 142
classes 152
classification
　neural networks, applying for 123, 124
　sensitivity measure 122
　specificity measure 122
classification, in MLPs 56, 57
classification problems
　foundations 118
cluster analysis 137
cluster evaluation 138
clustering 136
clustering task 136
cluster validation 138
coding, of neural network learning
　about 27
　class definitions 30-35
　learning parameter implementation 27, 28
　learning procedure 29, 30
common issues, in neural network
　　implementations 168
competitive learning 82-84
confusion matrix 121
cost function 21, 25
customer profiling
　about 142
　card credit analysis 143-149
　data, preprocessing 142, 143

D

data correlation 169, 170
data filtering 171
data preprocessing, weather forecasting
　　application
　about 104
　data equalizing 105, 106

data selection, weather forecasting application
  data filtering 103, 104
  input and output variables, selecting 103
  weather variables 102
data, types
  categorical 142
  numerical 141
Davies-Bouldin index 138
defined classes
  using 152, 153
delta rule 27
digit recognition 156
digit representation approach 157
dimensionality reduction 170, 171
disease diagnosis, with neural networks
  about 126
  ANN, used for diagnosing breast cancer 126-130
  NN, applying for early diagnosing of diabetes 131-133
Dunn index 138

E

Eclipse IDE
  code, running with 211
  debugging with 211, 212
encapsulation 12
epoch 30
error measurement 25
Euclidian distance algorithm 146
external validation 138, 154

F

feedback networks 10
feedforward networks 9

H

hands-on MLP implementation
  about 65-67
  backpropagation algorithm 68
  code, exploring 68-72

I

implementation, in Java
  card credit analysis, for customer profiling 143-149
inheritance 12
input selection
  about 168
  data correlation 169, 170
  data filtering 171
  dimensionality reduction 170, 171

J

Java implementation, weather forecasting application
  about 107
  charts, plotting 107
  data files, handling 108
  neural network, building 109-111
JFreeChart
  URL 107

K

Kohonen algorithm
  coding 90-92
Kohonen class
  exploring 92-95
Kohonen implementation
  animals, clustering 95-97
Kohonen neural network 140
Kohonen self-organizing maps (SOMs)
  1D SOM 85
  2D SOM 86, 87
  about 84
  step-by-step learning 88, 89
  using 89

L

layers, of neurons 7
learning
  about 20
  parameters 24, 25

learning ability, in neural networks 19
learning algorithms, examples
    about 26
    delta rule 27
    perceptrons 26
learning paradigms
    about 20
    supervised learning 20, 21
    unsupervised learning 21, 22
learning process, in MLPs
    about 60
    backpropagation algorithm 61, 62
    Levenberg – Marquardt algorithm 63, 64
learning process, neural networks 10, 11
learning, stages
    testing 23, 24
    training 23, 24
Levenberg – Marquardt algorithm
    about 63, 64
    implementation 72-74
logistic regression 119, 120

M

MLP applications
    about 56
    classification 56, 57
    regression 56-59
monolayer networks 8
multilayer networks 9
multilayer perceptrons (MLPs)
    about 52
    in OOP paradigm 55, 56
    properties 52
    weights 53, 54
multiple classes
    versus binary classes 120, 121

N

NetBeans
    code, running with 194
    debugging with 195-197
    download link 184
    environment, setting up 188-191
    installing 184-187
    programming with 194
    project, importing 191-193
neural network architectures
    about 8
    feedback networks 10
    feedforward networks 9
    monolayer networks 8
    multilayer networks 9
neural network architectures, applications
    about 37
    ADALINE (traffic forecast) 41-45
    perceptron (warning system) 37-40
neural network implementations
    common issues 168
neural network, of radial basis
        functions 139, 140
neural networks
    about 1, 119
    applying, for classification 123, 124
    applying, for early diagnosis
        of diabetes 131-133
    arranging 4
    discovering 2
    empirical design 112
    implementing 11-17
    learning ability 19
    learning process 10, 11
neural networks, for prediction
        problems 100, 101
neural networks, in pattern recognition
    applying 154, 155
    data, preprocessing 155, 156
neural networks, of empirical design
    about 112
    experiments, designing 113
    results and simulations 113-115
    training and test datasets, selecting 112
neural networks unsupervised learning 80
normalization 105
numerical data
    about 141
    examples 141

O

objects-oriented programming (OOP) 11
OCR problem
  about 156
  task, simplifying 156
online retraining
  about 172, 173
  application 176-179
  implementation 174
  stochastic online learning 174
Optical Character Recognition (OCR) 151
optical characters, recognizing
  about 157
  data, generating 158-160
  neural network, building 160
  results 163, 164
  trial and error 161, 162

P

pattern recognition
  about 152
  defined classes 152, 153
  examples, tasks 152
  undefined classes 153, 154
patterns 152
Pearson coefficient 169
perceptron
  about 26
  applications 48
  limitations 48
  linear separation 48, 49
  studying 48
  XOR case, analyzing 50, 51
perceptron (warning system) 37-40
polymorphism 12
practical application
  types of university enrolments 75-78
Principal Component Analysis (PCA) 170
Proben1
  about 126
  reference link 126
pseudo algorithm
  reference link, for source code 174

R

Radial basis functions (RBFs) 140
recurrent MLP 54
regression, in MLPs 58, 59

S

Self-Organizing Maps (SOMs) 79
single value decomposition (SVD) 142
stochastic online learning 174
structure selection 171
supervised learning 11, 20, 21
systematic structuring 22, 23

U

undefined classes 153, 154
Unified Modeling Language (UML) 16
unsupervised learning 21, 22
unsupervised learning algorithms
  about 80, 81
  competitive learning 82-84

W

weather forecasting application
  data preprocessing 104
  data, selecting 101
  Java implementation 107
weights 6

Thank you for buying
Neural Network Programming with Java

About Packt Publishing

Packt, pronounced 'packed', published its first book, *Mastering phpMyAdmin for Effective MySQL Management*, in April 2004, and subsequently continued to specialize in publishing highly focused books on specific technologies and solutions.

Our books and publications share the experiences of your fellow IT professionals in adapting and customizing today's systems, applications, and frameworks. Our solution-based books give you the knowledge and power to customize the software and technologies you're using to get the job done. Packt books are more specific and less general than the IT books you have seen in the past. Our unique business model allows us to bring you more focused information, giving you more of what you need to know, and less of what you don't.

Packt is a modern yet unique publishing company that focuses on producing quality, cutting-edge books for communities of developers, administrators, and newbies alike. For more information, please visit our website at www.packtpub.com.

About Packt Open Source

In 2010, Packt launched two new brands, Packt Open Source and Packt Enterprise, in order to continue its focus on specialization. This book is part of the Packt Open Source brand, home to books published on software built around open source licenses, and offering information to anybody from advanced developers to budding web designers. The Open Source brand also runs Packt's Open Source Royalty Scheme, by which Packt gives a royalty to each open source project about whose software a book is sold.

Writing for Packt

We welcome all inquiries from people who are interested in authoring. Book proposals should be sent to author@packtpub.com. If your book idea is still at an early stage and you would like to discuss it first before writing a formal book proposal, then please contact us; one of our commissioning editors will get in touch with you.

We're not just looking for published authors; if you have strong technical skills but no writing experience, our experienced editors can help you develop a writing career, or simply get some additional reward for your expertise.

[PACKT] open source
PUBLISHING
community experience distilled

Machine Learning with Spark

ISBN: 978-1-78328-851-9   Paperback: 338 pages

Create scalable machine learning applications to power a modern data-driven business using Spark

1. A practical tutorial with real-world use cases allowing you to develop your own machine learning systems with Spark.

2. Combine various techniques and models into an intelligent machine learning system.

3. Use Spark's powerful tools to load, analyze, clean, and transform your data.

Scala for Machine Learning

ISBN: 978-1-78355-874-2   Paperback: 520 pages

Leverage Scala and Machine Learning to construct and study systems that can learn from data

1. Explore a broad variety of data processing, machine learning, and genetic algorithms through diagrams, mathematical formulation, and source code.

2. Leverage your expertise in Scala programming to create and customize AI applications with your own scalable machine learning algorithms.

3. Experiment with different techniques, and evaluate their benefits and limitations using real-world financial applications, in a tutorial style.

Please check www.PacktPub.com for information on our titles

Mastering Machine Learning with scikit-learn

ISBN: 978-1-78398-836-5 Paperback: 238 pages

Apply effective learning algorithms to real-world problems using scikit-learn

1. Design and troubleshoot machine learning systems for common tasks including regression, classification, and clustering.

2. Acquaint yourself with popular machine learning algorithms, including decision trees, logistic regression, and support vector machines.

3. A practical example-based guide to help you gain expertise in implementing and evaluating machine learning systems using scikit-learn.

Clojure for Machine Learning

ISBN: 978-1-78328-435-1 Paperback: 292 pages

Successfully leverage advanced machine learning techniques using the Clojure ecosystem

1. Covers a lot of machine learning techniques with Clojure programming.

2. Encompasses precise patterns in data to predict future outcomes using various machine learning techniques.

3. Packed with several machine learning libraries available in the Clojure ecosystem.

Please check **www.PacktPub.com** for information on our titles

Printed in Great Britain
by Amazon